Postcard History Series

The Benjamin Franklin Parkway

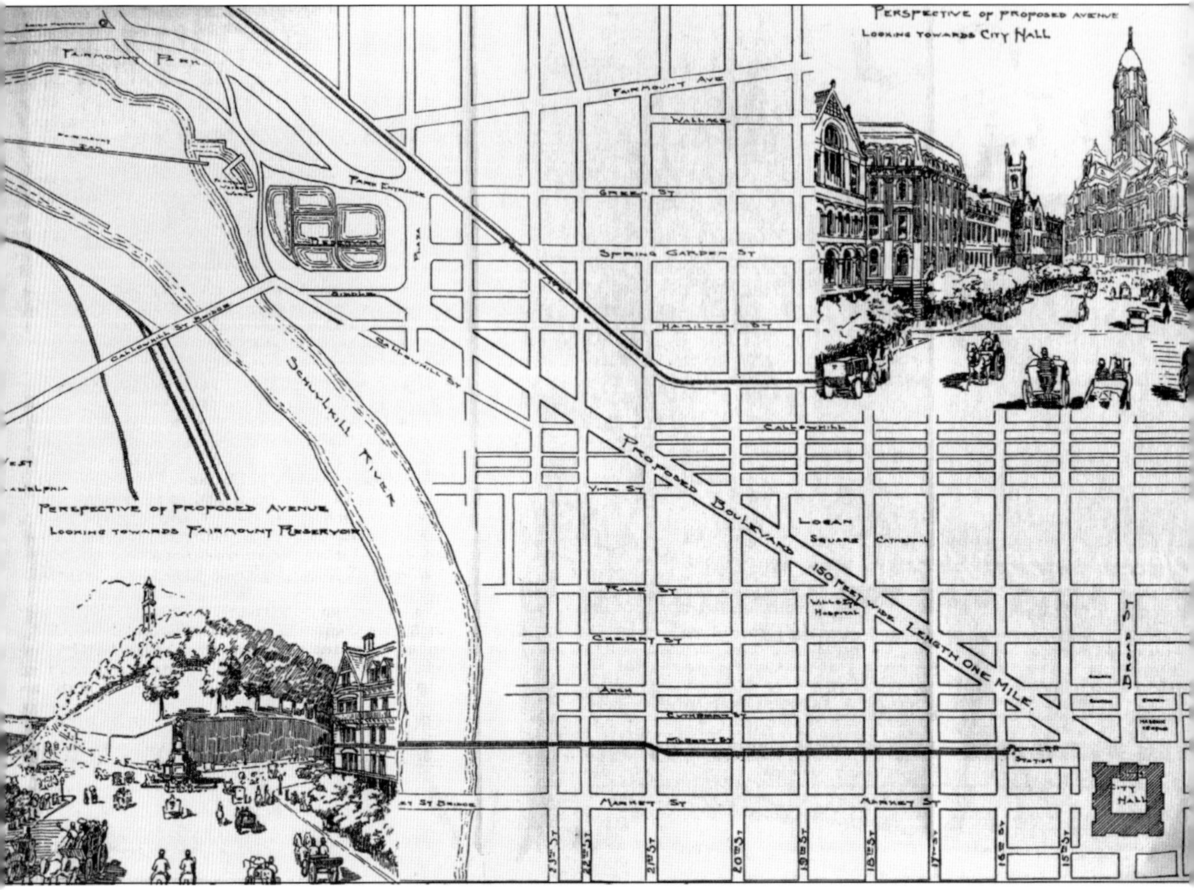

In the mid-1880s, real estate developer Charles Landis issued a prospective map advocating his proposal for a 150-foot-wide slanted thoroughfare from Philadelphia City Hall to the reservoirs of the Fairmount Water Works. His "Map of the Grand Avenue to the Park, Philadelphia" was amazingly prescient, as the Benjamin Franklin Parkway follows Landis's suggested course almost exactly. (The Free Library of Philadelphia.)

ON THE FRONT COVER: This postcard image was taken from the Philadelphia Saving Fund Society (PSFS) Building in 1937, the same year that the great boulevard's name was changed from Fairmount Parkway to Benjamin Franklin Parkway. The avenue disregards the city's checkerboard street grid, as it begins at Philadelphia City Hall and heads diagonally toward Logan Circle before reaching the Philadelphia Museum of Art. (K.F. Lutz, Philadelphia.)

ON THE BACK COVER: The Ben Franklin Parkway appears at night in this 1940 card. The caption on the back states, "This one mile-long boulevard at night turns into a 'white way' caused by the steady stream of passing automobiles and imposing buildings of the city in the background make this view from the Art Museum a most beautiful sight." In recent years, the "steady stream" has become more of a problem. (K.F. Lutz, Philadelphia.)

POSTCARD HISTORY SERIES

The Benjamin Franklin Parkway

Harry Kyriakodis

ARCADIA PUBLISHING

ISBN 978-1-4671-2153-8

Published by Arcadia Publishing
Charleston, South Carolina

Printed in the United States of America

Library of Congress Control Number: 2013950195

For all general information contact Arcadia Publishing at:
Telephone 843-853-2070
Fax 843-853-0044
E-mail sales@arcadiapublishing.com
For customer service and orders:
Toll-Free 1-888-313-2665

Visit us on the Internet at www.arcadiapublishing.com

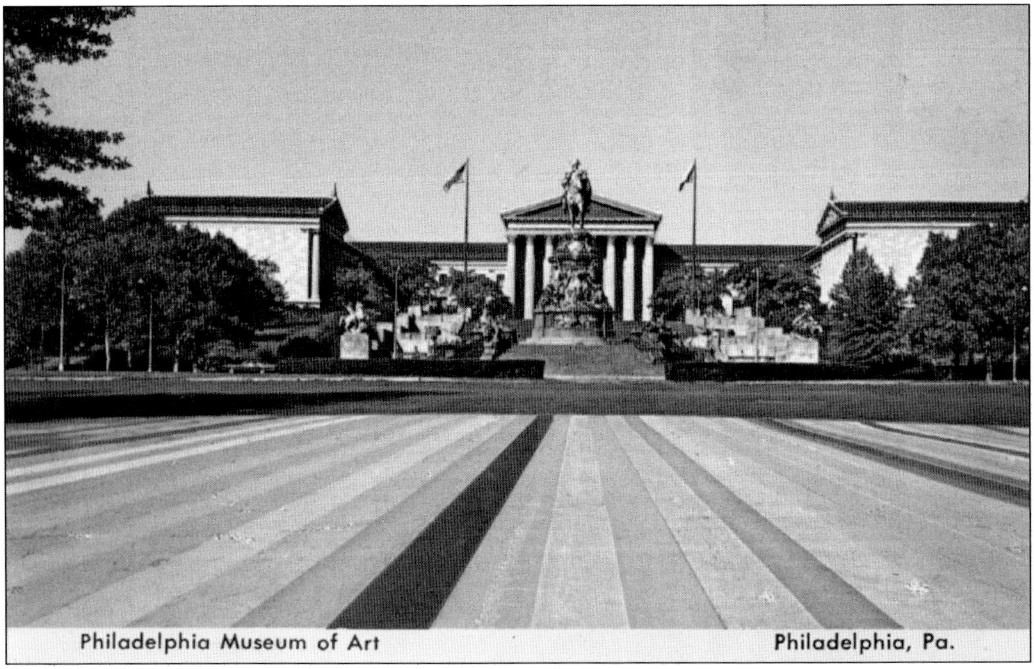

In 1972, the Philadelphia Museum of Art commissioned artist Gene Davis to paint a series of colored stripes on a stretch of the Parkway that had been abandoned due to the addition of Eakins Oval. Named *Franklin's Footpath*, the 38,000-square-foot street mural survived for a few years before eroding. This was supposedly the world's largest work of art at that time. The museum and the Washington Monument complete the scene. (Art Color Card Distributors.)

Contents

Acknowledgments

Let me thank the following people who helped me acquire images and who generally assisted me in researching this volume: Nicole Joniec (Library Company of Philadelphia), Ellen Trappey (Franklin Institute), Joelen Pastva (Moore College of Art), Greta Greenberger (Philadelphia City Hall), Judi Rogers (Parkway Council Foundation), Laura Griffith (Association for Public Art), Richard Boardman (Free Library of Philadelphia), Hyman Myers (on behalf of the Pennsylvania Academy of the Fine Arts), Sharon Hoffman, Amanda Mott, Cynthia Temple, Amy Singh, Paula Spilner, Mary Anne Eves, Thomas Keels, Rich Wagner, Bob Skiba, Rob Armstrong, Michael Weinberg, and David Brownlee. I am especially grateful to Gus Spector, who kindly invited me to his home and lent me several cards from his fantastic postcard collection. Lastly, I thank the team at Arcadia Publishing for guiding me through this process. Readers wishing to contact me may do so via my Facebook page or my LinkedIn page.

INTRODUCTION

The Logan Square neighborhood of the City of Brotherly Love occupies the northwest quadrant of center city (downtown) Philadelphia, extending from Broad Street to the Schuylkill River and from Market Street to Spring Garden Street. This locale consists of the Logan Square row home neighborhood, the Penn Center office core, upscale residential high-rises to the north and south, and the east bank of the Schuylkill River. To the north is the Philadelphia Art Museum and the Fairmount district.

Slicing through this entire quarter is the Benjamin Franklin Parkway. Named after Philadelphia's favorite son, the grand boulevard disregards the city's checkerboard street grid, as it begins at Philadelphia City Hall and heads diagonally toward Logan Circle before reaching the Philadelphia Museum of Art. The one-mile-long thoroughfare, with its unmistakable French influence, serves as the prime gateway to Philadelphia's glorious Fairmount Park and is the chief corridor for the city's most prominent cultural institutions—Philadelphia's "Museum Mile," as it were.

The notion that there should be a substantial street leading to Fairmount Park first emerged in the 1850s, as the park was being assembled. Such a road would link the harsh, congested city with the airy recreational park and would facilitate access to the park for all Philadelphians, especially laborers in the city's flourishing industrial districts.

Several proposals surfaced throughout the second half of the 19th century. In 1871, an unsigned pamphlet entitled "Broad Street, Penn Square and the Park" suggested two approaches, one to East Fairmount Park and one to West Fairmount Park, in anticipation of the Centennial International Exposition of 1876. Indeed, the difficulty of getting visitors to Fairmount Park during the centennial celebration underscored the need for direct access to the park. But nothing happened.

In the mid-1880s, real estate developer Charles Landis issued a prospective map advocating his proposal for a 150-foot-wide diagonal thoroughfare from Philadelphia City Hall to the reservoirs of the famed Fairmount Water Works. The construction of city hall had just started then, and the waterworks' basins were on the hill of Faire Mount, where the Philadelphia Museum of Art is today. Landis exuberantly declared, "A convenient approach to the park is a necessity. Why not make it something worthy of the magnificent city of Philadelphia?" Still, nothing happened.

In 1891, a group of eminent citizens presented the city government with a petition to create "a suitable and handsome avenue" to connect the center of Philadelphia to the park. Although city officials responded positively, this scheme, like the prior ones, gained little traction. A city ordinance placed the route on the city plan in 1893, but it was repealed two years later.

In 1900, an alliance of artists and designers called the Art Federation of Philadelphia revived discussion about the "Fairmount Park Parkway." This newfound interest had much to do with the Progressive Era's City Beautiful Movement, which was motivated by the Columbian Exposition of 1893 in Chicago. The City Beautiful approach to architecture and urban planning promoted classical beautification and monumental splendor for roadways.

The Art Federation helped organize a pool of businessmen called the Parkway Association for the purpose of generating publicity. That group distributed *The Proposed Parkway for Philadelphia: A Direct Thoroughfare from the Public Buildings to the Green Street Entrance of Fairmount Park* (1902), a descriptively titled volume that laid out a logical case for the concourse. The Art Federation was also joined by the City Parks Association and the Fairmount Park Art Association in lobbying for the Parkway.

All this must have helped, for the municipal government authorized the placing "on the city plan of an avenue or parkway between City Hall and Fairmount Park" on March 28, 1903. This was followed by a loan ordinance that committed the first public money appropriated for the Fairmount Parkway. Bonds were issued, and, from these, $1 million was allocated for acquiring property. The sum was huge for a city construction project of that period, but it would be followed in subsequent years by requests for more funding.

The boulevard's routing was confirmed shortly after this. Yet its planned axis tracked Pennsylvania Avenue, about a block farther north than where the Parkway would eventually come to be, so as to avoid disturbing a number of factories too costly to procure. This misalignment caused much trouble in the undertaking's early stages, since some buildings wound up being purchased and removed unnecessarily.

In any case, ground was finally broken on February 22, 1907, when the first brick was ceremoniously knocked off a house chimney at 422 North Twenty-second Street. Philadelphia mayor John E. Reyburn, taking office that April, ensured that the Parkway would be brought to fruition. He wholeheartedly supported the roadway and also made sure that its skewed bearing was corrected.

Architects Horace Trumbauer, Clarence C. Zantzinger, and Paul P. Crét produced a formal Parkway proposal for the Fairmount Park Art Association in December 1907. Their vision was for a wide diagonal lane fronted by monumental edifices as it proceeded en route to Fairmount Park. This pleasure drive, America's version of Paris's Avenue des Champs-Élysées, included an open vista from which to admire Philadelphia City Hall (never before viewable in its entirety) and an imperial plaza that would face the projected art museum atop Fairmount hill. Rendered by Paul Crét, the drawings laid out a direct axis between city hall and the future museum, thus ignoring Pennsylvania Avenue and mirroring the Parkway's final path.

The first city planning exhibition in America was held at Philadelphia City Hall on May 15–17, 1911, during the Third National Conference on City Planning. Among other things, the exhibition sought to educate Philadelphians about the city's plans for the Fairmount Parkway. It featured a 30-foot model of the drive that demonstrated what the spending of so much municipal money would accomplish. One conference speaker stated, "The whole improvement that the city proposes to make is not a street 140 or 250 feet wide, but a certain area of open space surrounded by buildings."

Much of the northwest sector of downtown Philadelphia was transformed over the next 20 years. The city ultimately condemned and demolished some two dozen city blocks—nearly 2,000 modest row homes, shops, and warehouses in all. It resold properties alongside the corridor to private developers to help fund the bold work. Meanwhile, stingy civic reformers tried to derail the undertaking, and a multitude of legal controversies and construction changes hindered progress. Graft and corruption also became entrenched in the project.

The Fairmount Park Commission, which was in charge of Parkway construction by 1917, later adopted a revised scheme set forth by Jacques Gréber, a French landscape architect and city planner. According to David B. Brownlee in his 1989 book *Building the City Beautiful: The Benjamin Franklin Parkway and the Philadelphia Museum of Art*, Gréber devised a sparse boulevard running through a wedge of parkland lined on either side with a few cultural edifices, unlike the dense urban avenue submitted by Trumbauer, Zantzinger, and Crét. Rather than bringing the packed metropolis out to Fairmount Park, he sought to bring the tranquil park into town.

Jacques Gréber drafted a set of large-scale drawings and watercolors for the Fairmount Park Commission that revealed two linear segments of the roadbed, with the narrower section running from Philadelphia City Hall to Logan Square and the wider portion (with median strips and outer drives flanked by secondary roadways) proceeding from the square to the planned Philadelphia Museum of Art. Additionally, his design for an elegant traffic circle within Logan Square was approved on June 12, 1918. Gréber imagined that this element would be comparable to the Place de la Concorde, a major public space in Paris along the Champs-Élysées.

The Fairmount Park Art Association soon published *The Fairmount Parkway: A Pictorial Record of Development from Its First Incorporation in the City Plan in 1904 to the Completion of the Main Drive from City Hall to Fairmount Park in 1919*. In this book, the organization's president stated that the Parkway furnished "a direct, dignified and interesting approach from the heart of the business and administrative quarter of the city, through the region of educational activities grouped about

Logan Square, to the great artistic center that is about to be developed around the Fairmount Plaza, at the entrance to Philadelphia's largest and most beautiful park."

Less indulgent observers noted that the Parkway was the most expensive mile of city street ever built anywhere. Costs had mounted to about $22 million by 1920. Nevertheless, the Parkway's construction was deemed—at least by Philadelphia boosters of the 1920s—as the greatest 20th-century accomplishment of any city in the world.

More than a few public fountains and works of art were installed along with the construction of the Parkway and its constituent buildings. These monuments and statuary include masterworks by artists like Auguste Rodin, R. Tait McKenzie, Albert Laessle, Augustus Saint-Gaudens, J. Otto Schweizer, Rudolf Siemering, Nathan Rapoport, Paul Manship, Emmanuel Frémiet, and three generations of the Calder family of sculptors. The esplanade therefore became a vast sculptural garden besides a mere transportation route, as art was integrated with architecture and landscape as City Beautiful aspects of the project.

Fairmount Parkway was the first of a series of radiating arteries proposed for William Penn's city by the Delaware River. Contemplated as far back as the 1880s, these broad diagonal thoroughfares were seen as a way to contend with the stiff orderliness of Philadelphia's gridiron layout. The avenues were intended to add European sophistication and grandeur to the metropolis and were considered the chief municipal components of Philadelphia's City Beautiful efforts. However, thoughts of these other slanted roadways were forgotten due to the Great Depression and World War II, as well as an overall lack of interest.

Civic indifference and poor economic conditions similarly induced many cultural and public institutions to abandon plans to move to the Parkway. Consequently, the street has never been regarded as truly finished, even though it was essentially complete by 1920 and many of its anticipated attractions were realized within a decade and a half.

Modifications have been made since the 1930s, such as the adding of Eakins Oval (a traffic loop), the subterranean slash of the Vine Street Expressway, and the replacement of original traffic fixtures, park benches, and aging paulownia trees along the way. Even the Fairmount Parkway's name was officially changed in 1937 to honor the city's most illustrious denizen, Benjamin Franklin. Still, the boulevard has proven remarkably resilient to revision, and laws protect its aesthetic values. Setback requirements and height limitations, for example, apply to structures within 200 feet of the concourse.

Local, national, and international visitors to the Parkway can see some of Philadelphia's most acclaimed institutions related to arts and science. The Philadelphia Museum of Art, the Academy of Natural Sciences, and the Franklin Institute Science Museum are the primary attractions of Museum Mile. Plus, the Barnes Foundation, with its superb collection of French impressionist and postimpressionist masterpieces, arrived in 2012. Along with the flags of countries from around the globe that line the route, the new Barnes museum has increased the international standing of Philadelphia's Champs-Élysées.

The Central Library of the Free Library of Philadelphia and its near twin, the former Philadelphia County/Family Court building, sit close. These two Beaux Arts palaces are joined by the Rodin Museum (another of Museum Mile's international gems), the Cathedral Basilica of Saints Peter and Paul (the oldest building on the Parkway), and the new Mormon Temple of Philadelphia (opening soon). Nearby are several other religious and educational institutions, including Race Street Friends Meetinghouse, Friends Select School, and Moore College of Art and Design. All of these venues help make the Benjamin Franklin Parkway one of the most culturally developed pieces of real estate in the world.

The string of impressive office buildings, hotels, condominiums, and apartment complexes lining the Parkway should not be overlooked, either. More residential structures are being erected throughout the Logan Square district as investment opportunities arise and the local population increases. Most recently, a $140-million combined apartment and supermarket complex has been approved for the Art Museum/Fairmount neighborhood. In addition, the Church of Jesus Christ of Latter-day Saints announced plans to build a high-rise residential tower in the area, and the old Family Court Building is set to be transformed into an $85-million Kimpton Hotel. When that happens, more people will be able to see the courthouse's collection of murals painted under the Works Progress Administration.

Even the world-famous "Rocky Steps" and the inspiring *Rocky* statue make their home on this stretch of distinguished road. Curiously, Philadelphia's most popular and world-renowned figures—William Penn, Benjamin Franklin, and Rocky Balboa—are united along the Parkway by the Parkway itself.

The Ben Franklin Parkway has been serving for years as Philadelphia's principal venue for music spectacles. The Made in America festivals are the latest sizable concerts to have been held on the esplanade, while the Million Woman March, in 1997, and Live 8 are singular national mega-events that have been observed there. An estimated 900,000 people jammed the Parkway on July 2, 2005, for the only Live 8 benefit concert held in the United States.

Philadelphia's Champs-Élysées also hosts the city's many ethnic celebrations and the oldest Thanksgiving Day parade in America. The annual Thanksgiving event sees the thoroughfare filled with giant balloons and floats, along with performers from dance groups, marching bands, and choirs. Plus, Santa Claus arrives to usher Philadelphia into the holiday season.

Regrettably, the Parkway's gradual transformation into a major commuter artery has compromised the regal ambiance and civic pride that it was initially meant to impart. Some 30,000 vehicles zoom up and down the street every day, making it more a multilane speedway leading into and out of town than a stately drive heading leisurely toward Fairmount Park. Worse yet is the virtual absence of pedestrian activity.

Various parties have proposed strategies to mitigate the avenue's inhospitable traffic issues and its lack of amenities west of Logan Circle. Penn Praxis, part of the School of Design at the University of Pennsylvania, has recently put forward a series of measures to enhance the Parkway as a commons for citizens to use and enjoy. The 2013 plan goes by the clever and fitting moniker, *More Park, Less Way: An Action Plan to Increase Urban Vibrancy on the Benjamin Franklin Parkway.*

Some 65 acres of open ground will soon be redesigned into usable green space, providing a variety of food kiosks, children's play areas, and other recreational zones for the 70,000 Philadelphians who live within a 10-minute walk. And the pedestrian experience of traversing the congested route will finally receive attention, for the plan incorporates improved crosswalks and traffic-calming features around Eakins Oval and other intersections. Bicycle lanes connecting Spring Garden Street to the multiuse trail along the Schuylkill River are envisioned as well.

A coalition of institutions and businesses called the Parkway Council Federation advocates for improvements like the ones outlined in *More Park, Less Way.* In 2003, the council created the Parkway Museum District to ensure that Philadelphia's Museum Mile realizes its role as a truly unique local, regional, and national cultural destination. This work has become critical as a celebration draws near to mark the Parkway's centennial in 2017.

Since 2000, the Parkway has already seen upwards of $80 million in public and private investment. The relocation of the Barnes and the renovation of the Rodin Museum are the foremost developments, but the recent makeovers of Dilworth Plaza, Three Parkway Plaza, Aviator Park, and Sister Cities Plaza—the latter two parks are within Logan Square, which was fully relandscaped by 2006—must also be mentioned. Add to this list the creation of Paine's Skatepark and the overhaul of Eakins Oval, which has already brought a temporary "pop-up" park to a rebranded space dubbed "The Oval." Love Park's revamping, the expansion of the Central Library, and the capping of parts of the Vine Street Expressway are still being planned. Altogether, this is the lively and ever-changing Benjamin Franklin Parkway of the 21st century.

The picture postcards and other images in this work show that the Parkway has been an integral part of Philadelphia's civic and cultural life for nearly 100 years. Taking decades to complete despite corruption, depression, and war, the tree-lined drive is a triumph in urban planning welcoming both natives and tourists. The splendid boulevard, at first so contentious, so expensive, and so foreign to the city and its inhabitants, has become a treasured part of the City of Brotherly Love.

One

Plans for the Fairmount Park Parkway

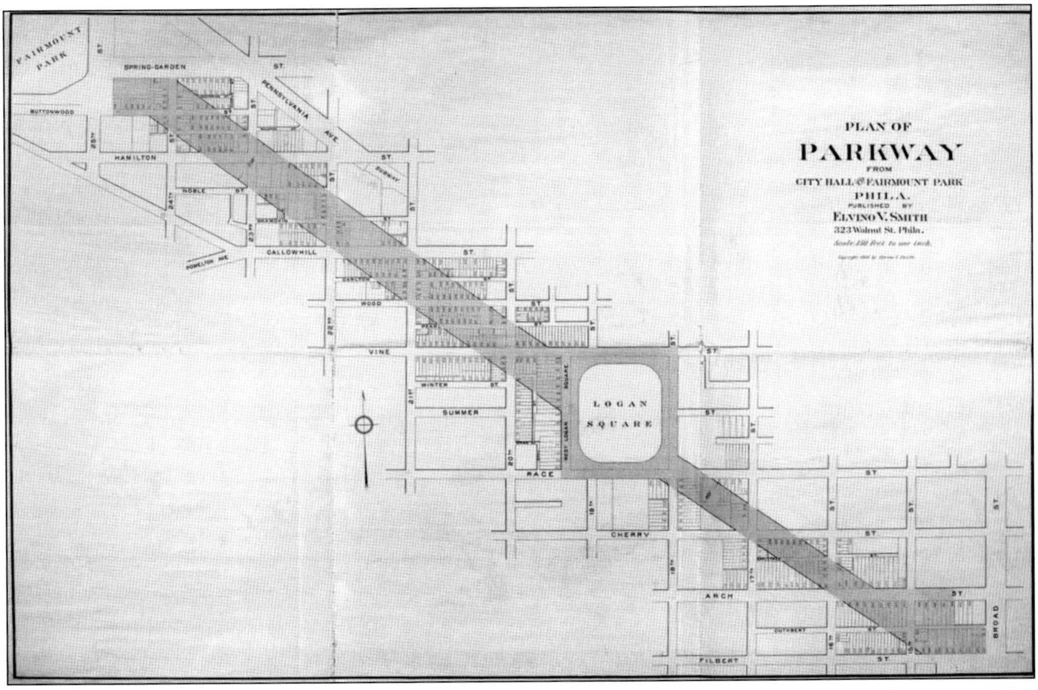

This 1904 "Plan of the Parkway from City Hall to Fairmount Park" shows an early view of the Fairmount Park Parkway's intended route. The trajectory goes through several city blocks that would eventually be eliminated. The roadway was also built much wider than what is manifest here. Not even a shadow of a trace remains of the many dwellings and shops that were removed. (The Library Company of Philadelphia.)

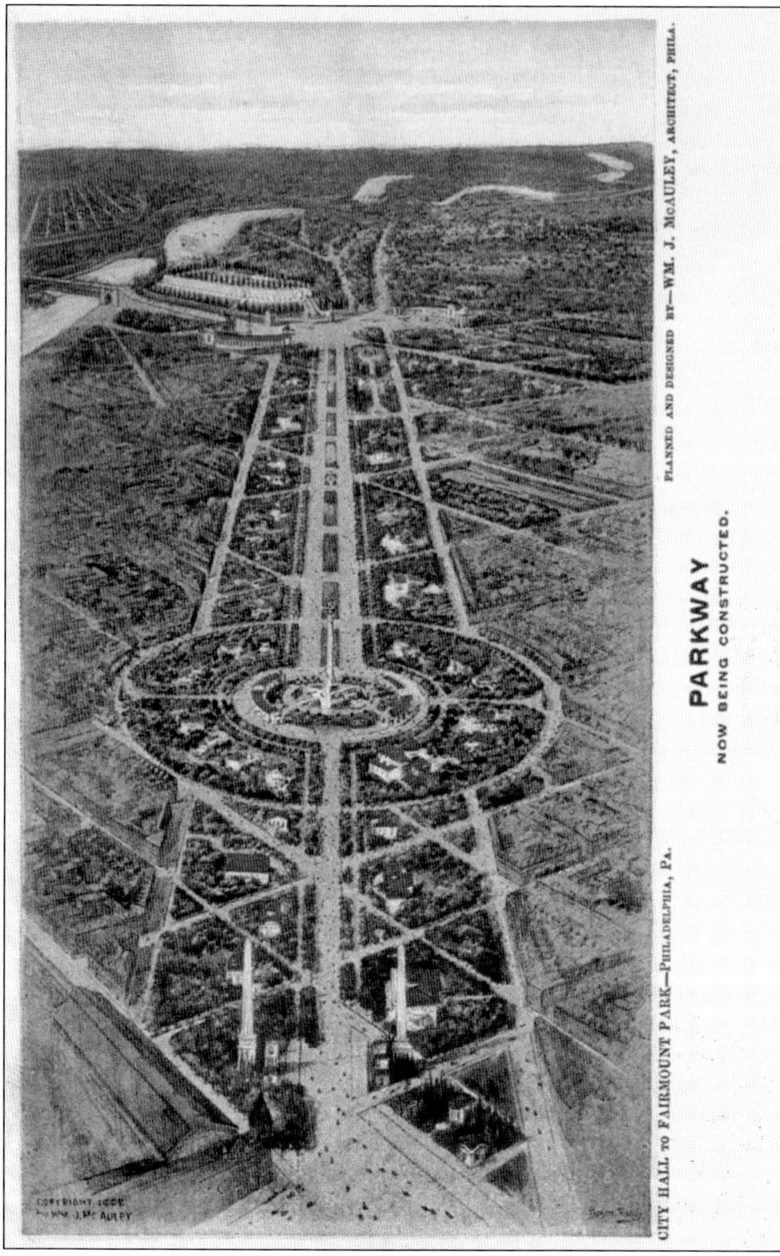

Various groups and individuals made proposals for the Fairmount Parkway in the late 19th and early 20th centuries. This grandiose design, released in 1902 and appearing on a crudely detailed postcard by 1907, is by Philadelphia architect William J. McAuley. The "McAuley Plan" exhibits a total disregard of extant conditions, as the roadway cuts from Philadelphia City Hall in a northwestern direction, albeit slightly north of the eventual route. It also shows Logan Square as a huge circle long before Jacques Gréber became involved in the Parkway project. An engineering journal of the day wrote, "The entire McAuley plan is too elaborate for the financial possibilities of the city at this time, but it is recognized as an artistic conception on a magnificent scale of what could and in future years may possibly be done." (Unmarked postcard; courtesy Gus Spector.)

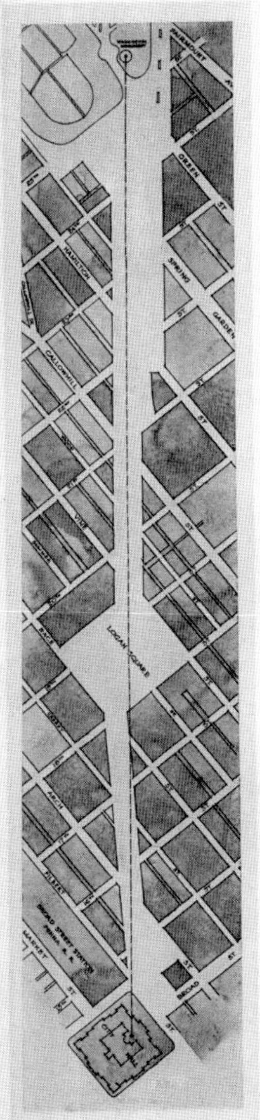

THE PARKWAY
as placed on the City Plan
April 9, 1906

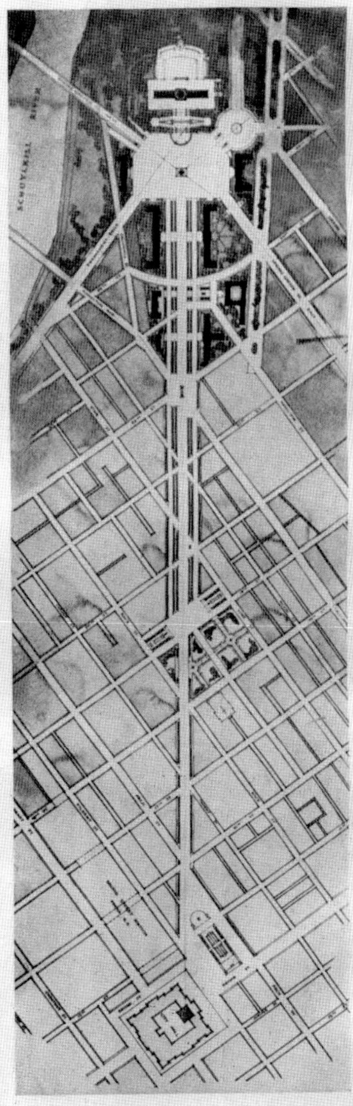

THE PARKWAY
as shown on plan made by Trumbauer,
Zantzinger and Cret for Fairmount Park
Art Association, December 9, 1907

The left drawing shows Fairmount Parkway as it was placed on the city plan on April 9, 1906. It indicates how uncertain the boulevard's path was in the early days of planning: the mile-long route veers north (incorporating Pennsylvania Avenue), and its northwestern terminus is Philadelphia's Washington Monument (at its original location near Green Street). The right diagram shows the thoroughfare as envisioned by architects Trumbauer, Zantzinger, and Crét, who designed a wide diagonal lane fronted by massive edifices. The road's final trajectory was basically established by December 9, 1907. This later drawing also suggests that a bridge over the Schuylkill River to connect with Powelton Avenue in West Philadelphia was contemplated. (Proposed as far back as 1869, this bridge has never been built.) Along with others in this chapter, this image is from *The Fairmount Parkway: A Pictorial Record of Development from Its First Incorporation in the City Plan in 1904 to the Completion of the Main Drive from City Hall to Fairmount Park in 1919.*

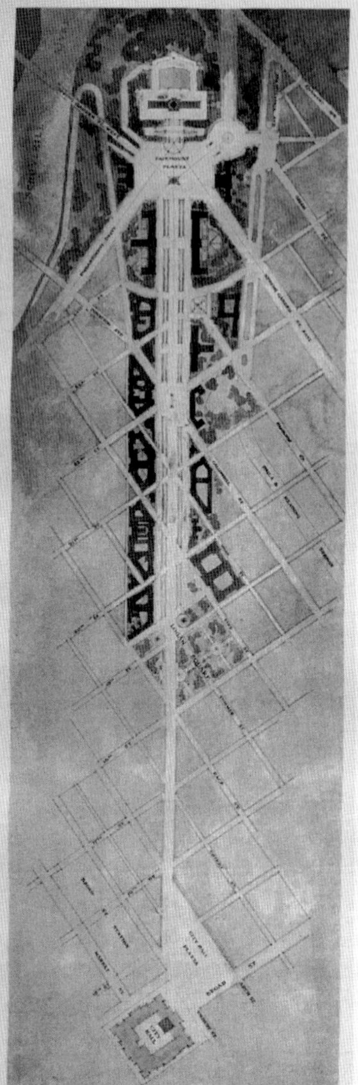

THE PARKWAY
as shown on revised plan recommended by
Mayor Reyburn in his annual message for 1908
and substantially placed on the City Plan in 1909

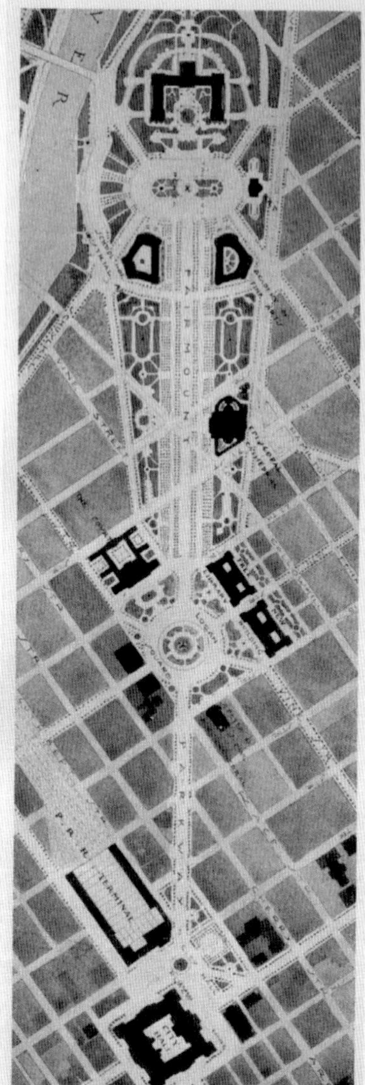

THE PARKWAY
as shown on plan made by Jacques Gréber
for the Commissioners of Fairmount Park in 1917
and now in course of construction

The Parkway's revised plan (left) was placed on the city plan in 1909 after being advocated by Mayor John E. Reyburn, a keen backer of the avenue. Cultural and educational institutions are shown lining the route, although most were never built. By 1917 (right), the Parkway had taken on the more open feel it has today with the work of a new designer, Jacques Gréber. Rather than bringing the city out to Fairmount Park, Gréber sought to bring the park into the city. Logan Square had also reached its projected size, and a substantial traffic island had materialized. This was Gréber's idea, as it mirrors the Place de la Concorde, a major public space in Paris along the Avenue des Champs-Élysées. An enormous Episcopal cathedral was to have been erected at Twenty-first Street, and the Pennsylvania Academy of the Fine Arts was to have moved to Twenty-third Street.

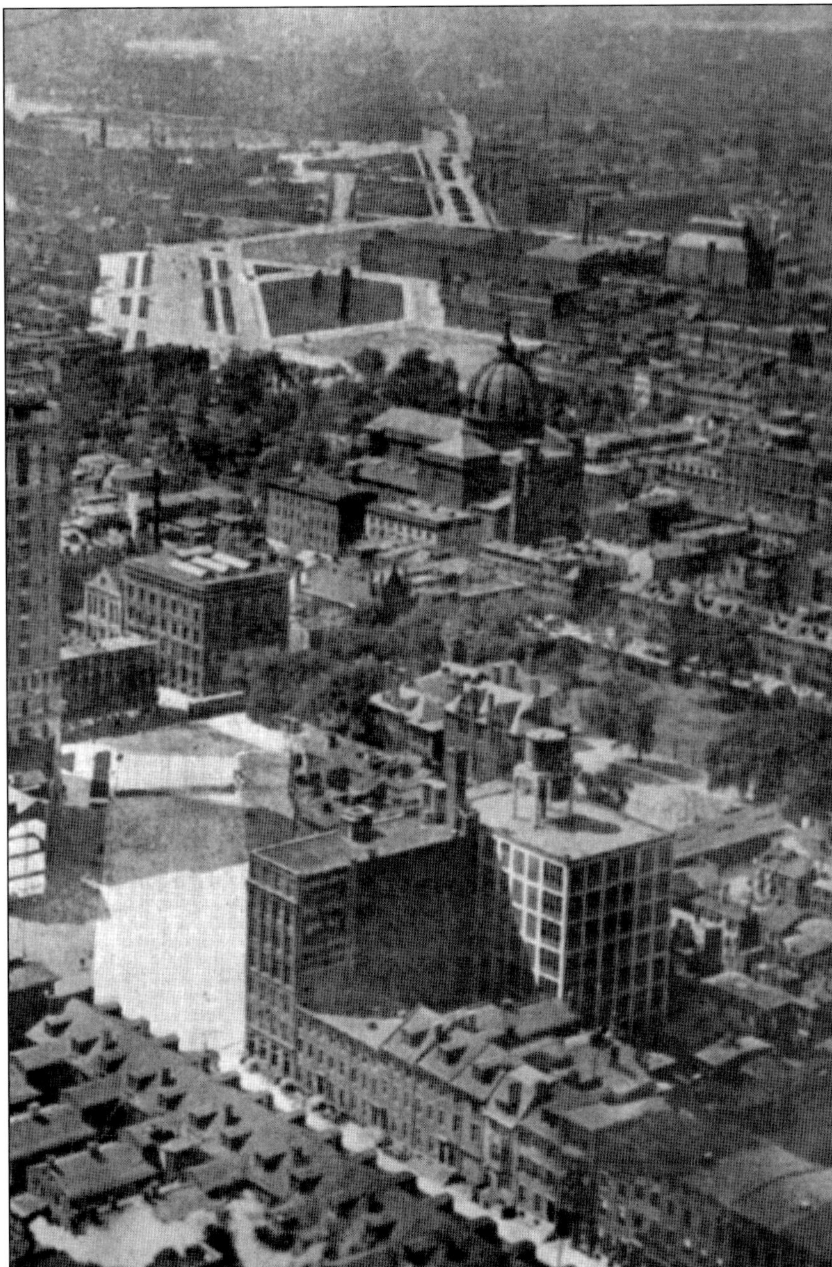

Some progress had been made in creating Fairmount Parkway by 1916, when this photograph was taken. The project was Philadelphia's earliest major attempt at slum clearance and urban renewal. A swath of some 1,500 Victorian row homes, grocery stores, churches, boardinghouses, corner bars, shops, and factories were taken down. Indeed, many expansive manufactories can be seen on the right (north) side of this image. The dome of the Cathedral of Saints Peter and Paul is visible in the upper center; it is one of the few structures pictured that still stands today. In the distance, the Philadelphia Museum of Art has yet to emerge on the site of the group of reservoirs that formerly served the Fairmount Water Works. To the right of that area is Pennsylvania Avenue, which was the Parkway's original course in the earliest years of its planning and construction.

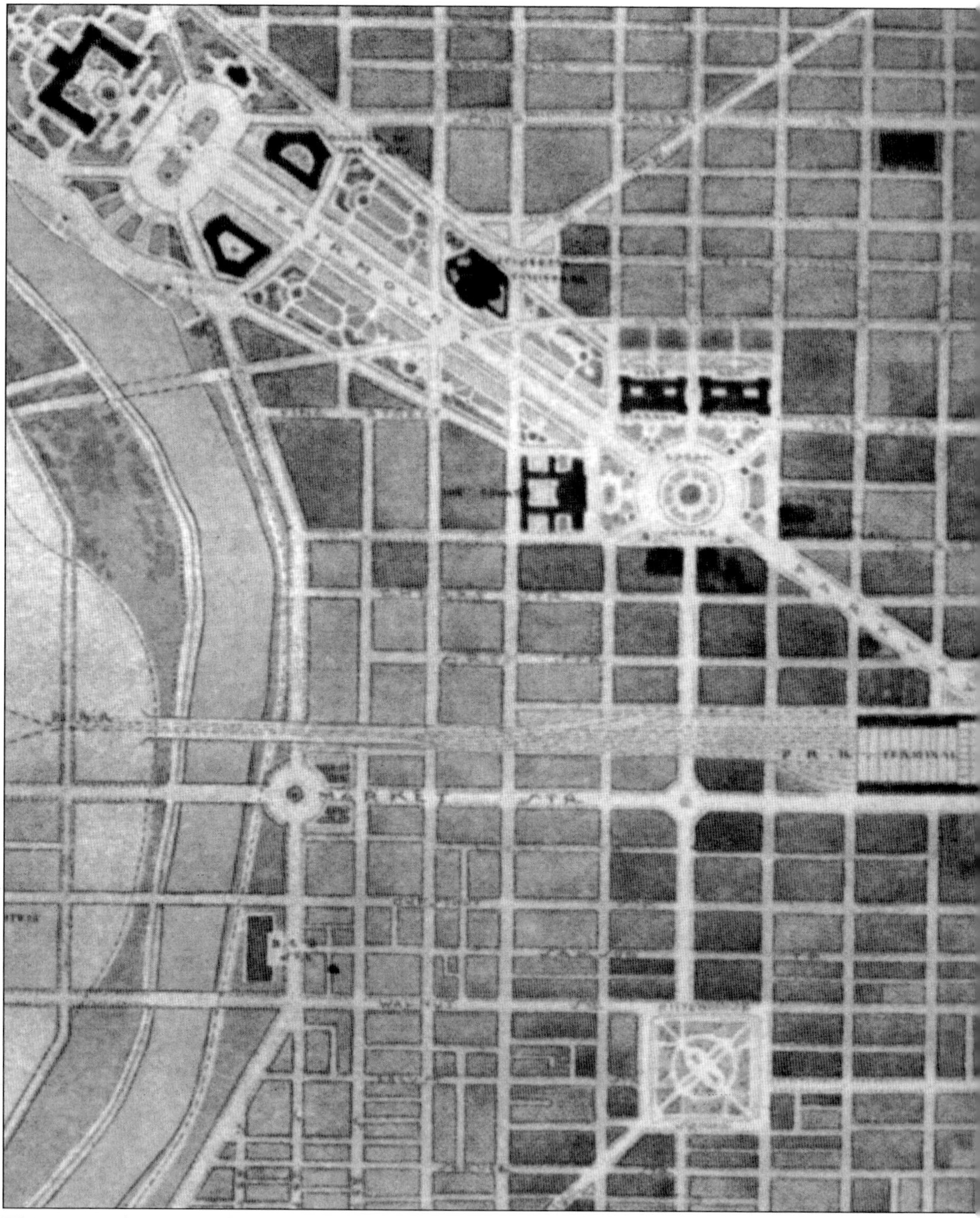

This cropped version of a 1917 Jacques Gréber watercolor illustrates the completed Parkway. It shows the roadway's western extremity, Fairmount Plaza, directly in front of the proposed museum of art. Gréber depicted Fairmount Plaza as an ornate place with the Washington Monument positioned between two fountains. In 1934, the first fount was installed alongside the fantastic equestrian memorial. As is evident, the plan was for all major streets in the area to connect to this large traffic device. Fairmount Plaza lasted for a few decades before being replaced with Eakins

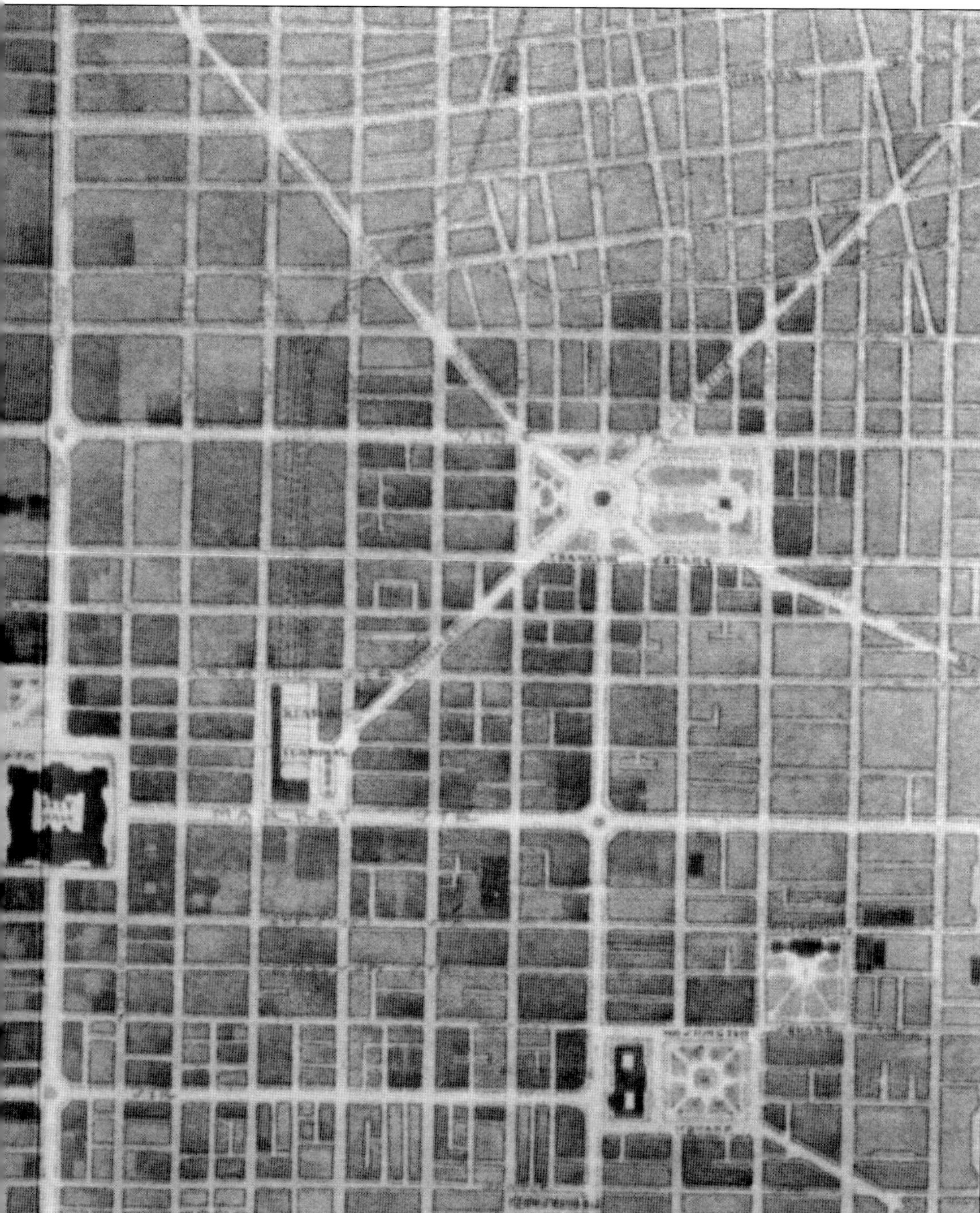

Oval, an even larger traffic device. This was in the 1960s, at which time the second fountain was installed. The watercolor also highlights some of the other slanting avenues proposed for Philadelphia under the City Beautiful Movement, the urban planning mindset fashionable at the time. Fairmount Parkway was the only such thoroughfare ever realized.

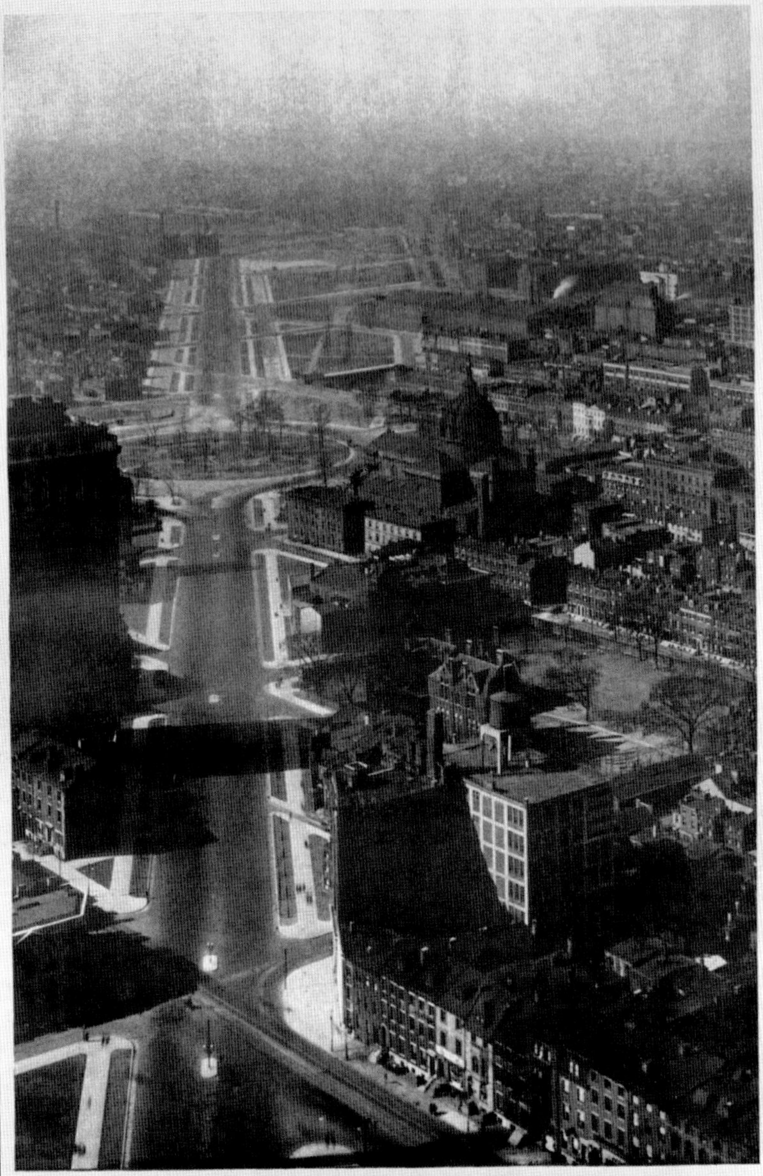

Photograph of the Parkway in course of construction
taken from top of City Hall tower in 1919

Fairmount Parkway's layout was more or less finished just three years later, although many buildings remained to be removed on either side of the boulevard between Philadelphia City Hall and Logan Square. Numerous buildings were trimmed and re-walled because the skewed roadway's construction extracted a wall or two (or more). Additionally, Logan Square had reached its current size by 1919, and a traffic circle has appeared, but Swann Memorial Fountain was not yet installed. On the horizon, the Philadelphia Museum of Art would soon rise on the site of the water-settling basins resting atop Fairmount hill. Oddly, this photograph taken from City Hall Tower shows no motor vehicles of any sort on the brand-new Parkway. This would certainly change in years to come.

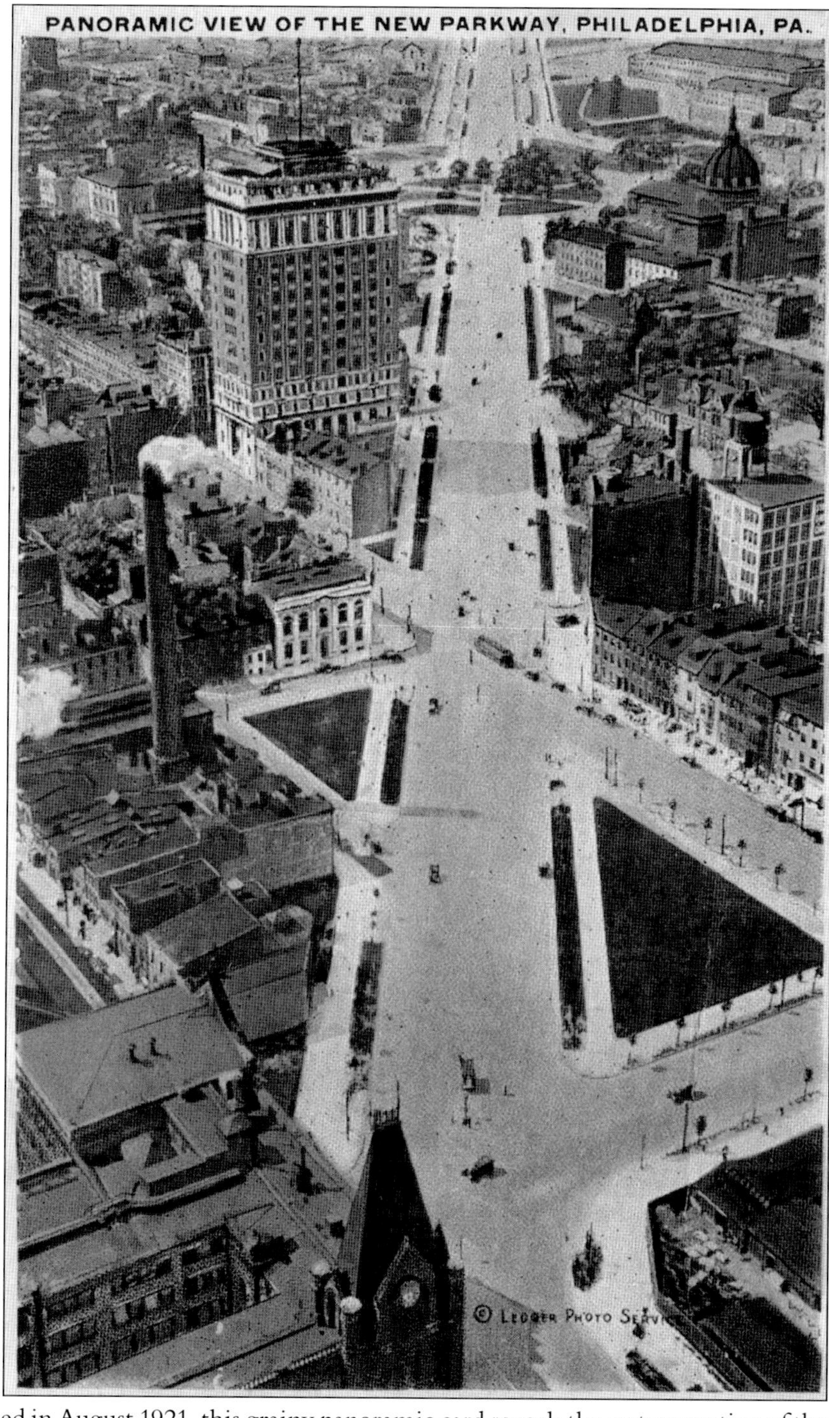

Postmarked in August 1921, this grainy panoramic card reveals the eastern section of the complete Fairmount Parkway. Many buildings flanking the wide avenue, however, are yet to be razed. The Pennsylvania Railroad's Broad Street Station is on the bottom left, clearly in the way of the Parkway's path approaching Philadelphia City Hall. It would be demolished years later because of this and other reasons. (Ledger Photo Service.)

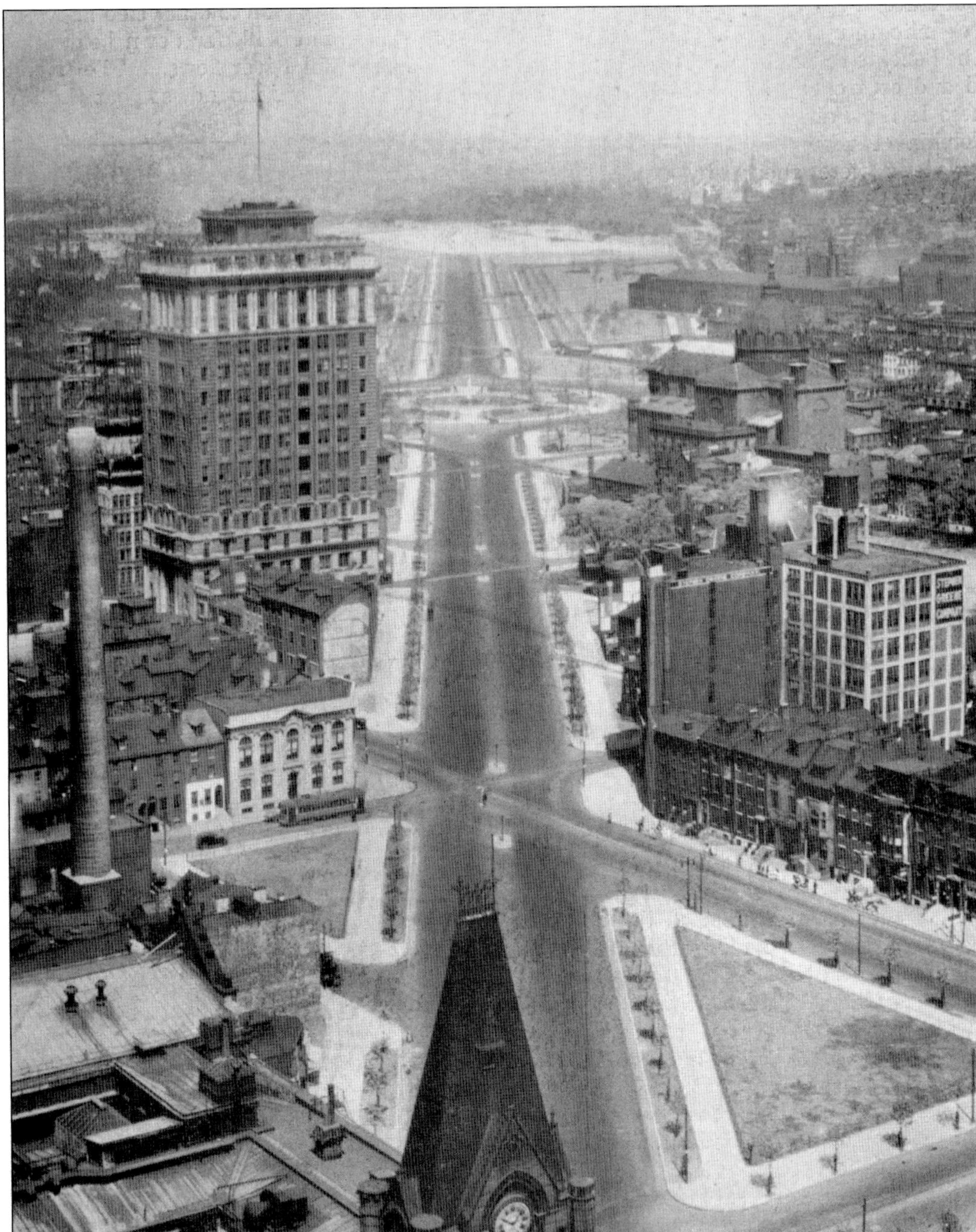

This 1922 photograph shows the Parkway looking new and inviting, but, again, not a single motor vehicle is on the street. Broad Street Station (and one of its towers) is conspicuously visible at the bottom. The Bell Parkway Building is on the left, and the Cathedral of Saints Peter and Paul is on the right, with Logan Circle in the center. Construction of the Philadelphia Museum of Art had not yet commenced. This image gives an idea as to how many worker homes and other buildings were torn down to create the Parkway.

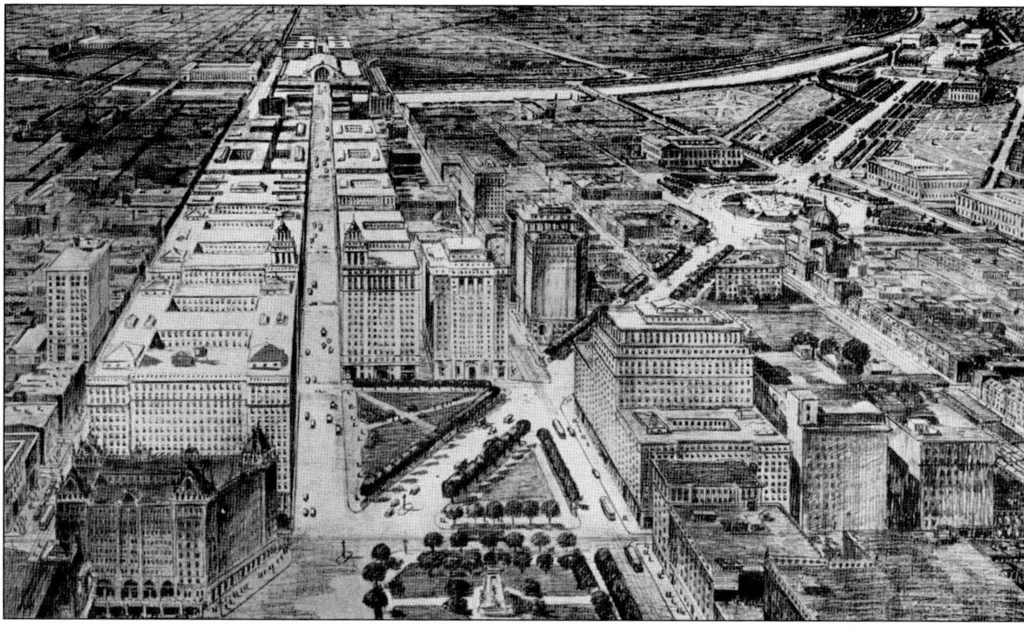

This late-1920s sketch falls under the City Beautiful urban planning movement. It portrays the northwest part of downtown Philadelphia as it was intended to become. The Parkway serves as a direct route toward Fairmount Park, while what became Penn Center is projected as a series of fine Beaux Arts office buildings leading to the Thirtieth Street Station (not yet built), across the Schuylkill River. (Thomas Keels.)

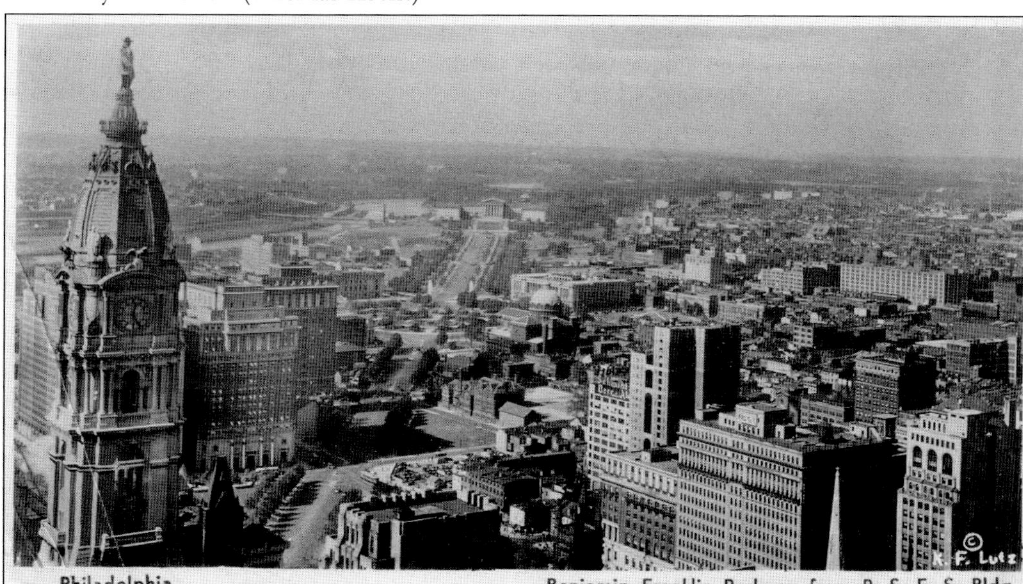

Taken from the renowned Philadelphia Saving Fund Society (PSFS) Building, at Twelfth and Market Streets, this photographic postcard shows the finished Fairmount Parkway and the Philadelphia Museum of Art at the upper center. The PSFS Building, now a Loews Hotel, is 491 feet high; the hat of the William Penn statue (left) atop Philadelphia City Hall is 547 feet high. The card is copyrighted 1937, the same year the Fairmount Parkway's name was changed to honor Benjamin Franklin. (K.F. Lutz, Philadelphia.)

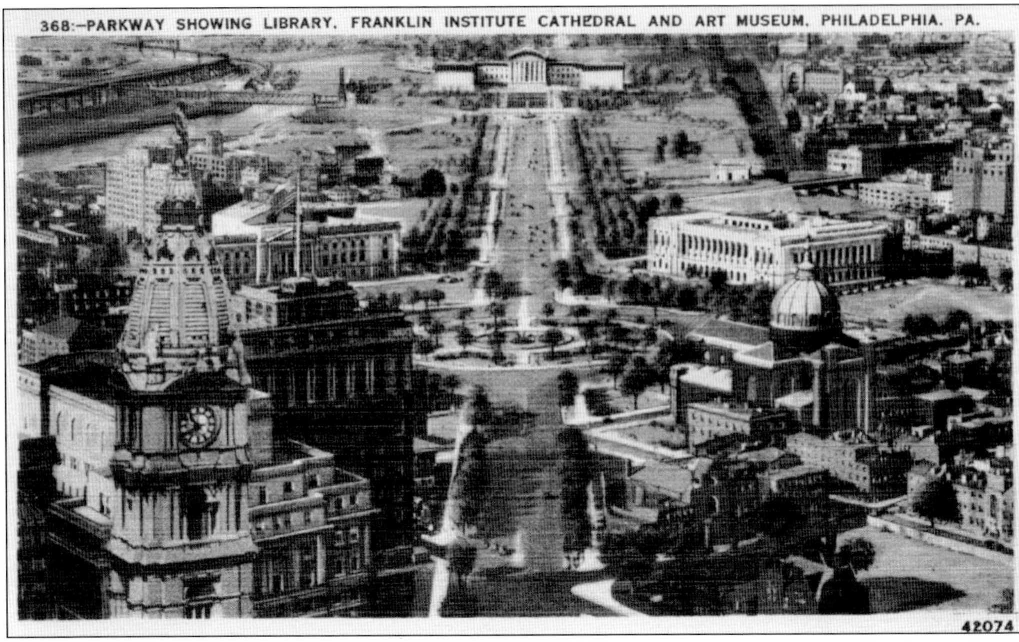

The Depression thwarted construction of many institutional buildings planned for the Parkway, so some dilapidated areas lingered on after the boulevard was completed. This 1930s postcard illustrates, in the center left, the last of the working-class homes, workshops, and warehouses removed for the undertaking. By 1959, that area had become the campus of the Park Towne Place Apartments. (Unmarked postcard.)

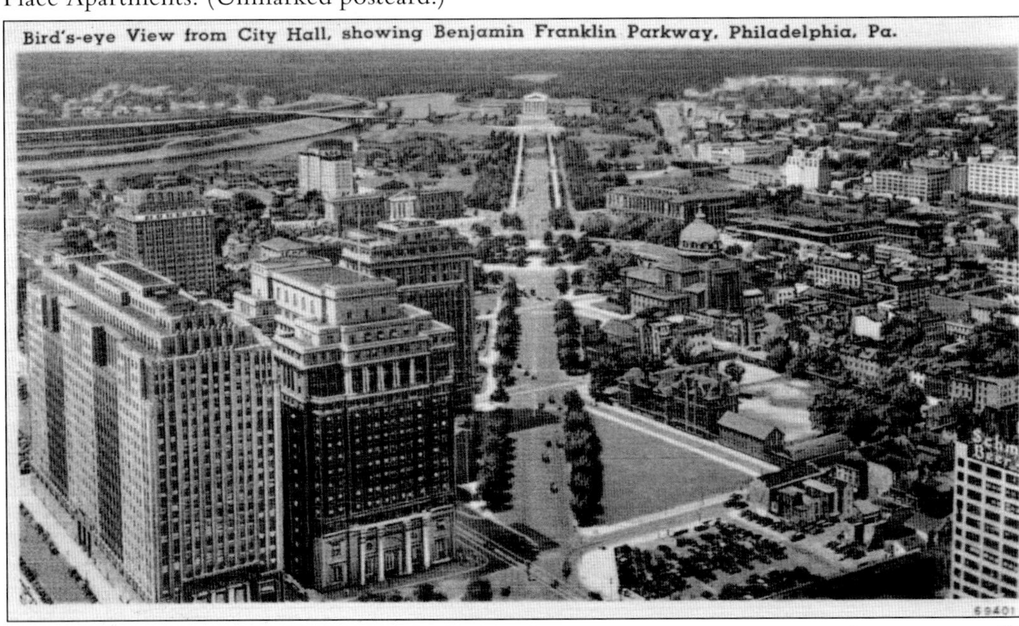

Work on the Family Court building is underway in this "Bird's-eye View from City Hall." Federal money and Works Progress Administration labor was used to raise the edifice, which was built for the Philadelphia Board of County Commissioners as its new courthouse for the Juvenile and Domestic Relations Branches of Municipal Court. This lush card must date to about 1939, since the building was complete in 1941. (Tichnor Brothers.)

Two

Philadelphia City Hall and Penn Square

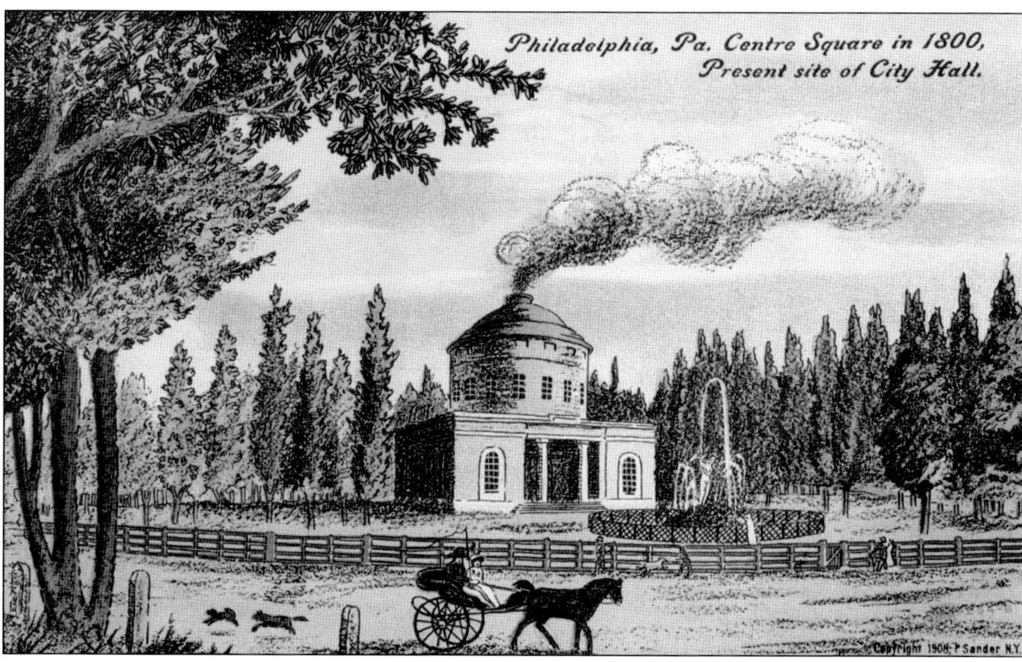

Penn (or Center) Square, the present location of Philadelphia's city hall, was once the site of the city's first waterworks. In 1799, the "Watering Committee" accepted the proposal of architect and engineer Benjamin Henry Latrobe to take water from the Schuylkill River and distribute it throughout the city. This was the nation's first municipal waterworks, completed in 1801. The steam engine of the Center Square Water Works, nicknamed "the pepper box" due to its circular shape, pumped water to an elevated tank from which it flowed by gravity throughout Philadelphia. This innovative system was abandoned in 1815 for a more capable water supply, discussed in chapter 10. Latrobe's marble pump house was dismantled in 1828–1829. (Unmarked postcard.)

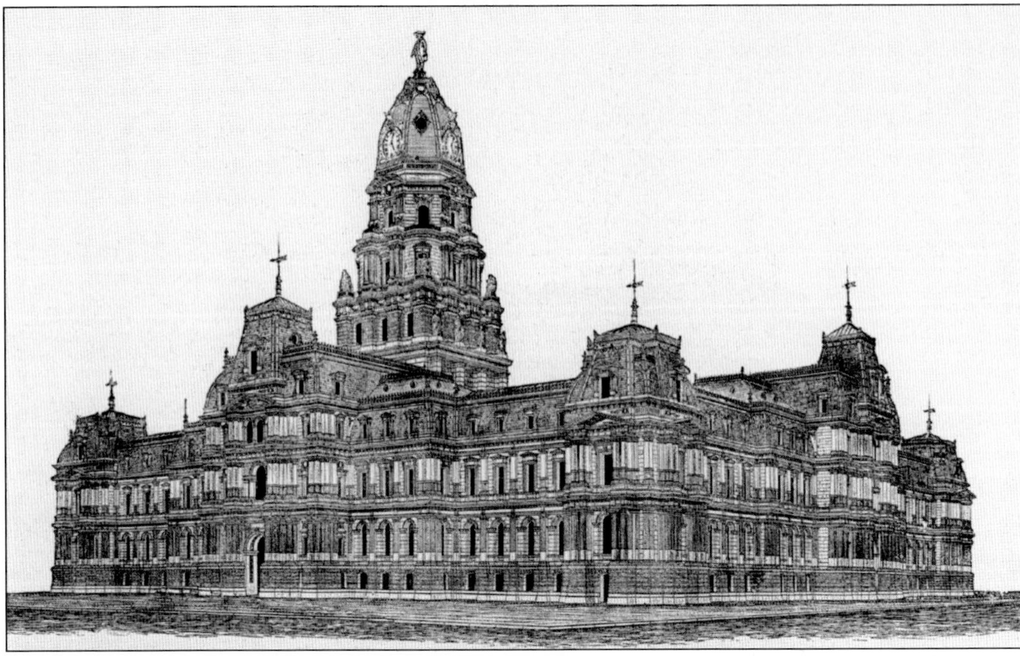

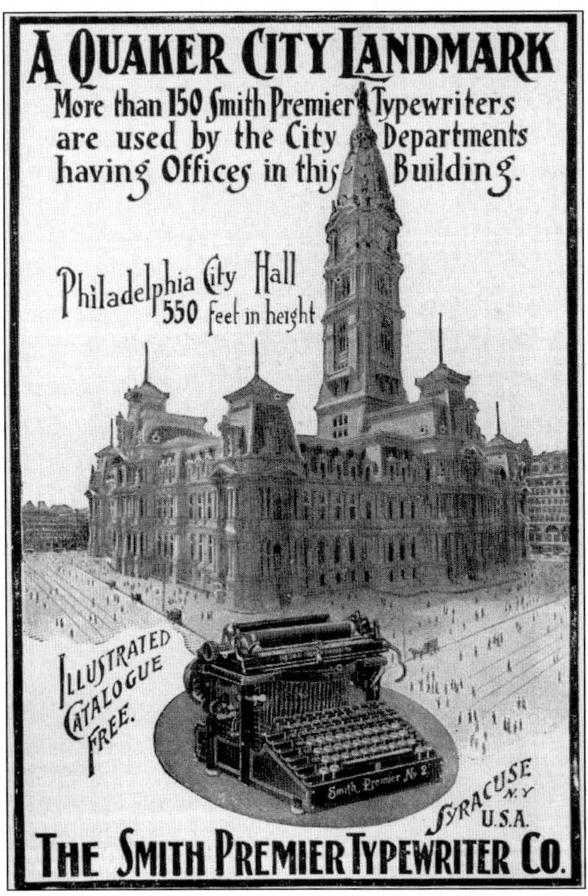

Erected at the intersection of Broad and Market Streets, Philadelphia City Hall (also known as "the Public Buildings") was designed by John McArthur Jr. and several other architects. They kept increasing the tower's height during construction with the hope that it would make city hall the world's tallest structure, which is why the tower looks undersized in this early drawing. The building's cornerstone was laid on July 4, 1874. (Author's collection.)

Philadelphia City Hall is the biggest and best example of French Second Empire architecture in America. It is also the largest governmental building in the nation, even bigger than the US Capitol in Washington, DC. The Public Buildings took some 30 years to build, complete with the usual charges of graft and corruption that public projects have often generated in Philadelphia. Here, the Smith Premier Typewriter Company is using the building's notoriety in this 1903 advertisement. (Author's collection.)

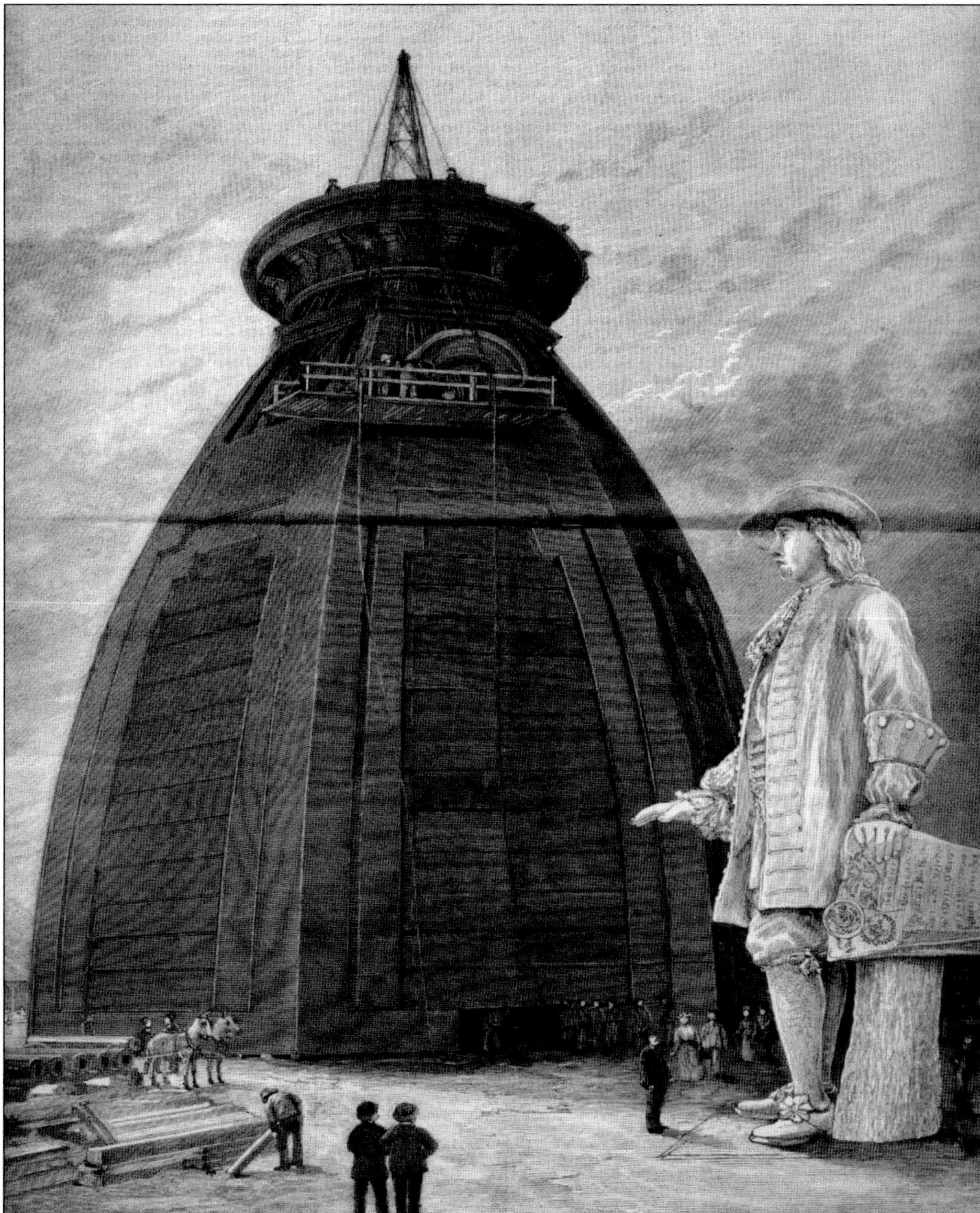

Despite Philadelphia's unpretentious Quaker roots, its city hall was contrived to be huge so as to make a statement about the city's wealth, industrial might, and future aspirations after the Civil War. The building's construction was national news for three decades during the later part of the 19th century. This image was on the cover of the October 29, 1892, issue of *Scientific American*. It shows the cast-iron dome of City Hall Tower and the mammoth statue of William Penn temporarily assembled at the Tacony Iron & Metal Company, where pieces were fitted before being brought to Penn Square by 1894. The bronze statue was "secured together . . . by bolts and rivets passing through inwardly projecting flanges." (Author's collection.)

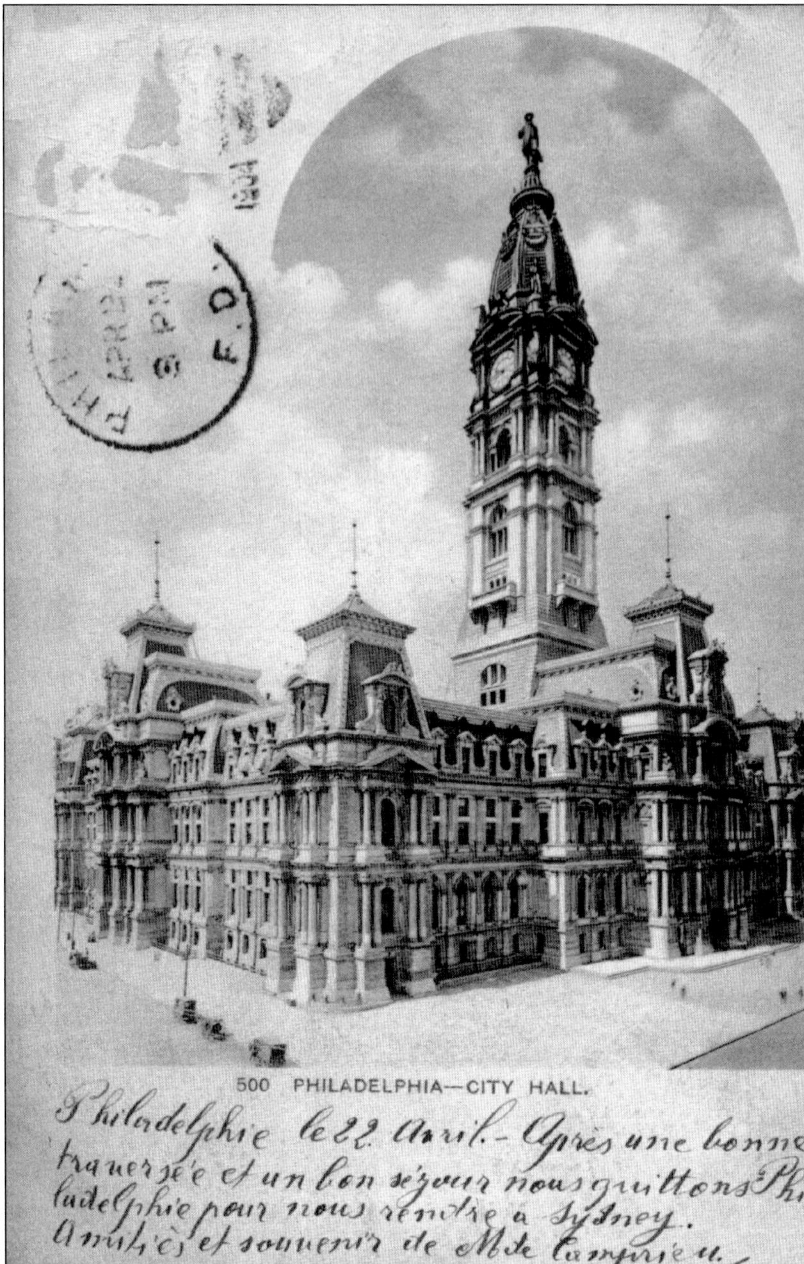

By the time work on the Public Buildings was finished in the early 1900s, the Victorian edifice was derided as a "monumental folly" and a "marble elephant," as well as the "ugliest building in America," a "chamber of horrors," the "great vampire," and worse. There were cries to demolish Philadelphia City Hall even before it was completed. Subsequent plans in the 1920s and again in the 1950s called for the entire structure to be taken down except for the tower, which would have been reclad in a more modern style. The sheer cost of demolition saved city hall at least once. The fabulous building has managed to survive and now flourishes as a beloved part of Philadelphia and its skyline. Note that the writing on this postal card is French; it was mailed to France in 1904. (Unmarked postcard.)

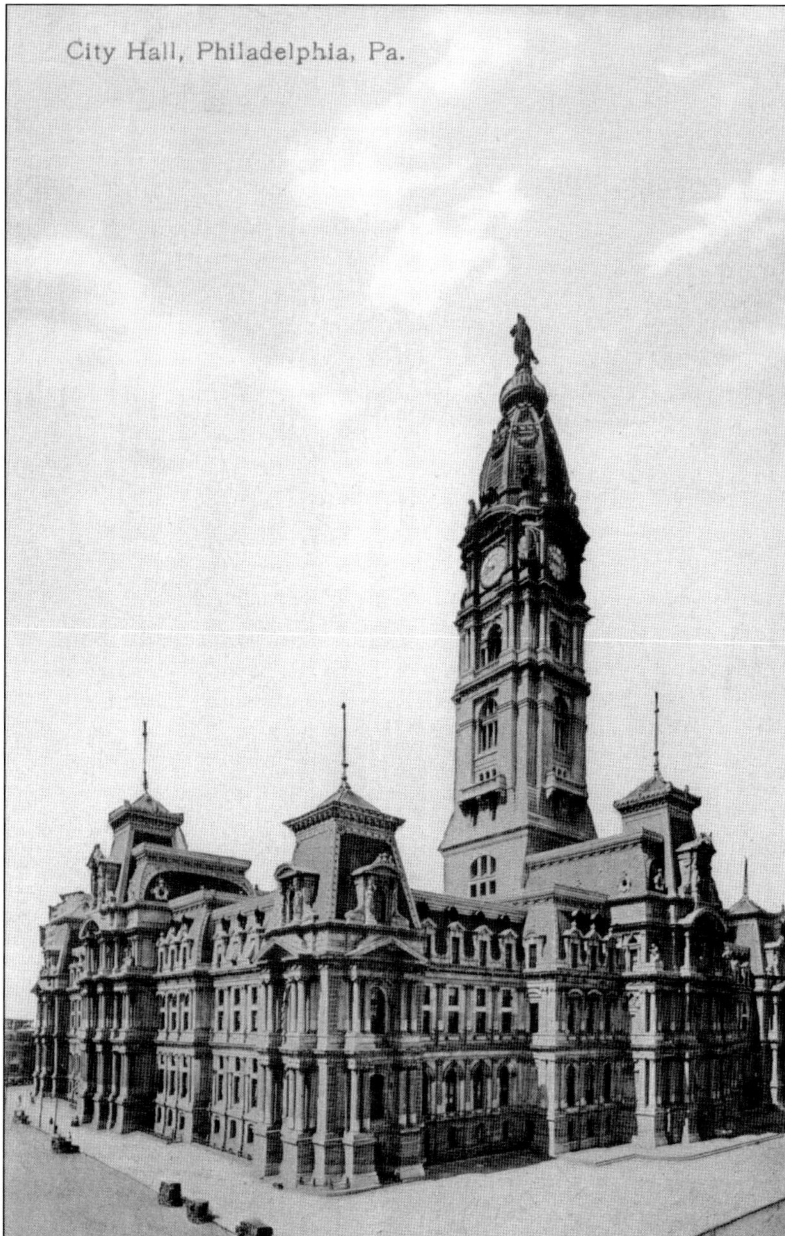

Philadelphia City Hall was at one time the tallest and largest working building in America, not to mention the most expensive—it cost over $24 million in the late 1800s. It became an integral part of the city's political life and a representation of Philadelphia, so much so that the building's image has been placed on countless souvenirs, postcards, and other items for over 100 years. With its mansard roofs, heavy stonework, and lavish ornamentation, the colossal pile mimics the Louvre in Paris. City hall has some 700 rooms, with the mayor's office on the second floor and city council and Pennsylvania Supreme Court chambers on the fourth. In its early years, the Public Buildings housed all departments of city government, including the Philadelphia Police Department. Paddy wagons brought criminals to and from the building via an entrance in the interior courtyard. (Busse Art Card Company, Philadelphia.)

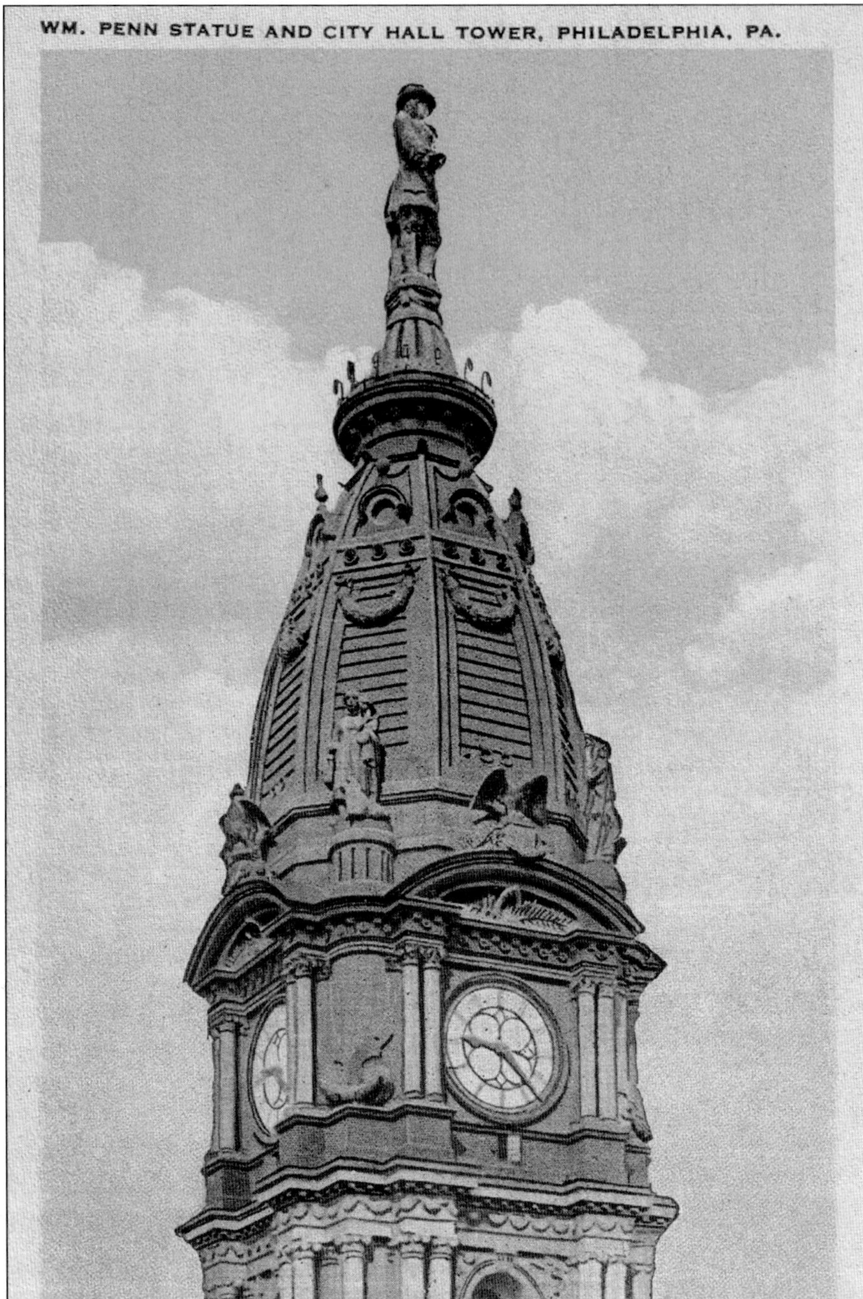

City hall's exterior displays one of the world's most elaborate collections of allegorical sculptures—over 250 pieces of artwork. Alexander Milne Calder was the sculptor of these, as well as the William Penn statue atop the tower. The tower clock consists of four 26-foot-diameter faces, which are among the widest on Earth and are actually larger than those of Big Ben (the Parliament Tower) in London. The minute hand is 15 feet long and weighs 225 pounds. What's more, the clock—at times called "Big Penn" in the distant past—was apparently the world's highest timepiece when it was activated, at midnight on December 31, 1898. (Union News Company.)

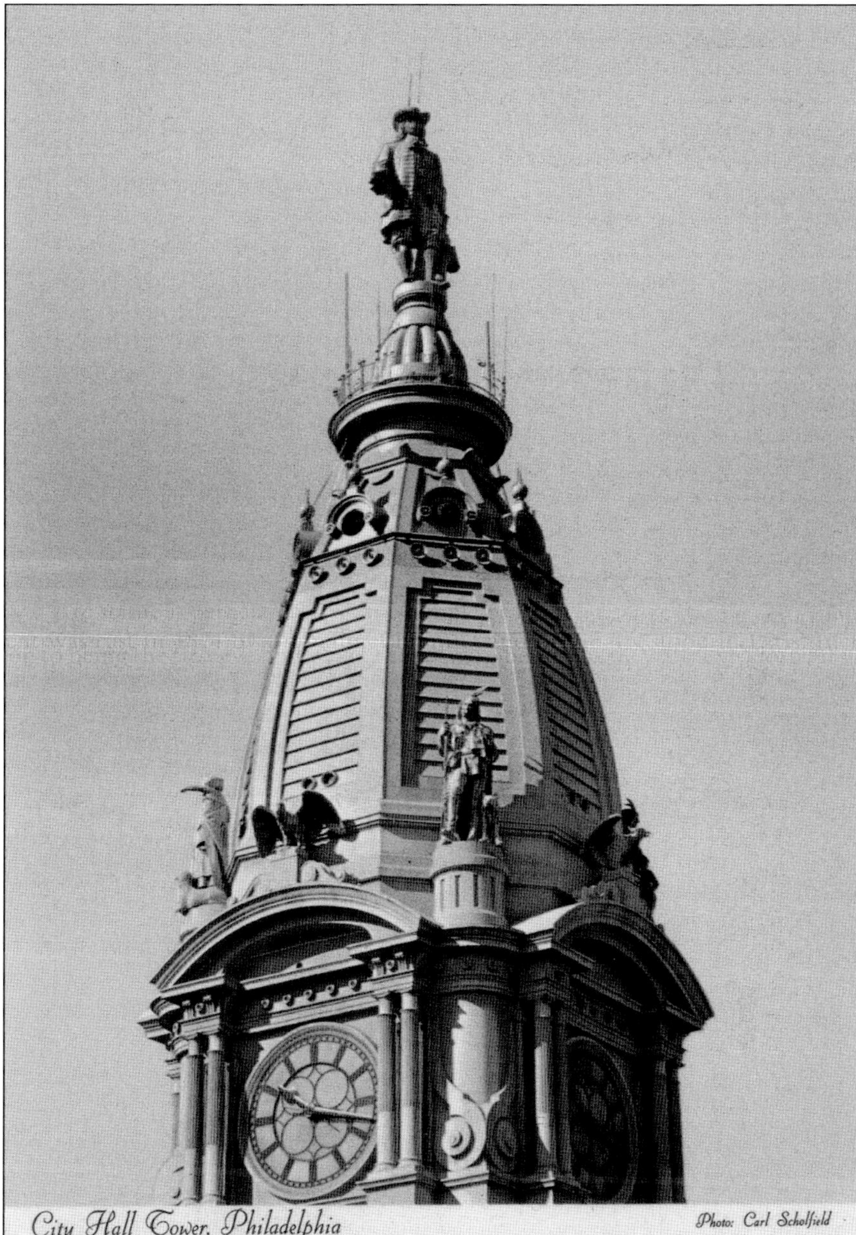

The sculptural collection adorning the Public Buildings, including the gigantic William Penn statue, was the work of Alexander Milne Calder. His son Alexander Stirling Calder designed Swann Memorial Fountain, in Logan Circle, and his grandson Alexander "Sandy" Calder installed the mobile *Ghost* at the Philadelphia Museum of Art. As these three works are all lined up along the Benjamin Franklin Parkway, a local wit once referred to them as "the Father, the Son and the Holy Ghost" (or possibly "Unholy Ghost"). Terrific vistas of Philadelphia can be seen from the tower's observation deck, at the base of the Penn statue (an elevator lifts visitors to just under William Penn's feet). This postcard shows the cluster of antennas that had been mounted in the late 1940s around the statue of William Penn—even, ignobly, on his head/hat. (Carl Scholfield.)

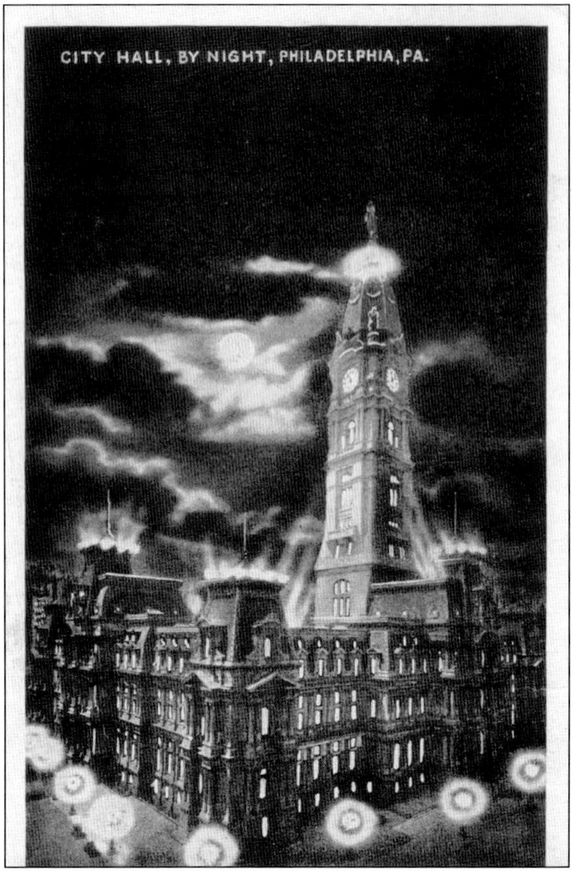

The William Penn statue topping city hall has become a celebrated social, political, and physical reference point for generations of Philadelphians. Early on, the work was encircled by arc lamps that lit the statue every night. The blazing light could be seen up to 30 miles away. This romantic yet somewhat unsettling card features the Public Buildings all lit up around 1919. (Unmarked postcard.)

Keeping an accurate timepiece was difficult in the days before radio, so the City of Philadelphia came up with an ingenious public service in 1906. The arc lamps of City Hall Tower were turned off three minutes before 9:00 p.m. and then re-lit exactly at 9:00, thus broadcasting the correct time once daily. Other accounts allege that the clock face lights were used for this purpose. Whatever the case, this tradition ceased in the 1930s. (Colourpicture.)

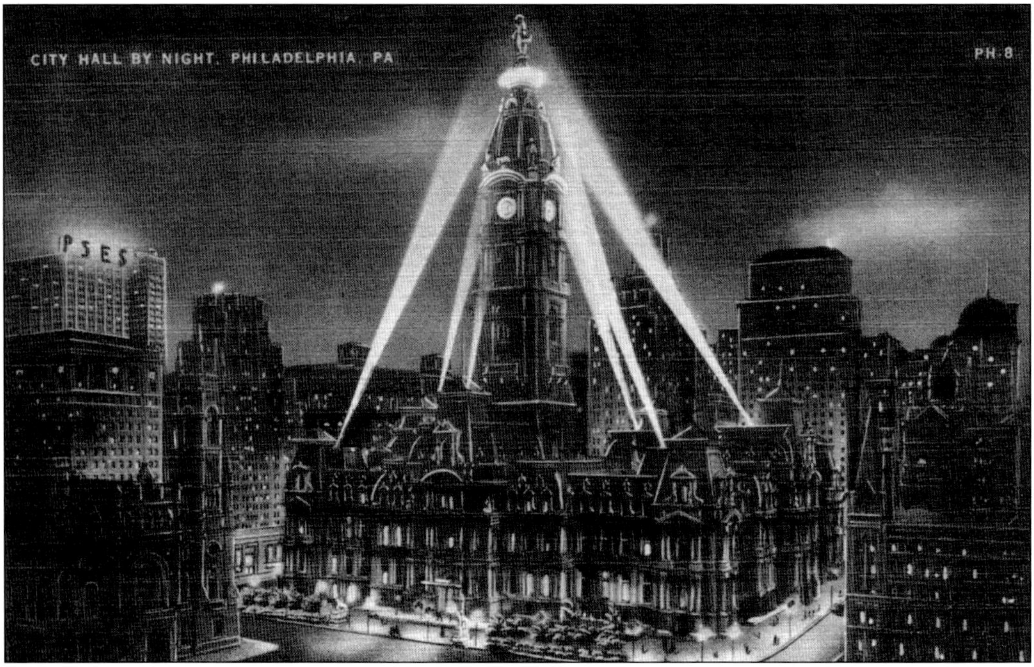

This 1906 card shows the Public Buildings lit in a different manner. The building has been decorated with lights, banners, and flags since the 1890s. One evening while it was under construction, Walt Whitman gazed upon the edifice. It presented "the Good Gray Poet" with "a majestic and lovely show there in the moonlight . . . silent, weird, beautiful." (Philadelphia Post Card Company.)

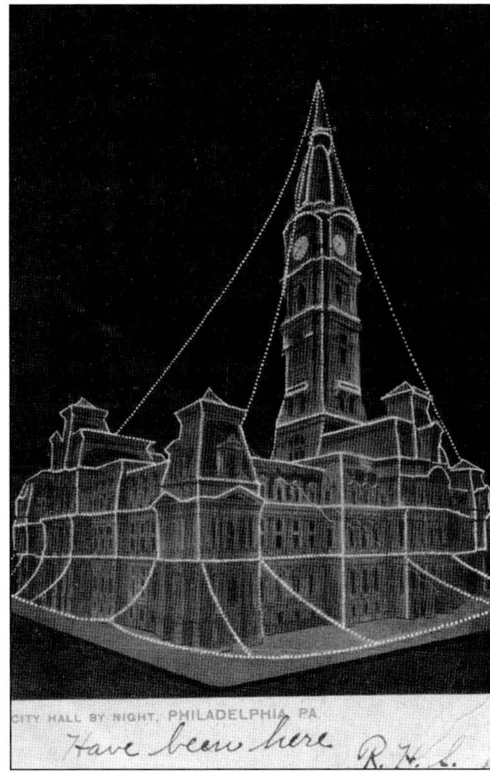

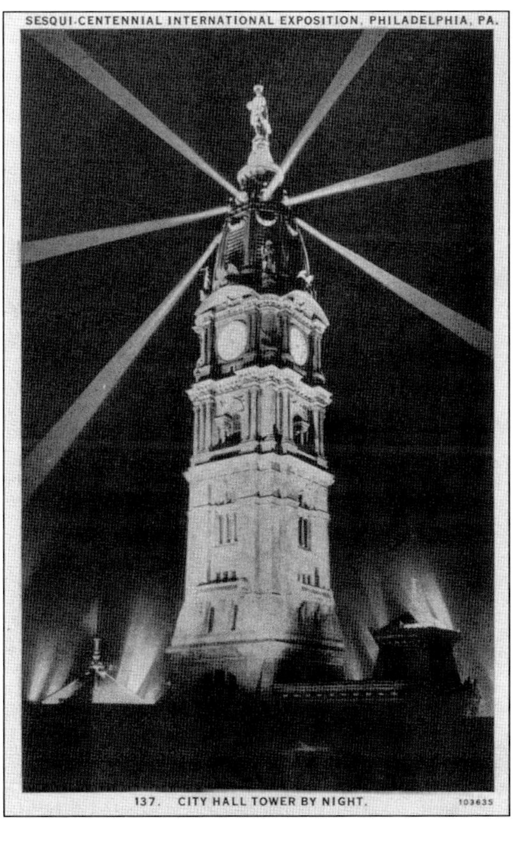

At 547 feet and 3.5 inches high, the tower was anticipated to make Philadelphia City Hall the highest building in the world. It was, however, surpassed during its construction by both the Washington Monument in Washington, DC, (550 feet) and the Eiffel Tower in Paris (984 feet). However, neither of those buildings are functional office space. The building still lays claim to being one of the tallest occupied masonry structures on Earth, if not the tallest. (John D. Cardinell.)

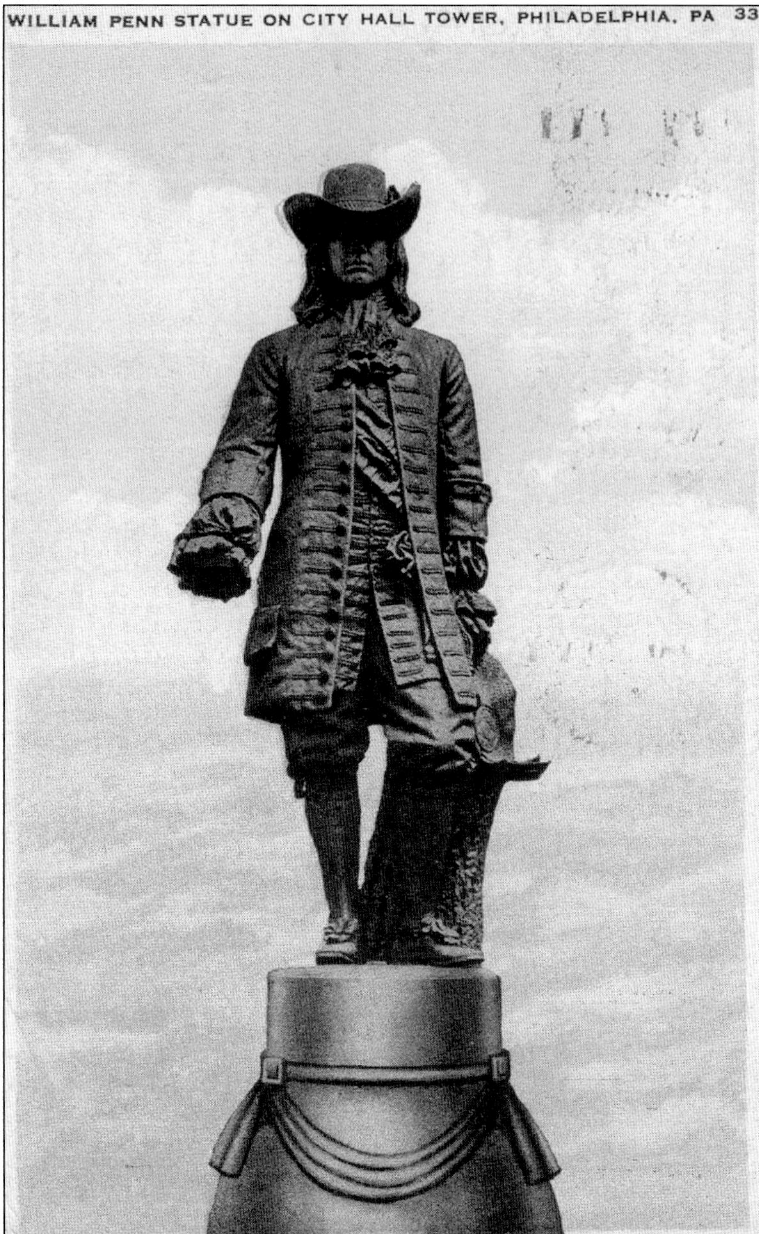

The William Penn statue atop City Hall Tower is perhaps the most widely recognized symbol of Philadelphia for visitors and Philadelphians alike, and can be seen miles away from every quarter of the city. For over 100 years, the figure has reminded city residents about the Quaker visionary who founded Philadelphia. The statue is the most famous of Alexander Calder's sculptures decorating the Public Buildings. Raised in pieces and assembled in November 1894, it represents William Penn at about 38 years old in period dress during his first trip to America. William Penn's left hand holds the Charter of Pennsylvania, which rests on a stump that suggests the first tree cut in Pennsylvania. His right hand appears to be making a gesture of blessing and welcome. The position of this hand is unfortunate, since the view from the Parkway makes it look as if Penn is relieving himself—or worse. (Buffalo Paper and Post Card Company.)

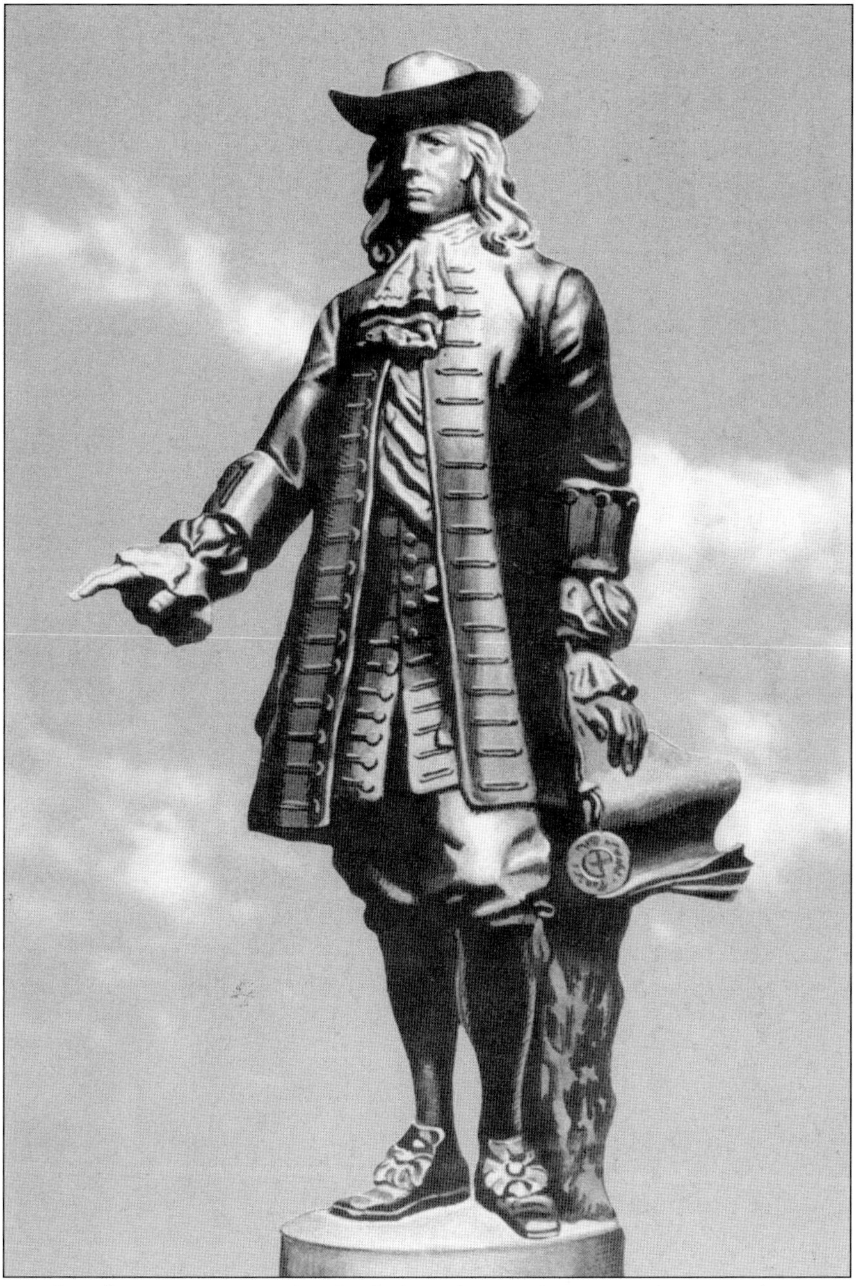

The statue of William Penn is 37 feet high from hat to shoes, weighs more than 27 tons, and faces northeast (therefore, the figure is in eternal silhouette). Some say that it looks toward Tacony, the place in Philadelphia where it was cast, while others say that the work gazes at Penn Treaty Park, where Penn made his legendary friendship accord with local Native Americans. At any rate, it is said to be the highest and largest sculpture on a building anywhere, as well as the largest sculpture ever cast in bronze. It has become an unofficial logo for Philadelphia and often challenges the Liberty Bell as the most recognizable symbol of the city. Until about 1986, a "gentlemen's agreement" among city planners and developers ensured that no building was to surpass the brim of William Penn's hat. (WYCO Products.)

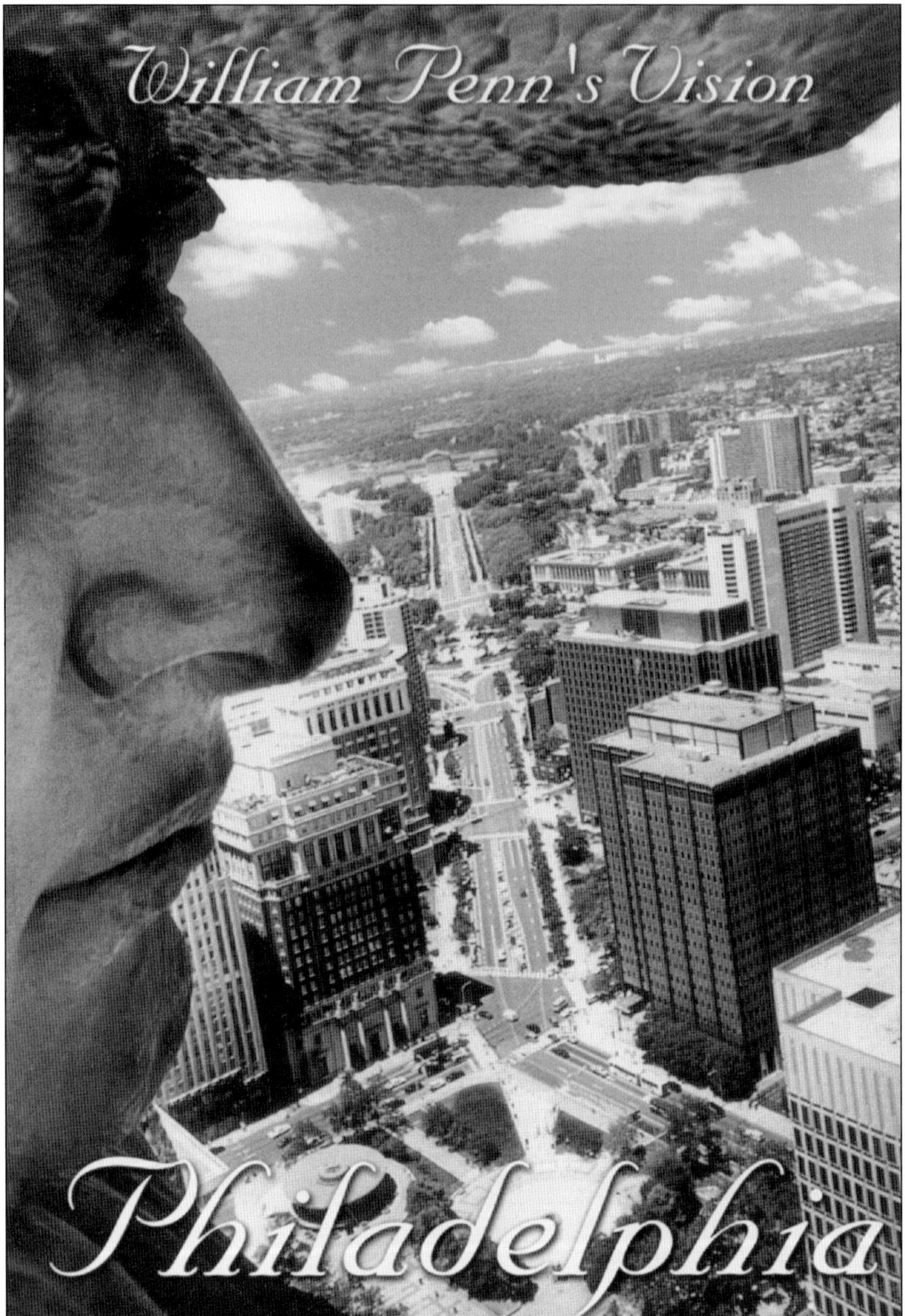

This striking postcard photograph, taken by a friend of this book's author, highlights the face of the William Penn statue with the Parkway receding toward northwest Philadelphia and Pennsylvania's Montgomery County. The unique image is not often duplicated. Compliments and kudos to the photographer, Marc A. Umile, who took a risk hanging from the brim of the statue's hat to get this terrific shot. (A narrow access tunnel through the statue leads to a hatch at the top of the hat.) (WYCO Colour Postcard.)

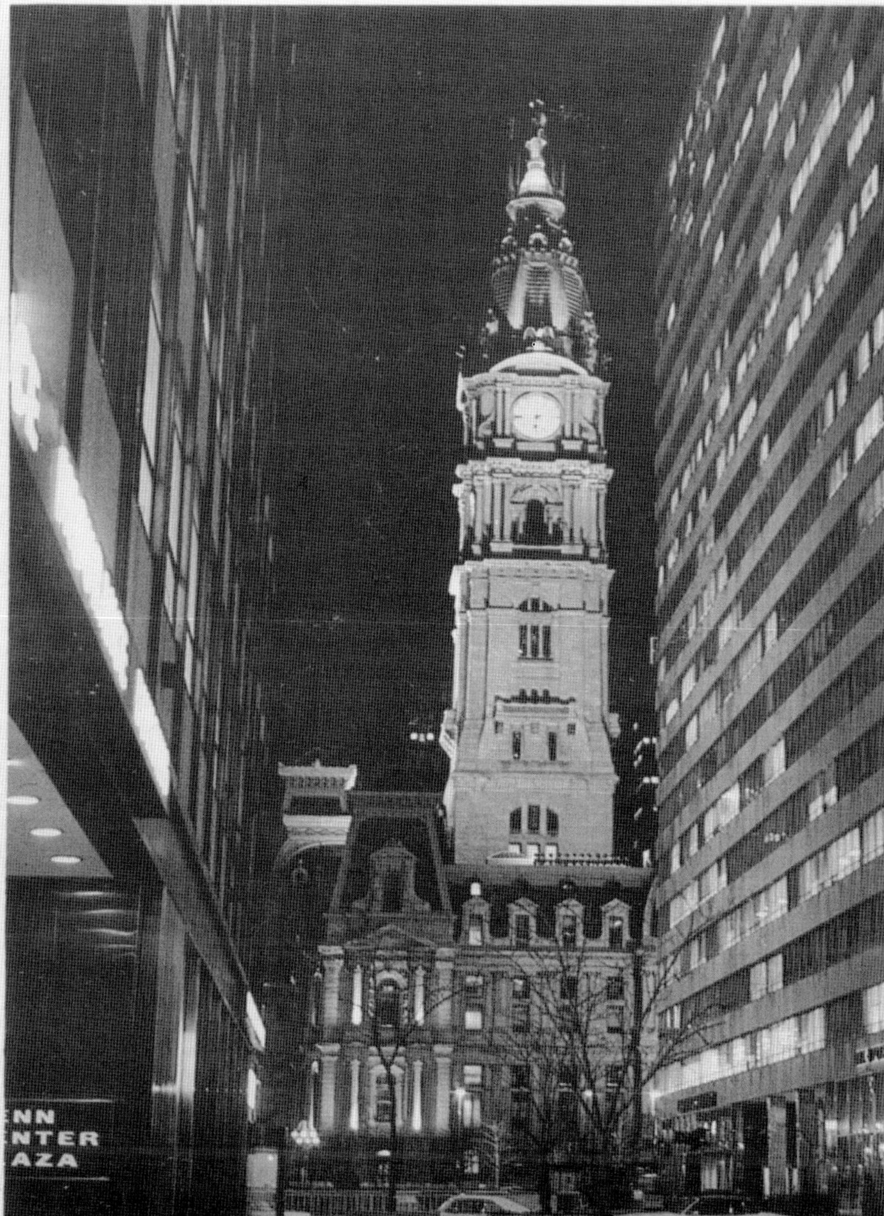

CITY HALL AT NIGHT PHILADELPHIA, PENNSYLVANIA

Philadelphia City Hall can be regarded as the pinnacle of conventional masonry construction. When engineers tunneled the Broad Street Subway in the mid-1920s, the underpinning of the building was the largest such procedure until that time. A total of 100,000 tons, or one-fourth of the building's mass, was shifted twice, with only a quarter inch of settlement. These days, subway trains traveling below cause no appreciable vibration inside. Across city hall on Market Street is a work of public art called *The Clothespin.* The immense rusting steel clothespin, the world's largest, was erected in 1976 to be purposefully out-of-character with city hall's Victorian ambiance. *The Clothespin* was created by sculptor Claes Oldenburg as both a commentary on art and a tourist attraction. (Philadelphia Post Card Company.)

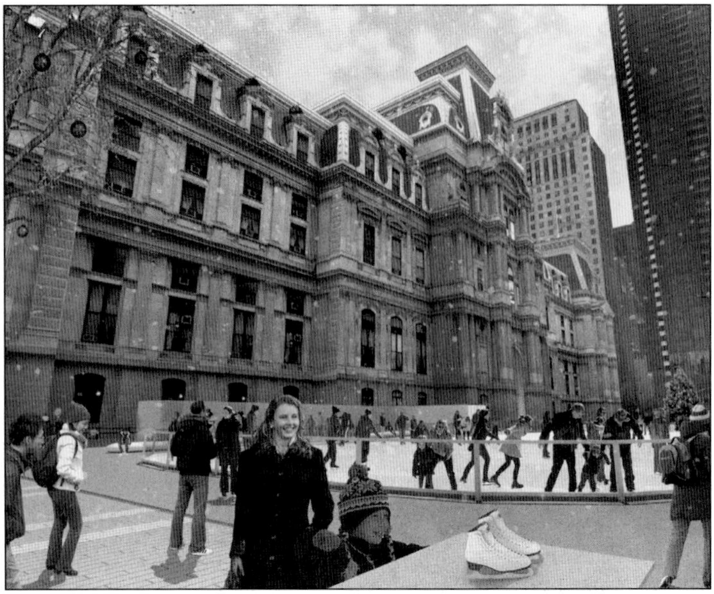

Dilworth Plaza, on city hall's west side, is named after Richardson K. Dilworth, Philadelphia's mayor from 1956 to 1962. A $55-million facelift has recently transformed the courtyard into a green public space offering easy access to the subway lines below. Trees, a café, and an ice-skating rink have also been added. The northwest end of Dilworth Plaza looks in the Ben Franklin Parkway's direction. This conceptual view is courtesy of the Center City District.

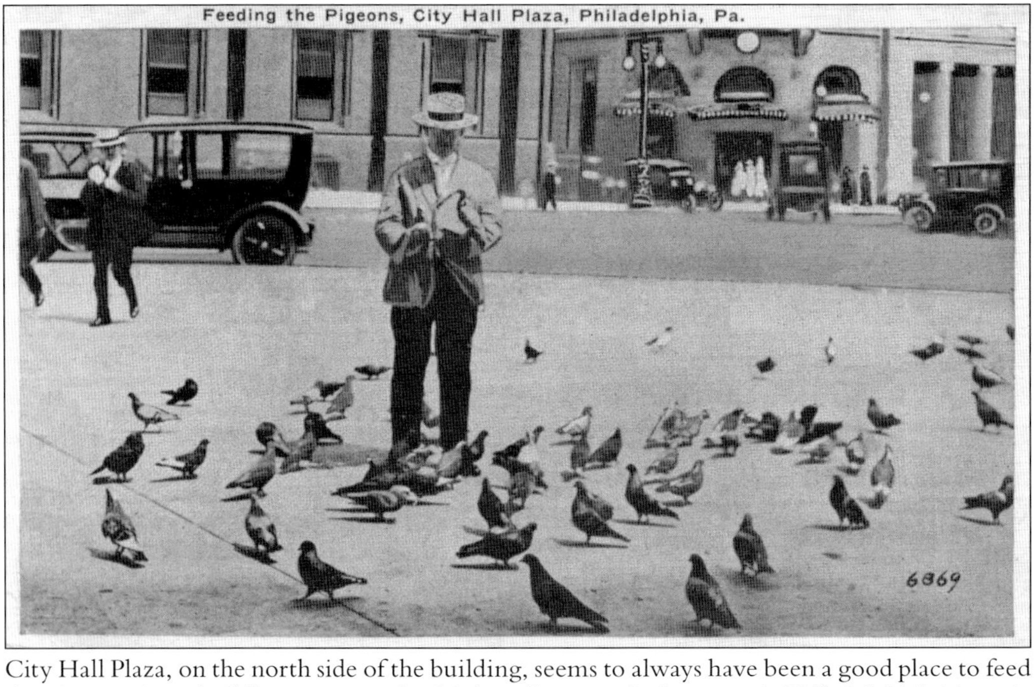

City Hall Plaza, on the north side of the building, seems to always have been a good place to feed the pigeons. Two buildings are seen in this heavily retouched postcard: Philadelphia's Masonic Temple (left) and the old headquarters of the *Philadelphia Bulletin* newspaper, which was supplanted in the 1990s by the Philadelphia Criminal Justice Center. (P. Sander, Philadelphia.)

130—City Hall, Philadelphia, Pa., Masonic Temple in Left Foreground

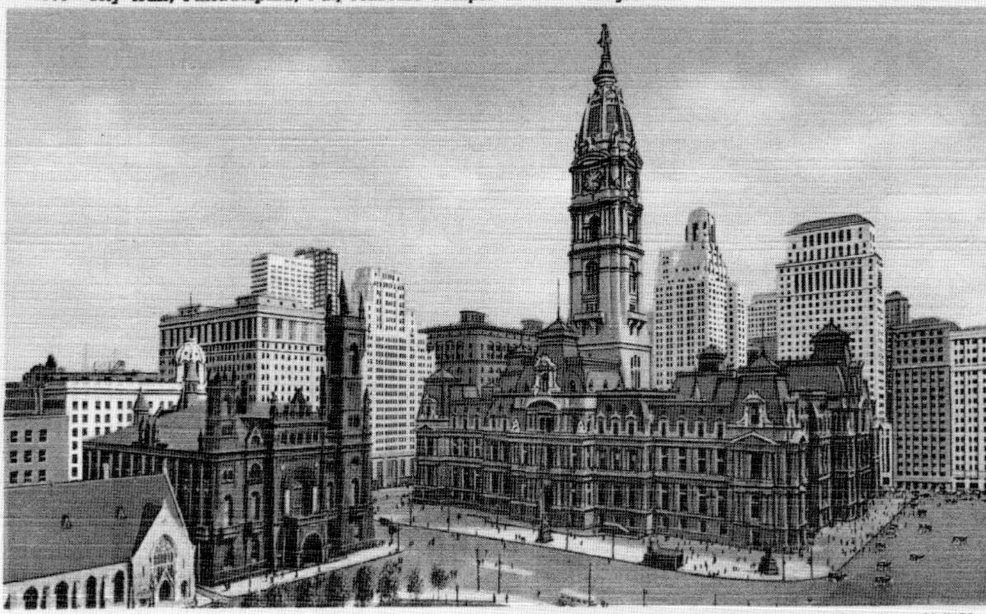

3A-H575

The Philadelphia Masonic Temple is seen here along with its longtime neighbor, Philadelphia City Hall, in this beautiful 1940s postcard. Among the world's largest Masonic lodges, the Romanesque/Norman–style temple is one of the best examples of post–Civil War architecture in North America. It opened in 1873, a year before the Public Buildings were started, and remains the nation's preeminent shrine of American Freemasonry. (C.T. Art-Colortone.)

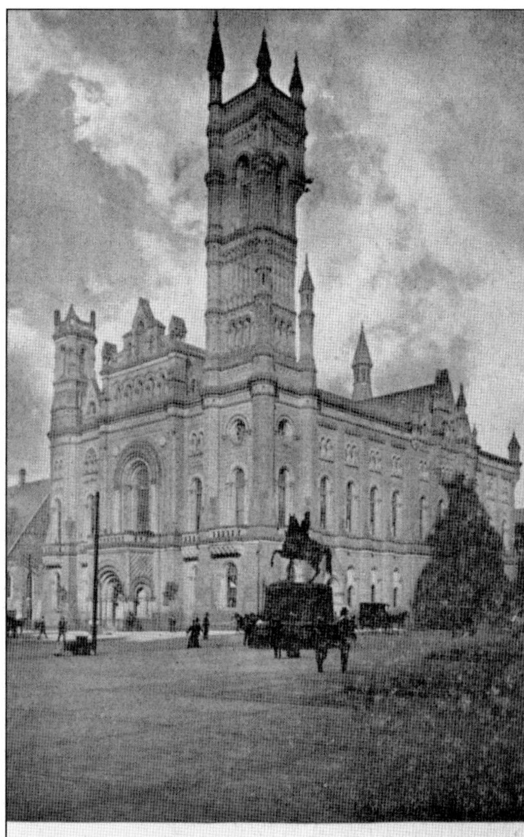

Masonic Temple—Philadelphia.

Designed by James H. Windrim, the temple serves as the Grand Lodge of Free and Accepted Masons of Pennsylvania and contains an exquisite collection of paintings, statuary, and furnishings. Windrim was the director of Philadelphia's Department of Public Works and in 1892 produced an early perspective of the Parkway. The equestrian statue is of Maj. Gen. John Fulton Reynolds of Civil War fame, completed in 1884 by John Rogers. It's still there, as is another Civil War–era statue (not shown), that of Gen. George B. McClellan, completed in 1891 by Henry Jackson Ellicott. (Unmarked postcard.)

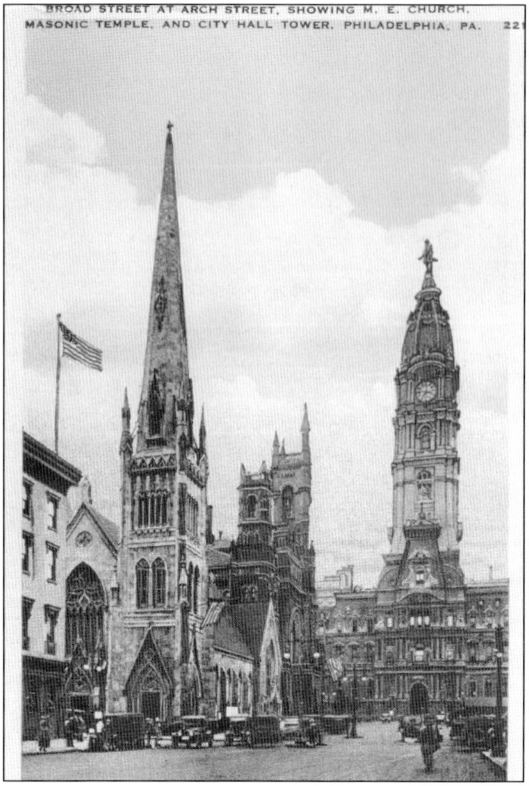

Next to the Masonic temple is Arch Street United Methodist Church, Philadelphia's finest example of Gothic Revival architecture. It was founded in 1862 after younger members of Union Methodist Church believed a violin should set the pitch for singing hymns. Older worshipers, refusing to accept "the devil's music," insisted on using a tuning fork. The disagreement led to raising this church at Broad and Arch Streets. (Philadelphia Art Company.)

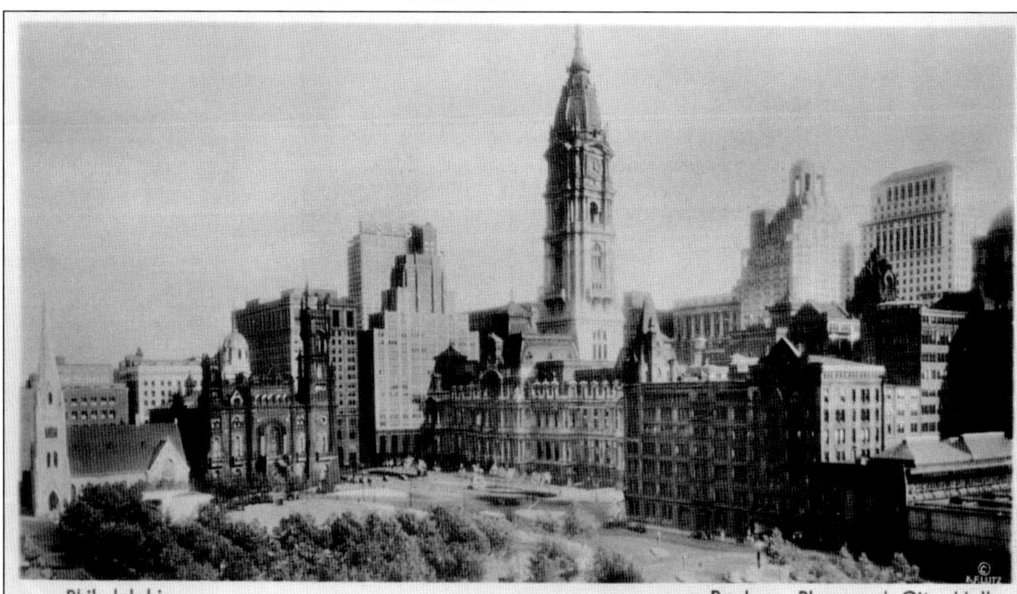

This 1937 photographic card shows scores of buildings, including Arch Street Methodist Church (left), the Masonic Temple, Philadelphia City Hall, and Broad Street Station (right). The train station was scheduled to have been demolished with the completion of Thirtieth Street Station and Suburban Station, but the Depression and World War II delayed this until the 1950s. The greenery at the bottom is Reyburn Plaza. (K.F. Lutz, Philadelphia.)

Three

JOHN F. KENNEDY PLAZA (LOVE PARK) AND VICINITY

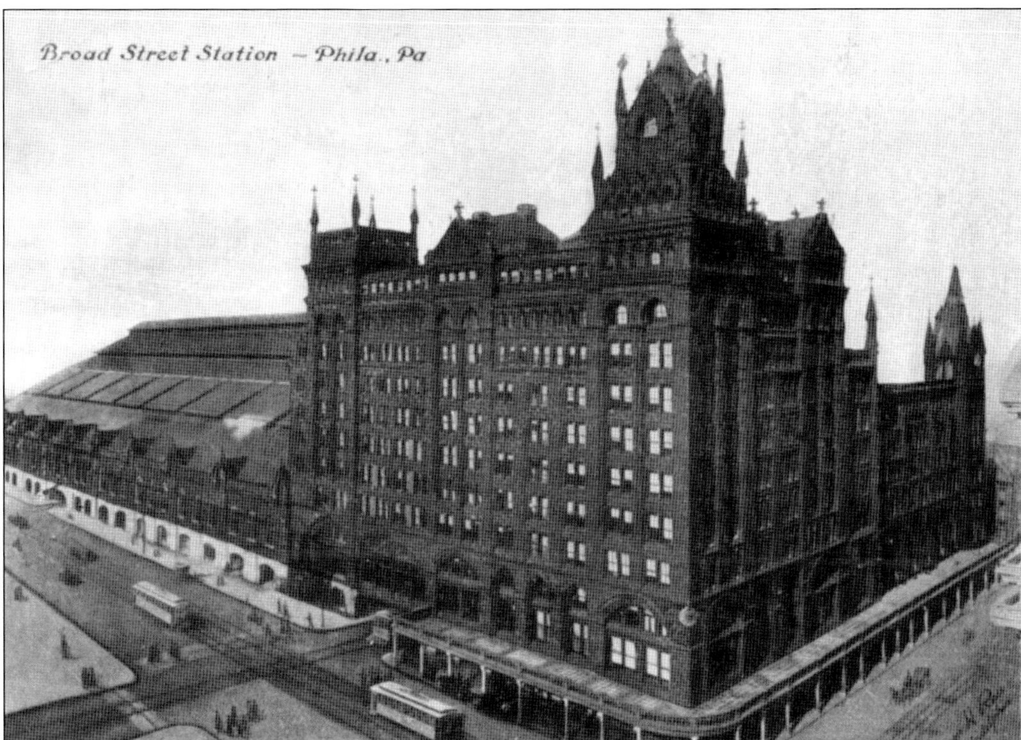

Broad Street Station was one of the most famed passenger stations in the world. This marvelous Victorian pile brought the Pennsylvania Railroad's tracks into Philadelphia, directly across from city hall. Designed by Joseph and John Wilson and opened in 1881, the terminal became among the world's largest railroad stations when it was expanded by Frank Furness in the 1890s. The Wilson brothers at that time also added a colossal train shed over the terminal's 16 tracks. (Unmarked postcard.)

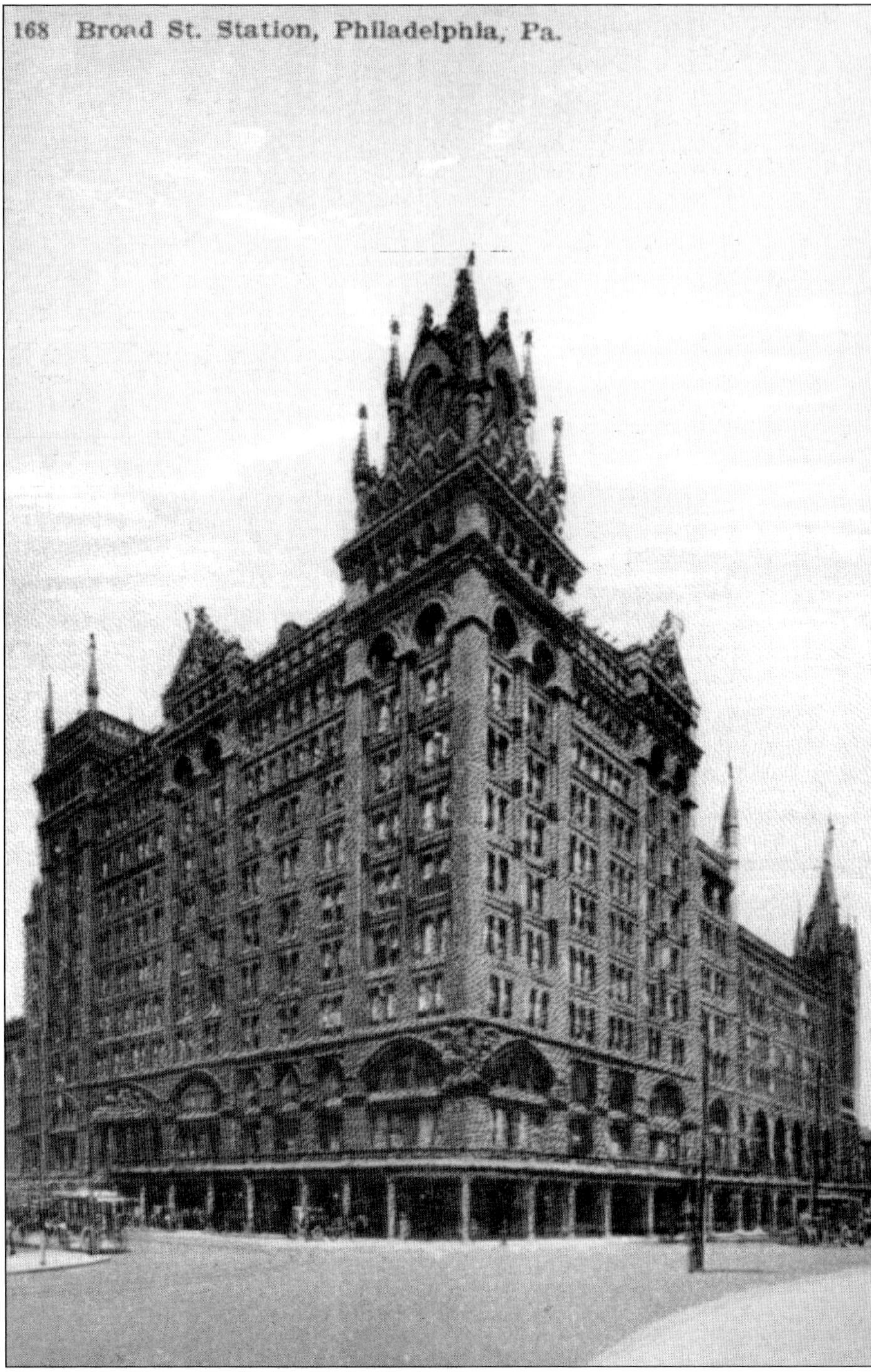

The train shed burned down in 1923 in one of Philadelphia's most serious blazes and was not replaced. Since the Benjamin Franklin Parkway was being built around then, the thought was that the entire station should be removed as part of the City Beautiful Movement. The elevated tracks leading to Broad Street Station would be removed, too. Philadelphians dubbed that structure the "Chinese Wall" because it was reminiscent of the Great Wall of China. (Unmarked postcard.)

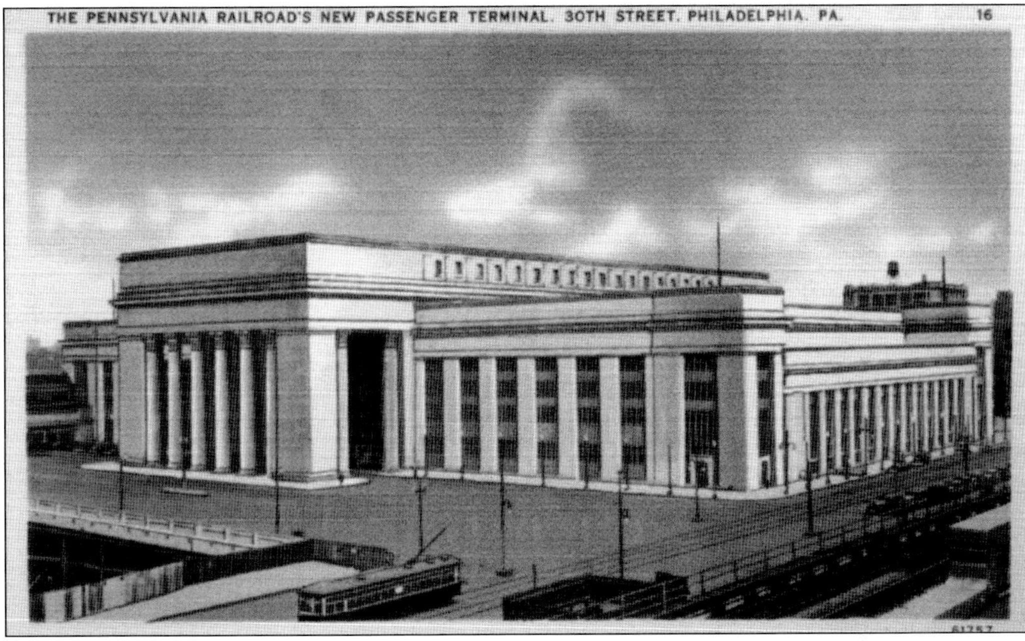

This chic postcard features the Pennsylvania Railroad's Thirtieth Street Station, opened in the early 1930s on the west bank of the Schuylkill River. The Classic Revival station was an element of the city's beautification efforts that engendered the Parkway; it was also the last great train station built in the United States. Thirtieth Street Station still serves as Amtrak's passenger station in Philadelphia. (Union News Company.)

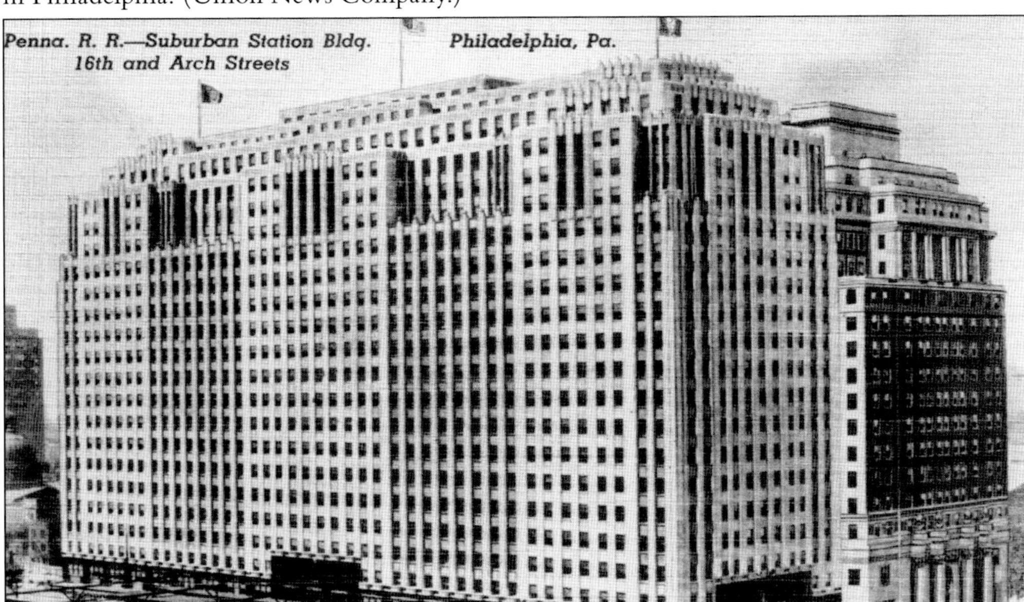

On September 28, 1930, the Pennsylvania Railroad opened Broad Street Suburban Station, a sprawling underground terminal for regional rail traffic. The art deco edifice above the station is a model of an integrated office building and passenger terminal. Located at Sixteenth Street and John F. Kennedy Boulevard, the 21-story structure is now called One Penn Center at Suburban Station. It is listed in the National Register of Historic Places. (Colourpicture.)

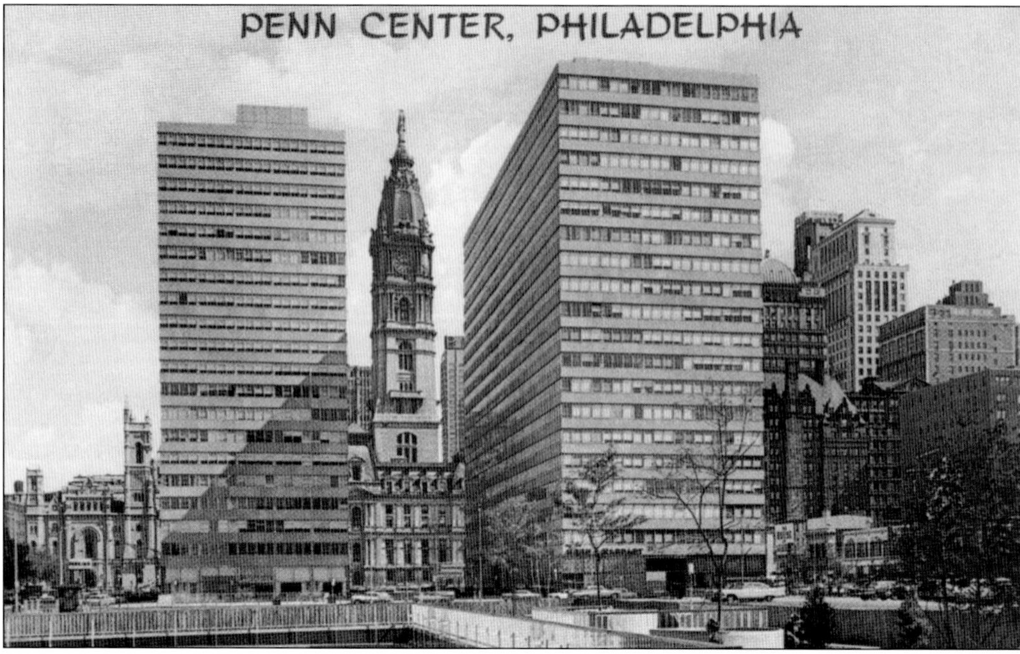

Penn Center is Philadelphia's version of Lower Manhattan, a canyon of office buildings from city hall to Twentieth Street along both JFK Boulevard and Market Street. Built from the 1950s through the 1970s, Penn Center occupies space formerly taken up by the Pennsylvania Railroad's elevated tracks (the "Chinese Wall"). The underground concourse system throughout this area is particularly noteworthy. (WYCO Products.)

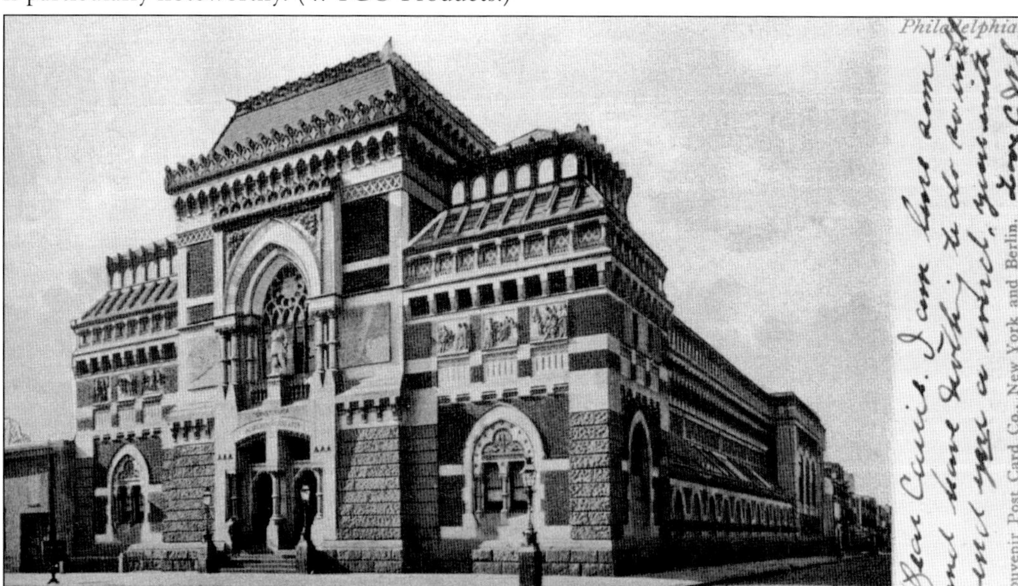

The Pennsylvania Academy of the Fine Arts (PAFA) is a member of the Parkway's group of cultural institutions despite being located at Broad and Cherry Streets. Established in 1805 as the first art school and art museum in the nation, PAFA is recognized internationally for training artists from around the globe and for its eminent collections of 18th-, 19th-, and 20th-century American artwork. (Souvenir Post Card Company.)

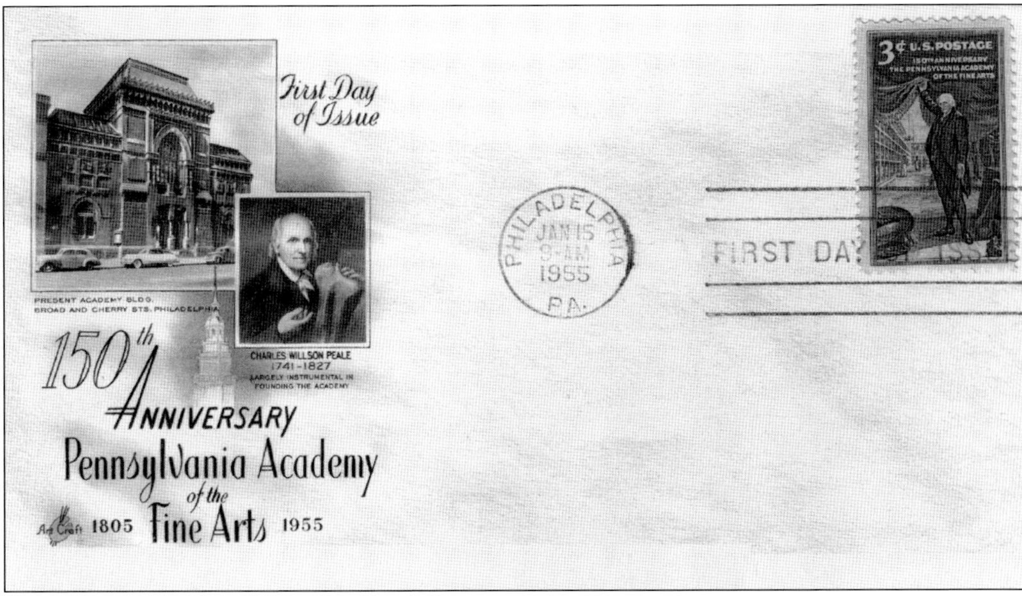

Dating from 1876, the PAFA building provides a wonderful setting for the academy's collection of art and for its many exhibitions. It was designed by Frank Furness and George Hewitt and is one of the finest examples of Victorian Gothic architecture in America. The National Historic Landmark was restored in 1976. This First Day of Issue cachet was one of several released in 1955 for the academy's 150th anniversary. (Author's collection.)

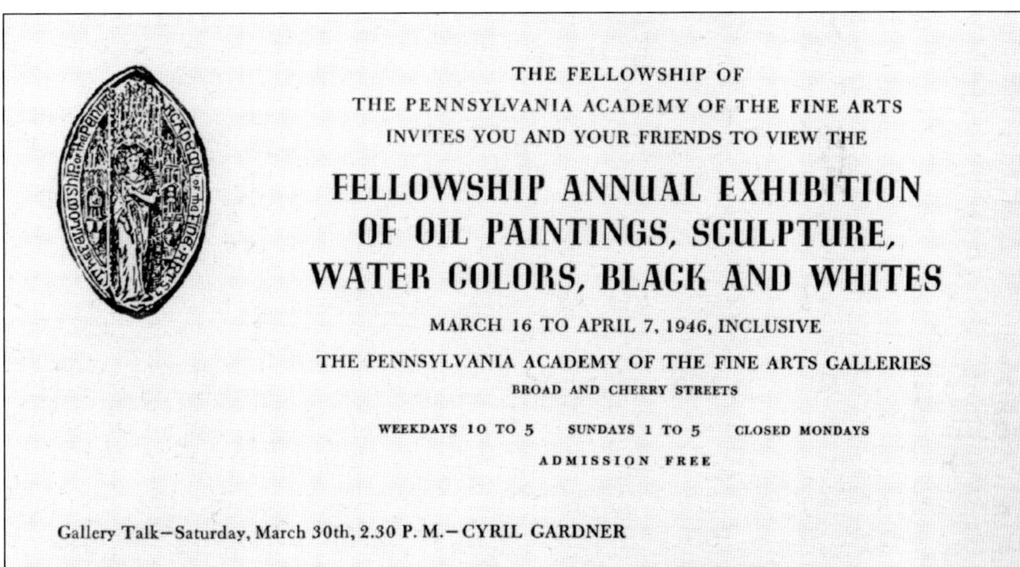

THE FELLOWSHIP OF
THE PENNSYLVANIA ACADEMY OF THE FINE ARTS
INVITES YOU AND YOUR FRIENDS TO VIEW THE

FELLOWSHIP ANNUAL EXHIBITION
OF OIL PAINTINGS, SCULPTURE,
WATER COLORS, BLACK AND WHITES

MARCH 16 TO APRIL 7, 1946, INCLUSIVE
THE PENNSYLVANIA ACADEMY OF THE FINE ARTS GALLERIES
BROAD AND CHERRY STREETS

WEEKDAYS 10 TO 5 SUNDAYS 1 TO 5 CLOSED MONDAYS
ADMISSION FREE

Gallery Talk—Saturday, March 30th, 2.30 P. M.—CYRIL GARDNER

PAFA has many art exhibits during the year. The annual student exhibition displays more than 1,000 student works from the academy's drawing, sculpture, and printmaking disciplines. Some 10,000 people have attended the student show, which dates back to 1879. This is a postcard invitation to the 1946 Fellowship Annual Exhibition. (Unmarked postcard.)

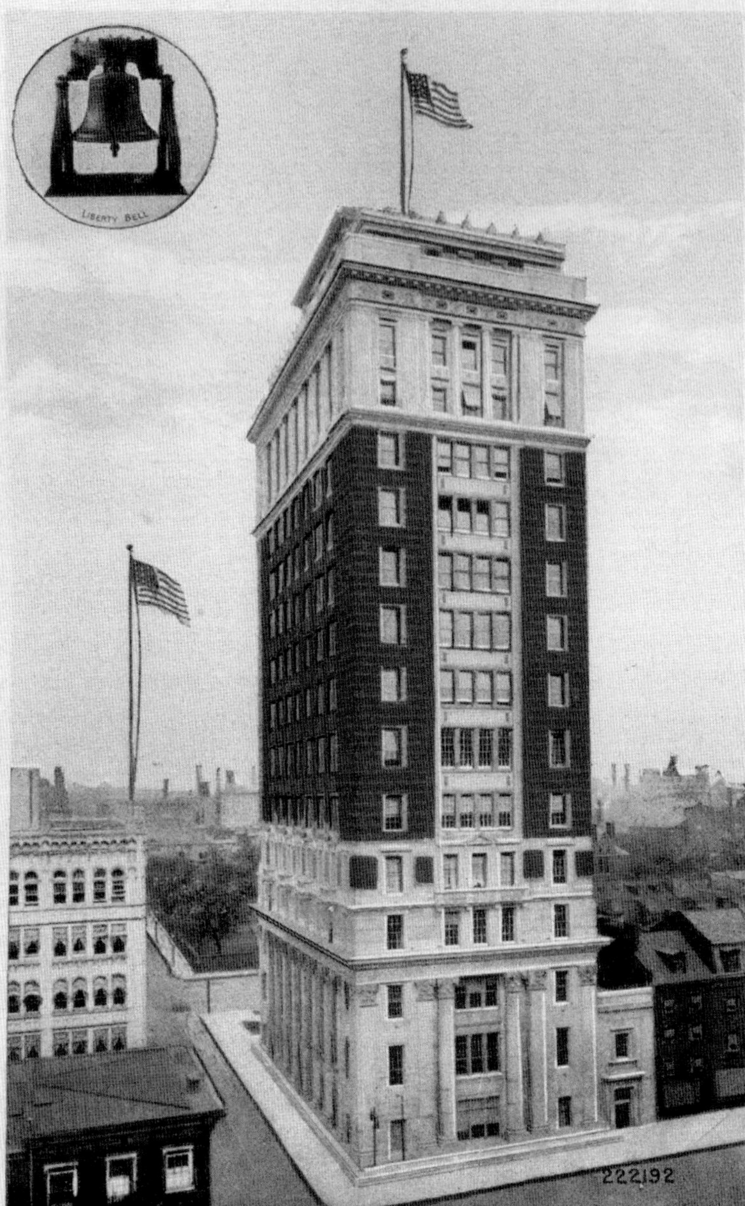

BELL TELEPHONE BUILDING, 17TH AND ARCH STREETS, PHILADELPHIA, PA.

Completed in 1915, the Bell Parkway Building, at Seventeenth and Arch Streets, once housed the headquarters of the Bell Telephone Company of Pennsylvania and Associated Companies. An article in the *Proceedings of the Engineers' Club of Philadelphia* revels in the structure's handsome looks: "From the great Corinthian capped corners and pilasters of the limestone base to the stone-like, gray terra-cotta that forms its upper colonnade of Ionic columns, [the building] is distinctive. Four sides, each as ornamental as the other, does it present to the four points of the compass; for this is one of very few buildings in Philadelphia which has no wall to mar its appearance from any angle from one may look." Logan Square is visible in the background of this card. (Unmarked postcard; courtesy Gus Spector.)

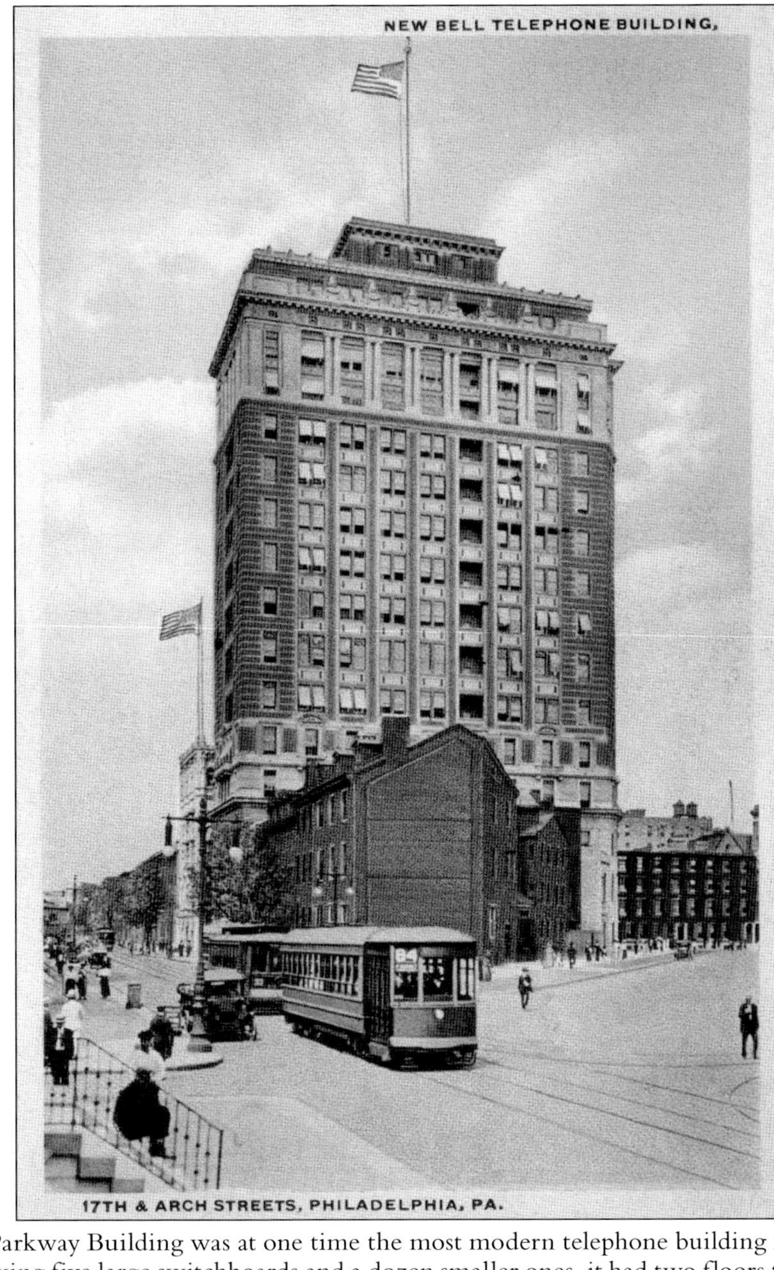

The Bell Parkway Building was at one time the most modern telephone building in the world. Besides having five large switchboards and a dozen smaller ones, it had two floors that served as dining and rest areas for the operators who routed calls there. Bell had 1,150 employees in the building, including some 700 female operators. Now approaching its 100th year, the building continues to serve as a telephone switching hub and office space for Verizon Communications. (Bell Atlantic and GTE merged to become Verizon in 2000.) Not shown in this card are two other Bell Telephone skyscrapers along the Parkway. The Bell Telephone Company Building, with its distinctive stainless steel facade, is on Sixteenth Street. Finished in 1961, it was renamed One Parkway years ago. And the red granite Bell Atlantic Tower was completed in 1991 on Arch Street. The 55-story edifice has been renamed Three Logan Square. (Unmarked postcard; courtesy Gus Spector.)

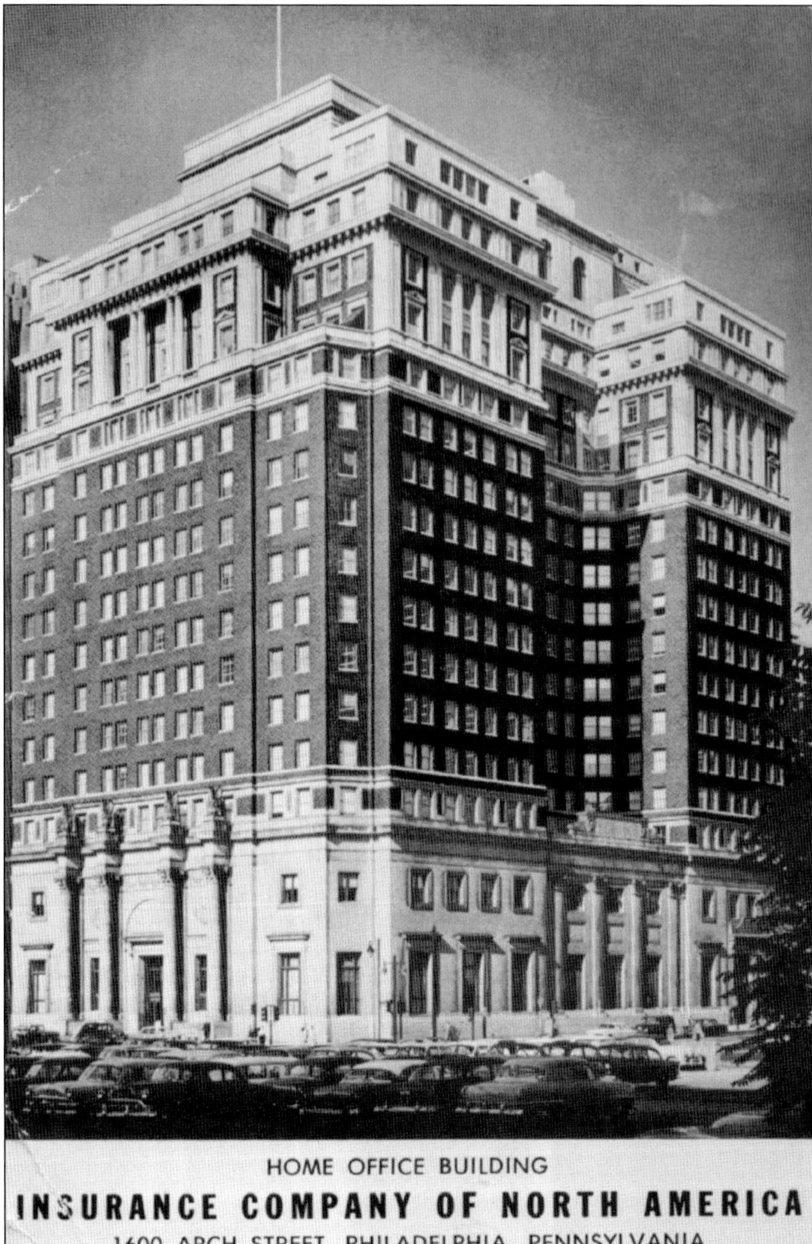

This building at Sixteenth Street and the Parkway was previously the center of operations for the Insurance Company of North America (INA). The firm was formed in 1792 as the first marine insurance company and the first joint stock company in the United States. By the 20th century, INA was one of the nation's largest property insurance companies, which gave it the self-assurance to move into this enormous 20-story pile by 1925. The Georgian Colonial Revival building was erected as "the Gateway to the Parkway." INA Corporation and Connecticut General Insurance Corporation later merged and became CIGNA, a health services organization based in Connecticut. In 2007, the old INA building was converted into an elegant condominium called the Phoenix. (Conti-Print Post Card, Philadelphia.)

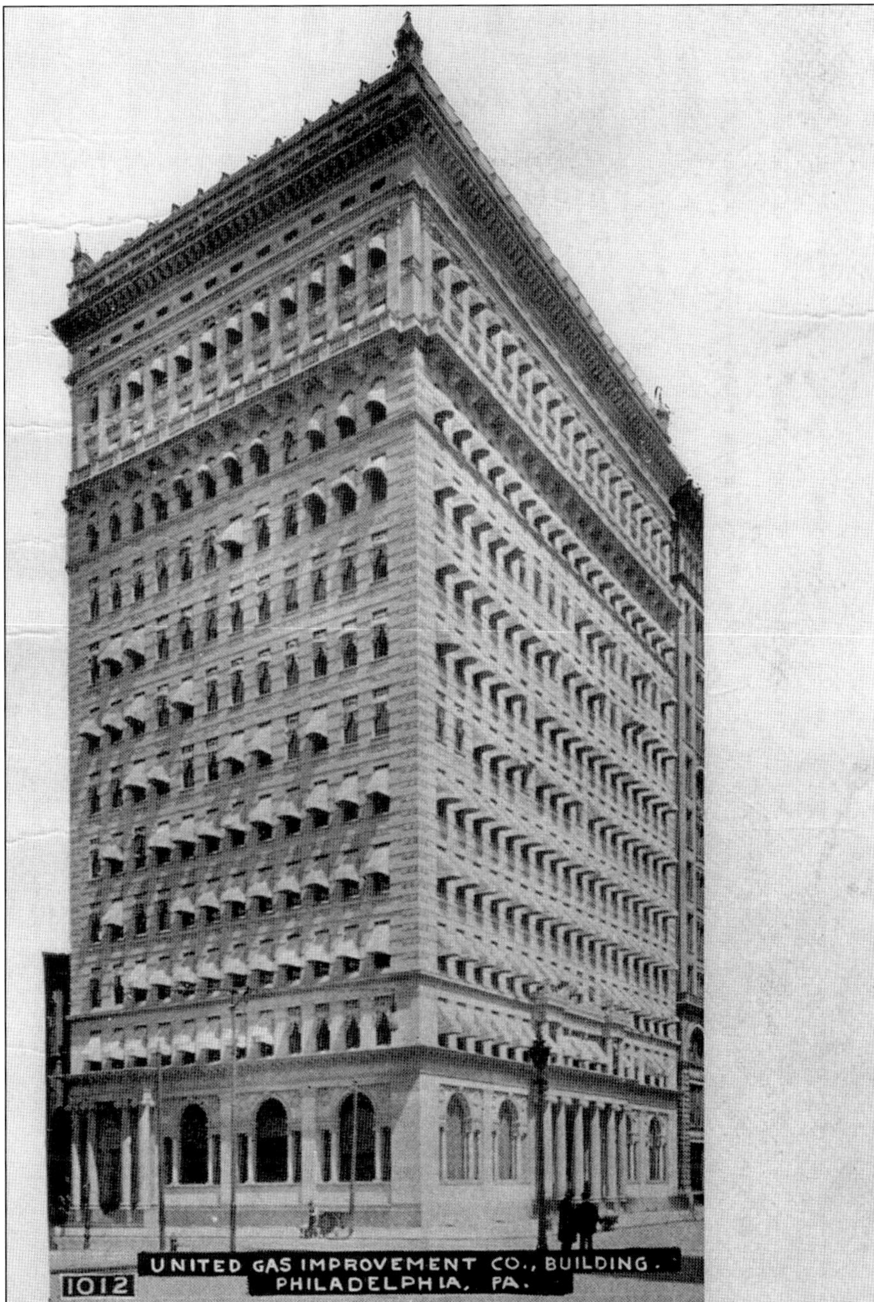

The United Gas Improvement (UGI) Building, now named One City Plaza, is at the northwest corner of Broad and Arch Streets. Constructed in 1899 after designs by the Wilson brothers, the edifice was subsequently enlarged toward the west and is now twice as wide as it looks in this postcard. UGI was established in Philadelphia in 1882 as the world's first utility holding company. Now based in Valley Forge, Pennsylvania, UGI Corporation is a Fortune 500 business and one of the biggest gas companies in the world. One City Plaza is used as office space today. (Illustrated Postal Card Company.)

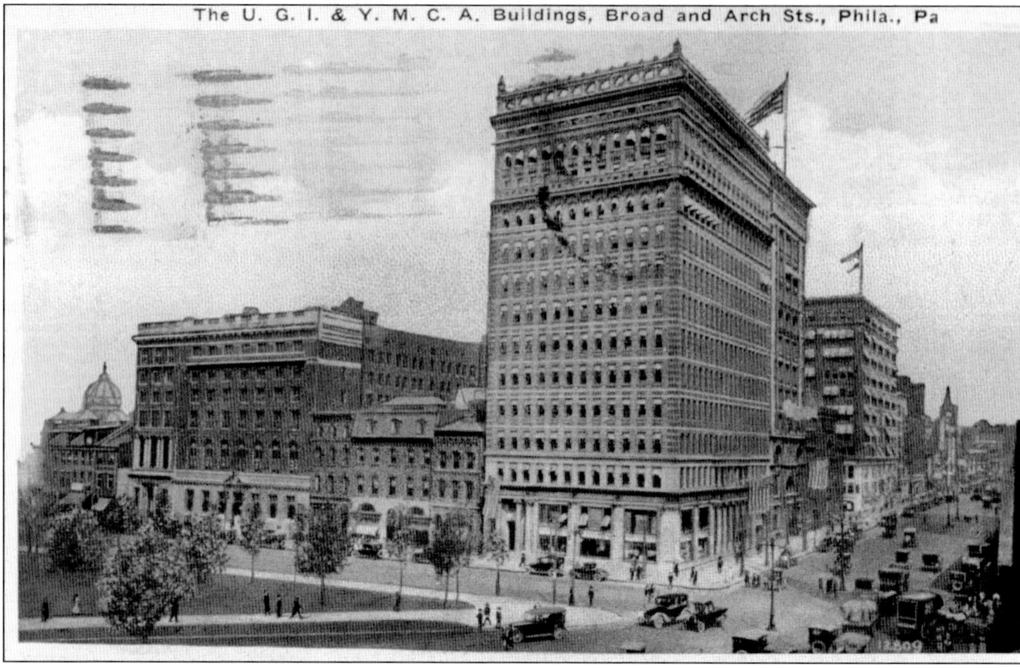

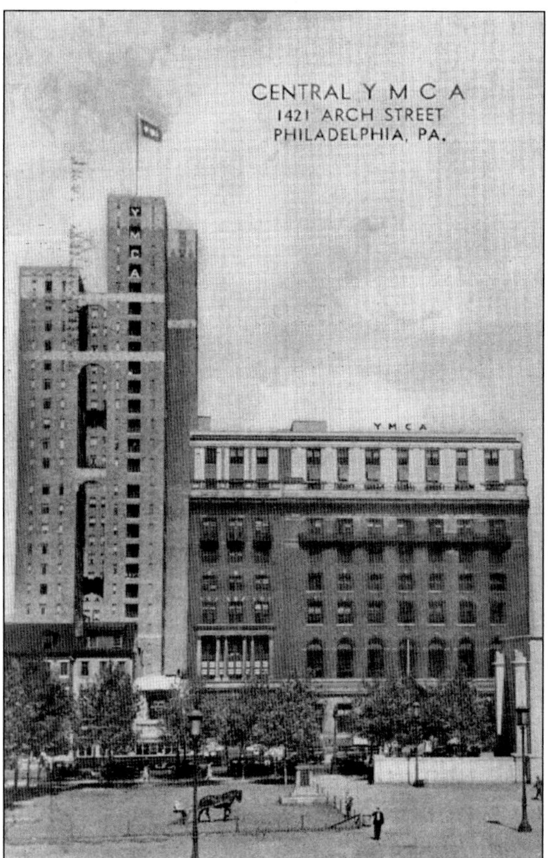

Girl Scout cookies were first commercially sold at the UGI Building. In November 1932, the Girl Scouts of Greater Philadelphia Council persuaded the Philadelphia Gas Company to allow its Scouts to bake shortbread cookies in company ovens on the first floor. Passersby on Arch Street were soon enticed by the aroma and then begged to buy the cookies. So was inaugurated a national tradition. Here, the Central YMCA is adjacent the UGI Building. (P. Sander, Philadelphia.)

The Central YMCA of Philadelphia was the world's largest YMCA in the 1920s and 1930s. Designed by architect Horace Trumbauer and built in 1906–1907, the 10-story brick and limestone building on Arch Street quickly expanded into a 26-story tower next door. The Philadelphia YMCA supplied friendship under a Christian motif that youthful newcomers to the city knew from their small-town churches. (Ruth Murray Miller, Philadelphia.)

In its heyday, the Central YMCA offered hundreds of rooms for young male students, single women, married couples, sailors stationed at the Philadelphia Naval Shipyard, and others. The Y nicknamed itself "Youthadelphia" and claimed to be a city-within-a-city "Where Young Men and Women Live and Play." (Unmarked postcard.)

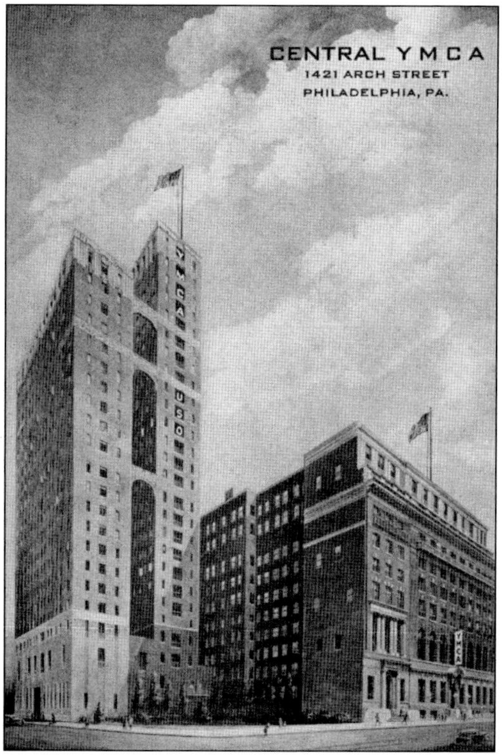

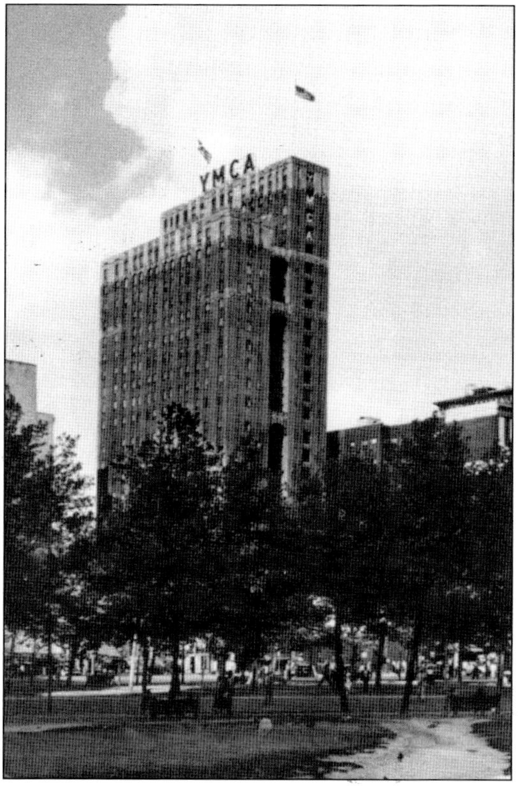

As residents turned increasingly poor or mentally ill by the 1960s, the camaraderie of Youthadelphia became a vestige of earlier times. The YMCA lost its appeal and its residences were shuttered in the 1980s. It became a mere health club before closing in 2003. The high-rise is now the Metropolitan Apartments, and a Le Méridien Hotel occupies the smaller building. (K.F. Lutz, Philadelphia.)

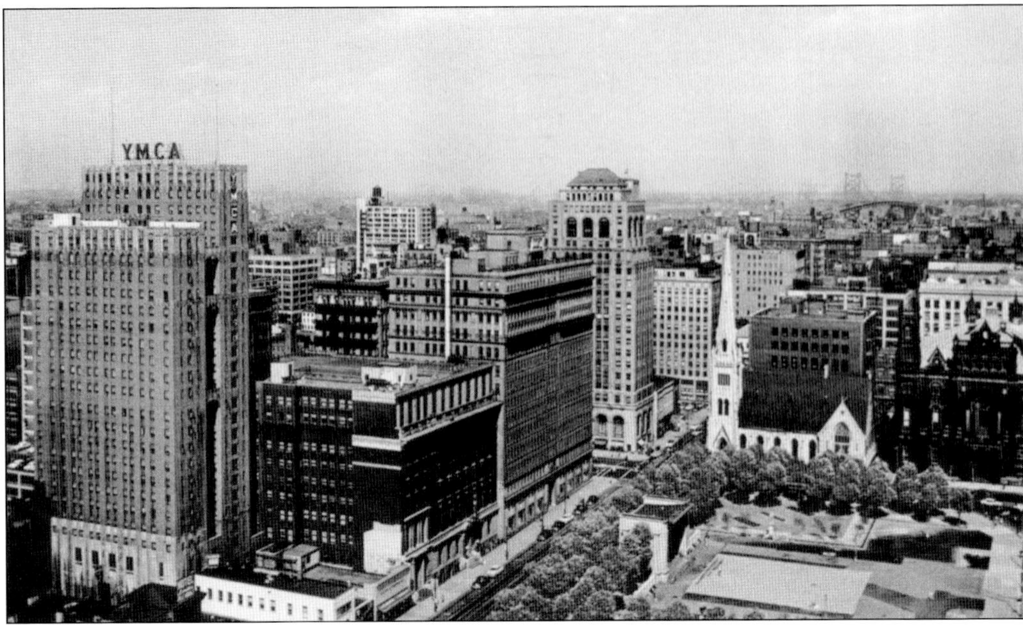

John E. Reyburn was an ardent Parkway booster who served as mayor of Philadelphia from 1907 to 1911. A plaza named after him was constructed between city hall and Arch Street as part of the Parkway project. This included the razing of a row of once-elegant townhouses along Arch Street in 1915. Reyburn Plaza, with its bandstand, built in 1928, became the setting for political events; Pres. Harry Truman spoke there on October 21, 1952. (Curteichcolor.)

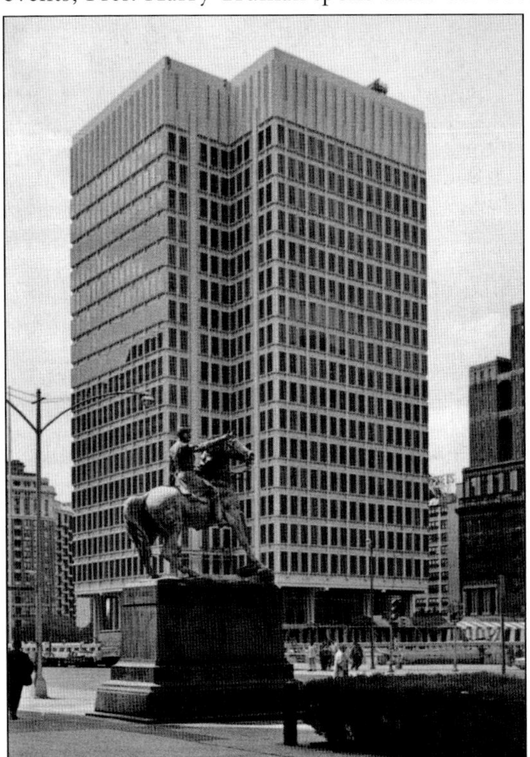

The Municipal Services Building (MSB), designed by Vincent Kling & Associates, replaced Reyburn Plaza in 1962–1963. The city's construction of the 16-story building gave private developers confidence to build other modern office towers in the Penn Center zone near city hall. The statue of Maj. Gen. John Reynolds is in the foreground. A statue of 1970s mayor Frank Rizzo, waving toward city hall, was installed at MSB Plaza (a.k.a. Thomas Paine Plaza) in 1999 (not seen here). The larger-than-life work, by sculptor Zenos Frudakis, shares the plaza with large metal and fiberglass board game pieces from a whimsical public art installation called *Your Move*. (Art Color Card Distributors; courtesy Gus Spector.)

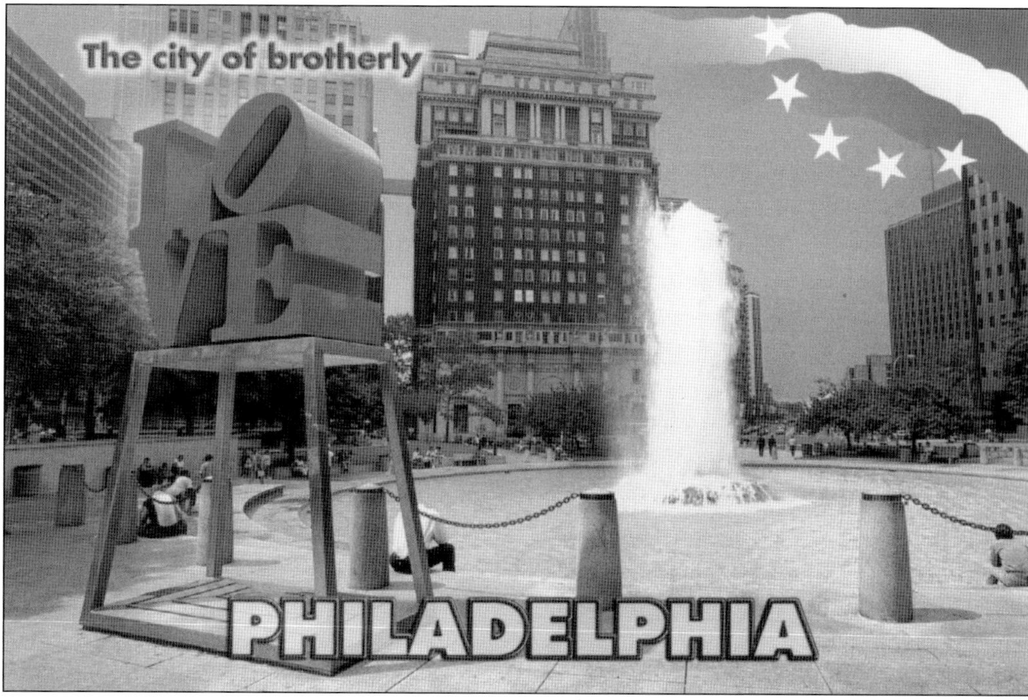

Devised by city planner Edmund N. Bacon as the Parkway's eastern terminus, the open space west of the MSB was dedicated in 1967 as John F. Kennedy Plaza. The square, with its eye-catching fountain and pool, is better known as Love Park after the globally famous *Love* sculpture. Versions of this pop art work are all around the nation and the world, but the City of Brotherly Love's example is probably the most prestigious. The red aluminum work was placed in Kennedy Plaza as part of the city's US bicentennial celebration. Supposedly, the *O* is tilted because love is imperfect. (The Postcard Factory.)

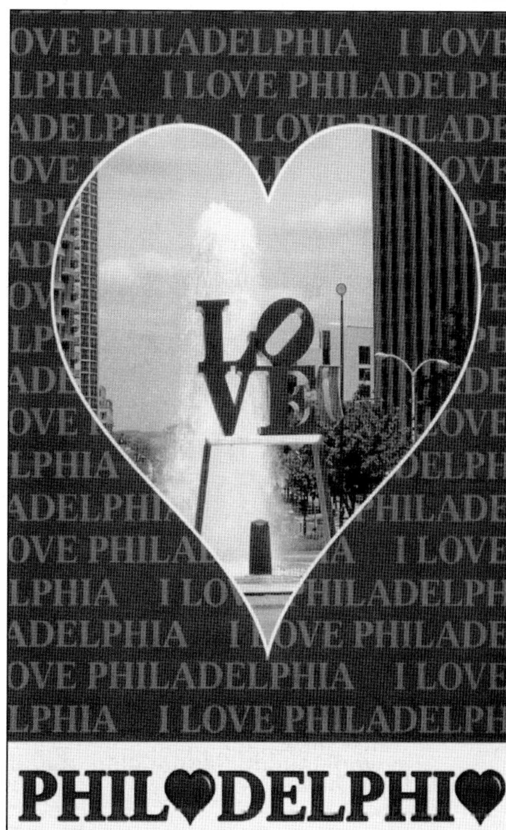

Love has been reproduced in countless ways and is one of the most plagiarized pieces of artwork in America. Love Park, meanwhile, became an internationally renowned skateboarding spot by the 1990s, but soon after lost this status when the city added wooden benches and greenery to make the place more welcoming for office workers and tourists. The city is planning to further renovate Love Park and sell the crumbling parking garage beneath it. Several cafés and restaurants may also be added. (Frank Burd, Americana Souvenirs and Gifts.)

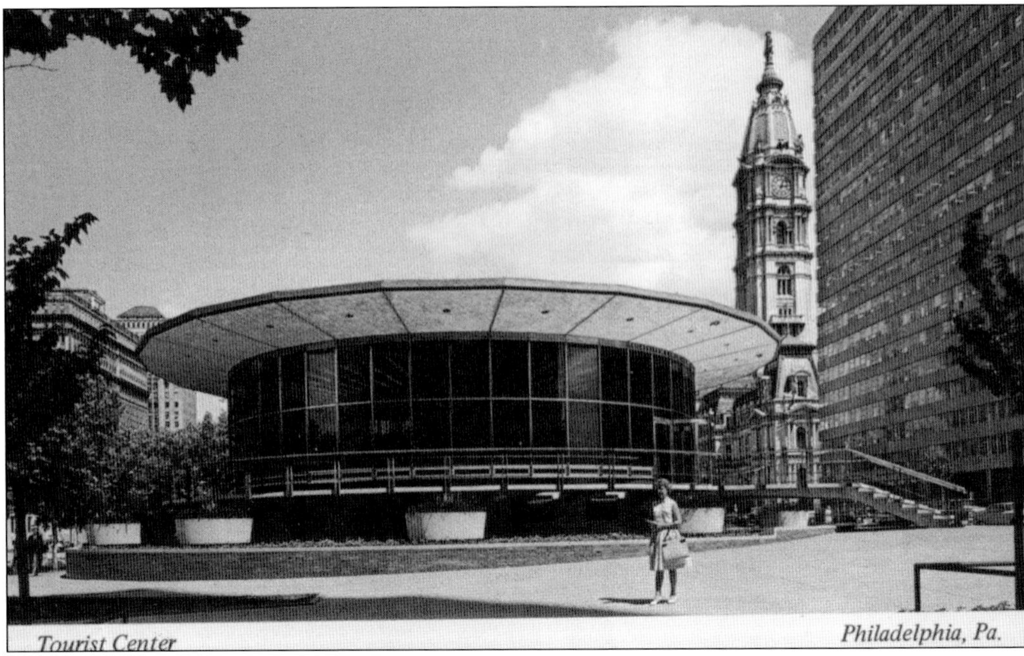

The flying saucer–shaped building within Love Park was built in 1961 as the Hospitality Center of the Philadelphia Convention and Visitors Bureau. An advertisement in a 1962 issue of *Architectural Record* proclaimed that the tourist facility "helps express this city's dynamic and tasteful approach to urban renewal." In 2006, the avant-garde structure became the Fairmount Park Welcome Center, although its fate is uncertain at this time. (Art Color Card Distributors.)

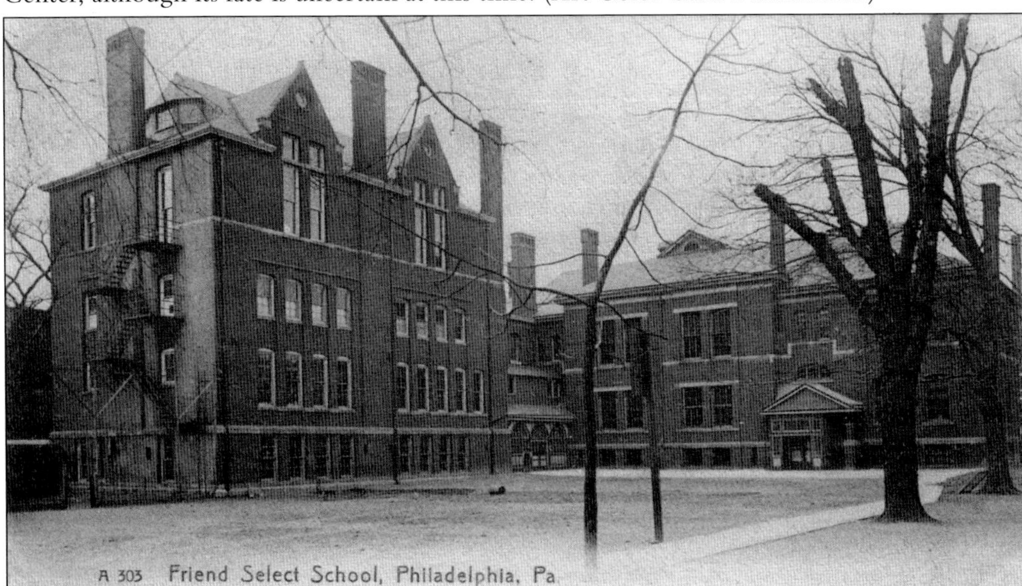

Friends Select School was formed when a Quaker girls school and a Quaker boys school moved to 140 North Sixteenth Street in 1885–1886 and eventually merged. The combined school was built on a burial ground owned by the Society of Friends. Today, Friends Select is a college-preparatory school that occupies a large 1960s building—with a rooftop schoolyard—at practically the same location, 1651 Benjamin Franklin Parkway. (Unmarked postcard; courtesy Gus Spector.)

Four

Logan Square/Circle
East Side

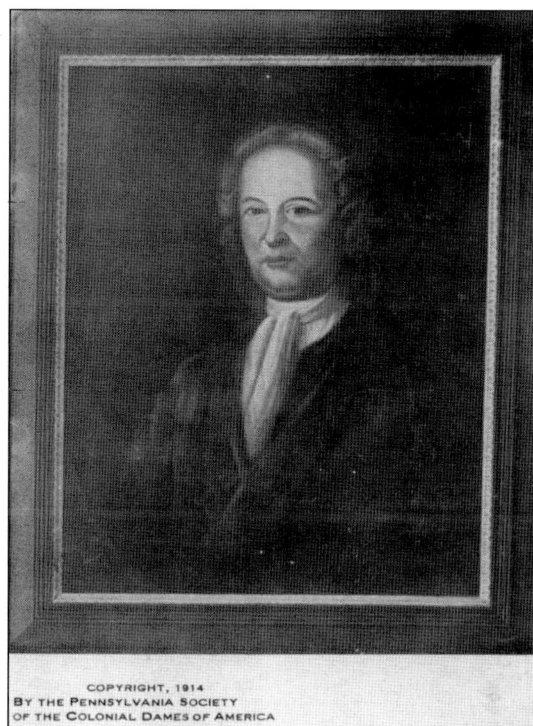

James Logan (1674–1751) distinguished himself as a businessman, politician, and scholar. He was William Penn's secretary and confidant, a mayor of Philadelphia, and an acting governor of Pennsylvania. Logan Square, originally called North West Square, was one of five areas that Penn designated as public commons in the city. It was used as a potter's field and a setting for public hangings until 1825, when it took on the colonial statesman's name. (Unmarked postcard.)

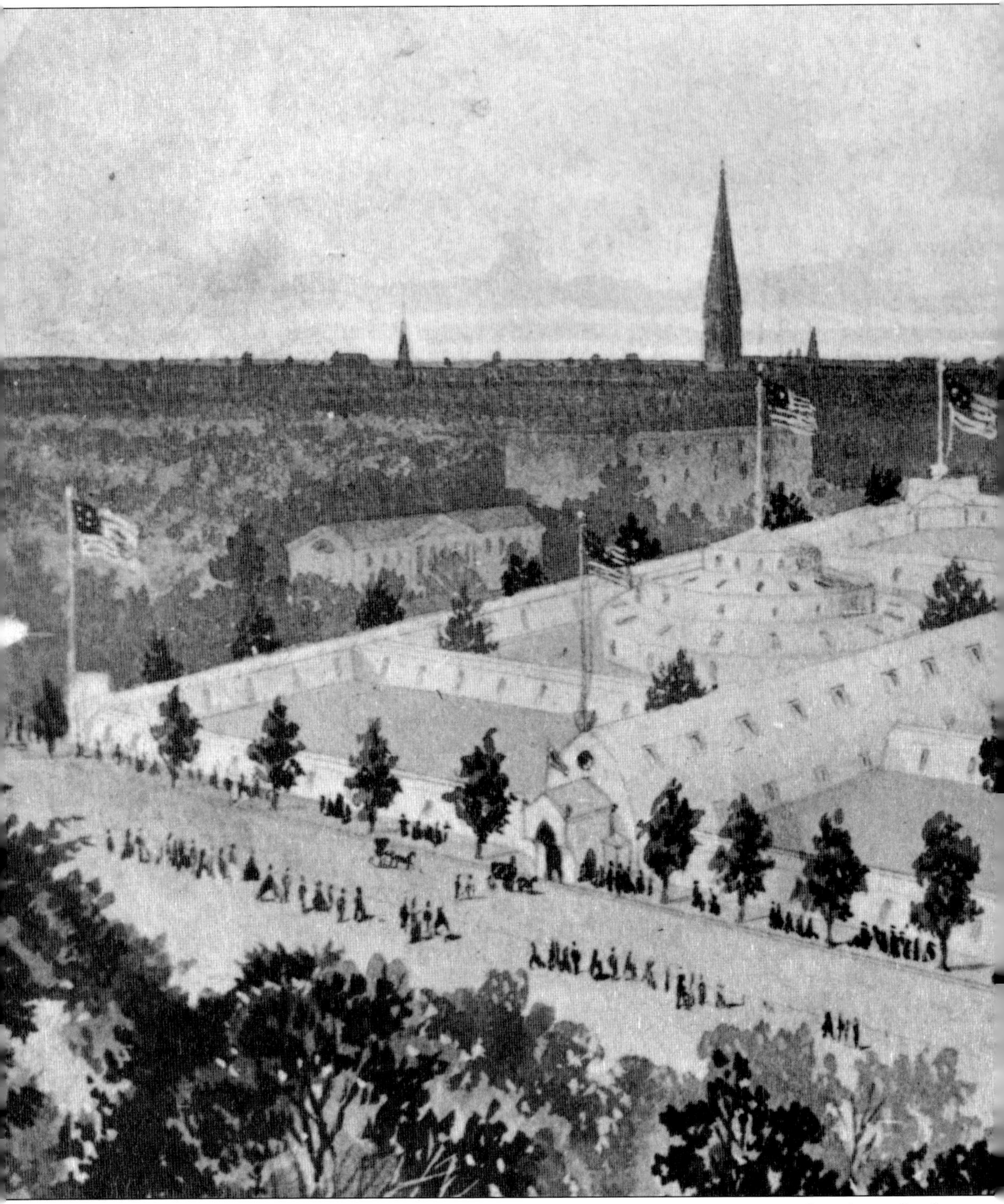

During the Civil War, Northerners formed the US Sanitary Commission to distribute food, clothing, and medicine to battle-weary troops and to establish rest homes for convalescing soldiers. To raise funds, "Sanitary Fairs" were organized. Philadelphia's Great Central Sanitary Fair was held at Logan Square from June 7 to June 28, 1864. Although the structures were temporary,

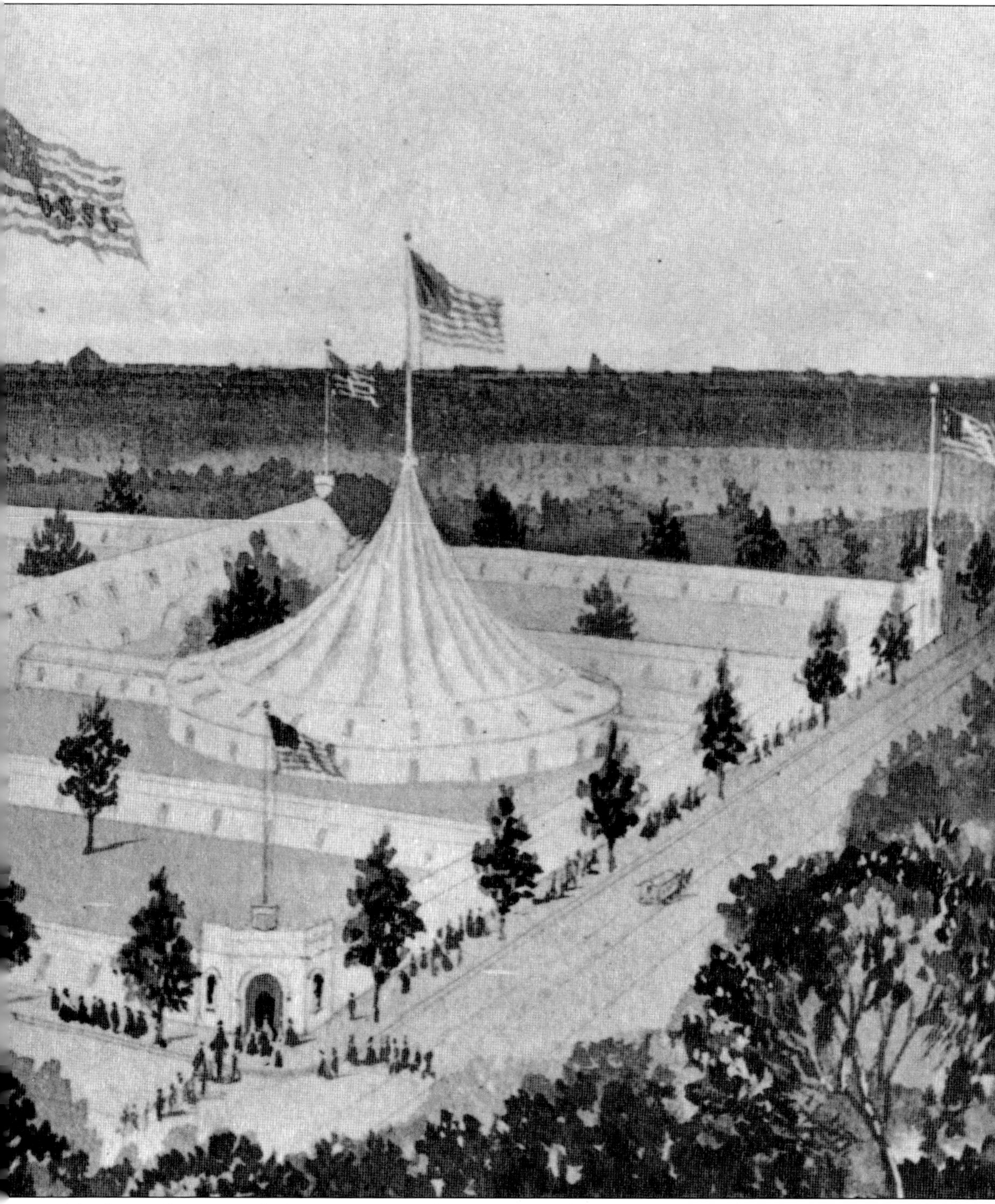

this charity bazaar included a restaurant that could accommodate 1,000 people. Pres. Abraham Lincoln and his wife attended the fair on June 16. His speech caused such an outpouring of emotions that officials decided it would be dangerous for him to attend another Sanitary Fair. This view is to the southwest. (Library of Congress; published by A. Winch.)

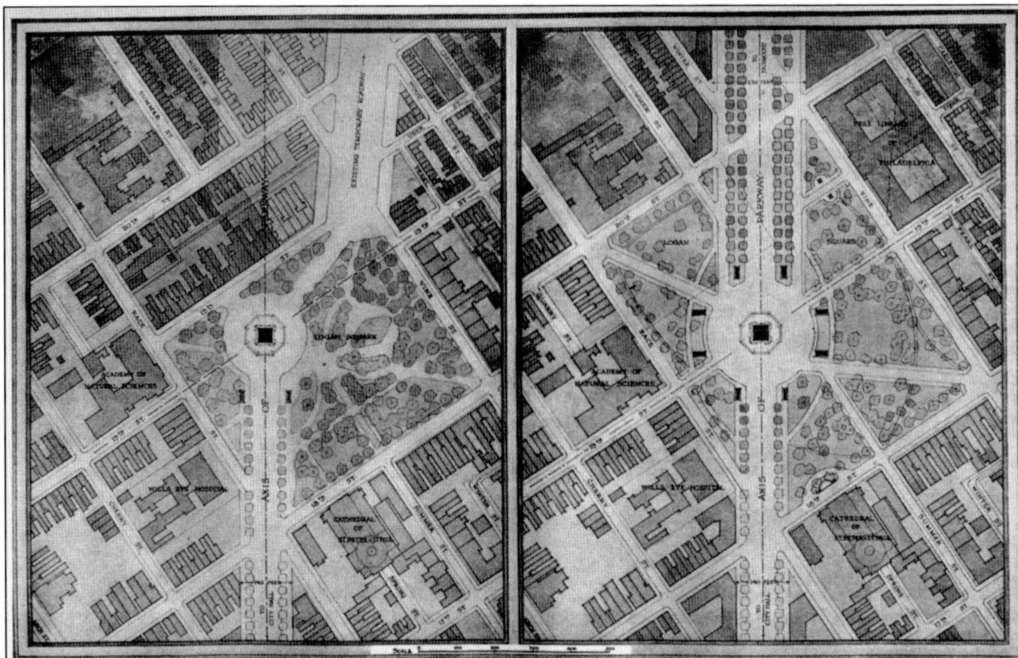

Plan of Logan Square
showing site for Soldiers and Sailors Monument
to conform with the Parkway as placed
on the City Plan in 1906

Plan of Logan Square
showing site for Soldiers and Sailors Monument
to conform with the Parkway as recommended
by Mayor Reyburn in 1909

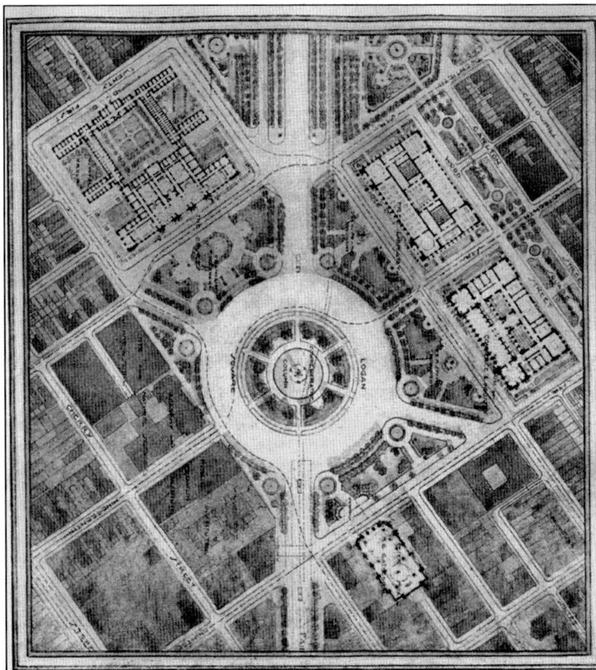

Plan of Logan Square
as shown on plan of Jacques Gréber
approved by the Commissioners of
Fairmount Park June 12, 1918

These plans for Logan Square appear in the 1919 publication *The Fairmount Parkway.* The left drawing shows the plaza as planned in 1906, with the Parkway's irregular routing. Note the "Existing Temporary Roadway" label on the path of Pennsylvania Avenue. The 1909 diagram indicates that row homes would be eliminated to expand Logan Square to the west, and that many trees would ultimately be planted throughout it.

Landscape architect Jacques Gréber envisioned a circular Logan Square, similar to the Place de la Concorde in Paris. His plan closely approximates today's Logan Circle, except that a "commemorative column" appears where Swann Memorial Fountain came to be, and "The Court" complex is where the Franklin Institute is now. This plan is also from *The Fairmount Parkway.*

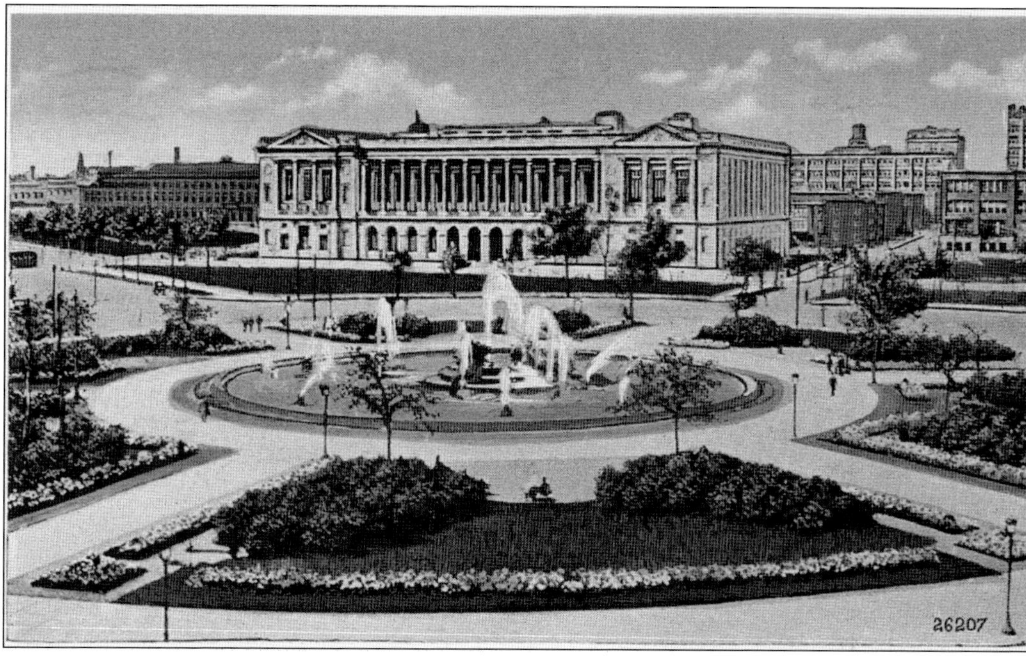

Logan Square is one of the most photographed locales in Philadelphia. The plaza is usually called Logan Circle, since it has hosted a huge, European-style traffic circle since the 1920s. Yet referring to the park as Logan Square is still absolutely correct, since its overall shape is a quadrangle. The Central Library of Philadelphia is featured in this 1930s prospect. (Unmarked postcard.)

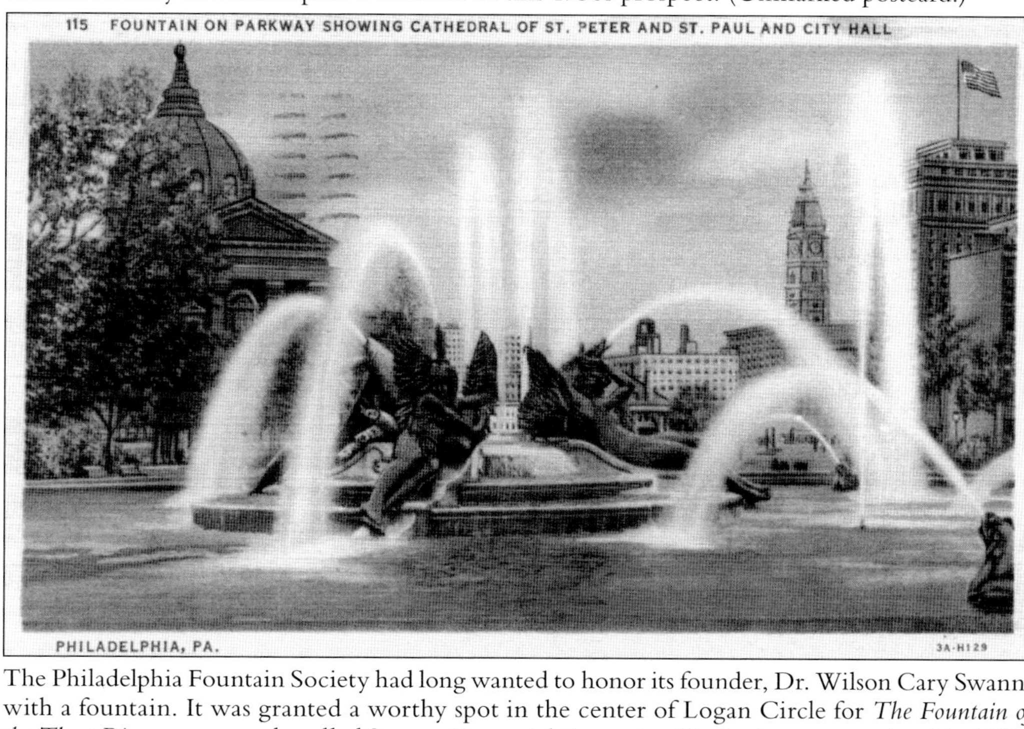

The Philadelphia Fountain Society had long wanted to honor its founder, Dr. Wilson Cary Swann, with a fountain. It was granted a worthy spot in the center of Logan Circle for *The Fountain of the Three Rivers*, commonly called Swann Memorial Fountain. The basin was completed in 1920, but it took four more years to finish the sculptures. (Lynn Boyer, C.T. Art-Colortone.)

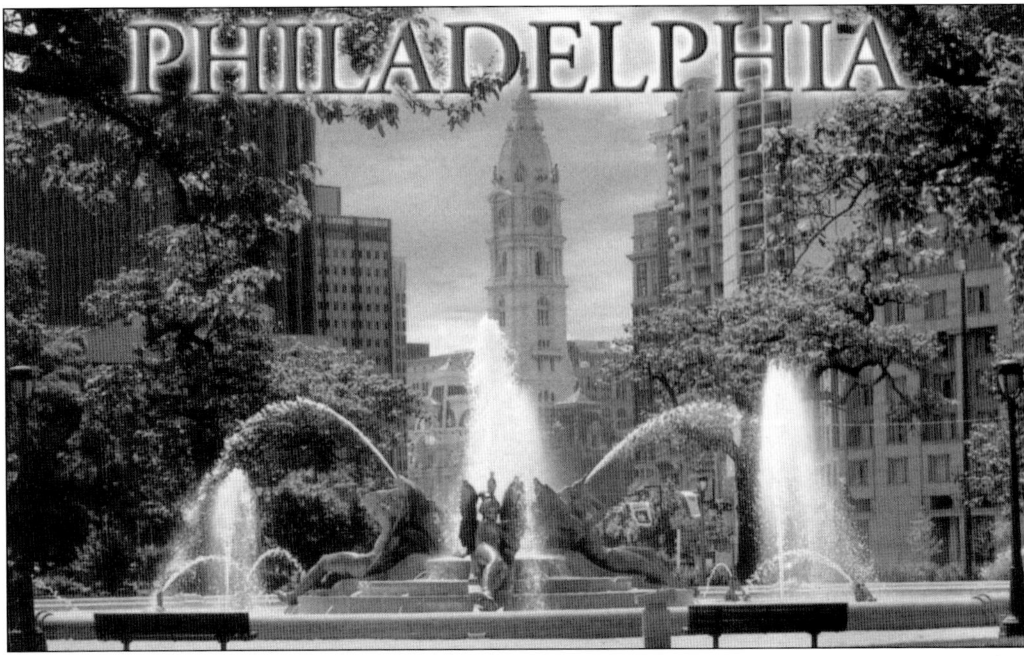

Architect Wilson Eyre Jr. designed the Swann Memorial Fountain, including the central jet that spurts water more than 50 feet high. Sculptor Alexander Stirling Calder created the playful bronze turtles and frogs that spray water, together with the three Native American figures. City Hall Tower stands tall in the background of this modern postcard. (John Hinde Curteich, Americana Souvenirs and Gifts.)

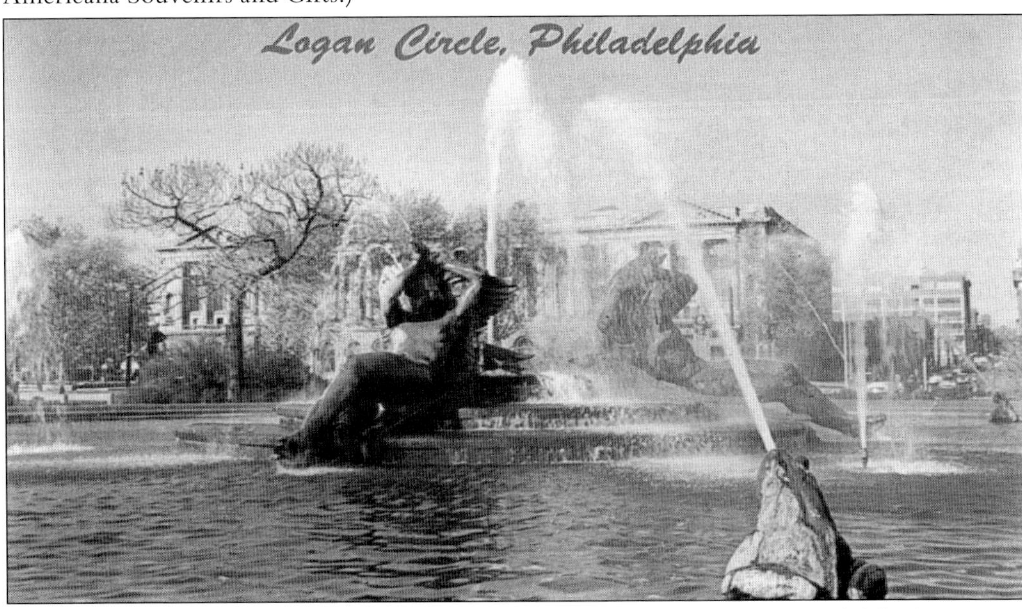

As stated by Alexander Calder, the Native Americans correspond to Philadelphia's principal waterways: the mature woman holding the neck of a swan personifies the Schuylkill River; the male reaching for his bow embodies the Delaware River; and the girl leaning against a swan symbolizes Wissahickon Creek. The use of swans was an obvious pun on Dr. Swann's name. (Charles F. Williams, C.T. Art-Colortone.)

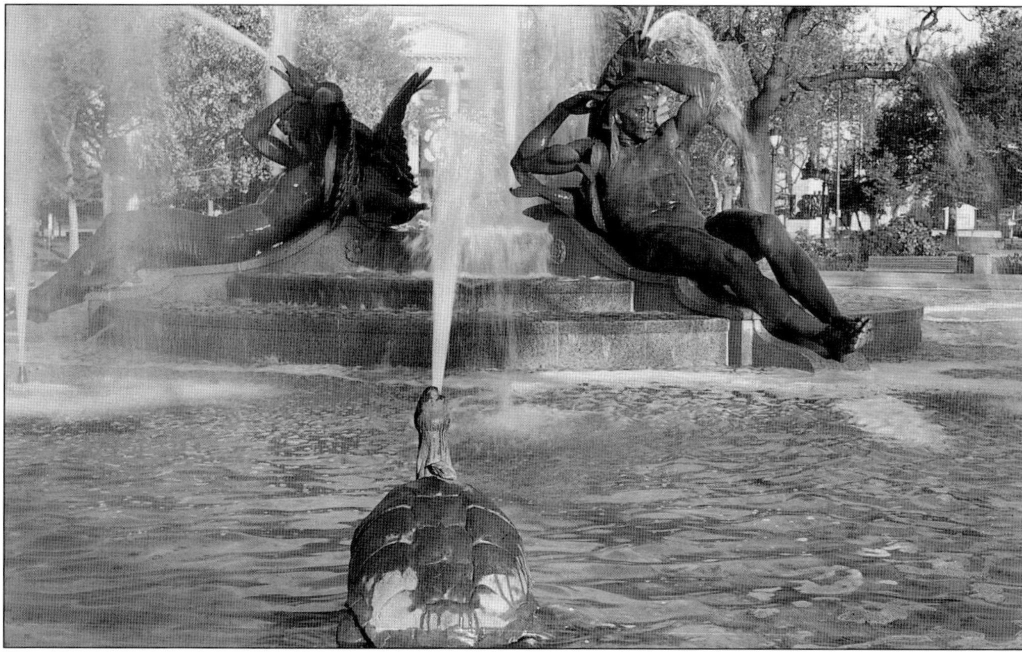

A crowd of 10,000 citizens danced in the surrounding streets when the fountain opened on July 23, 1924. These days, kids in street clothes and bathing suits wade alongside the Native American figures, but the works provoked criticism in the 1920s because of their nudity. (Library of Congress.)

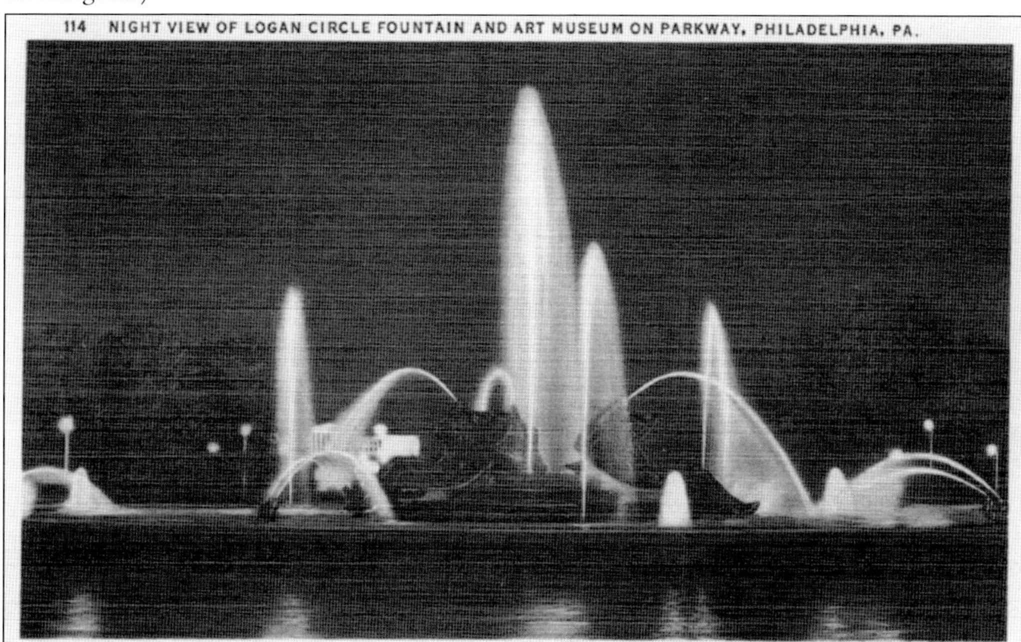

Alexander Stirling Calder's father designed the William Penn statue and the allegorical sculptures embellishing city hall. His son Alexander "Sandy" Calder installed the mobile *Ghost* at the Philadelphia Museum of Art. Alas, despite being proposed years ago, a museum focusing on forms produced by Sandy Calder did not set up shop on the Ben Franklin Parkway. (WYCO Products.)

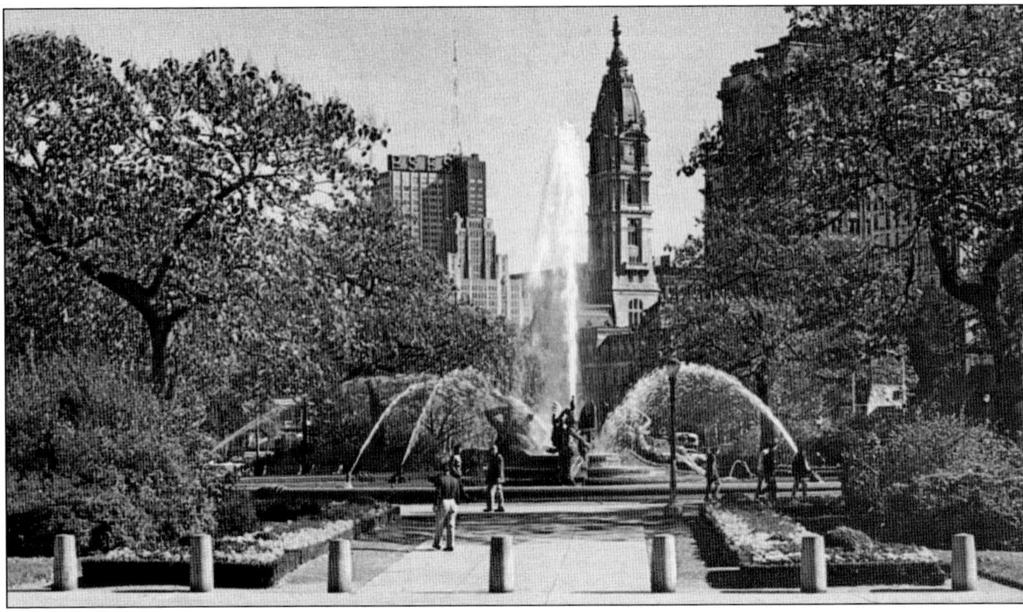

Besides serving as the centerpiece of Logan Circle, Swann Memorial Fountain is the midpoint of the entire Parkway. Few people a century ago could have imagined the insidious impact of automobiles on the avenue. Today, Logan Circle is perilous to drive around, let alone walk across. This 1976 postcard highlights two iconic Philadelphia buildings: city hall and the PSFS Building. (WYCO Products.)

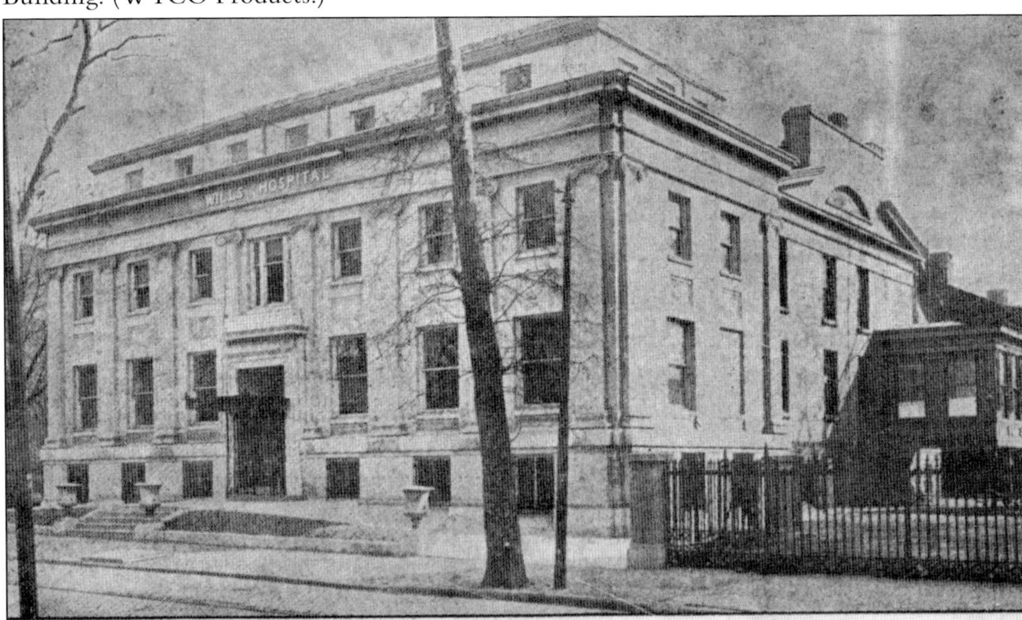

WILLS HOSPITAL, Race Street between 18th and 19th, Philadelphia, Pa.

Wills Eye Hospital once faced Logan Square on the south side. In 1832, Quaker merchant James Wills bequeathed $108,000 to establish a hospital "for the Relief of the Indigent Blind and Lame." The 70-bed institution, designed by Thomas Ustick Walter, extended from Sassafras (now Race) Street to Cherry Street, west of Schuylkill Fifth (now Eighteenth) Street. (Unmarked postcard; courtesy Gus Spector.)

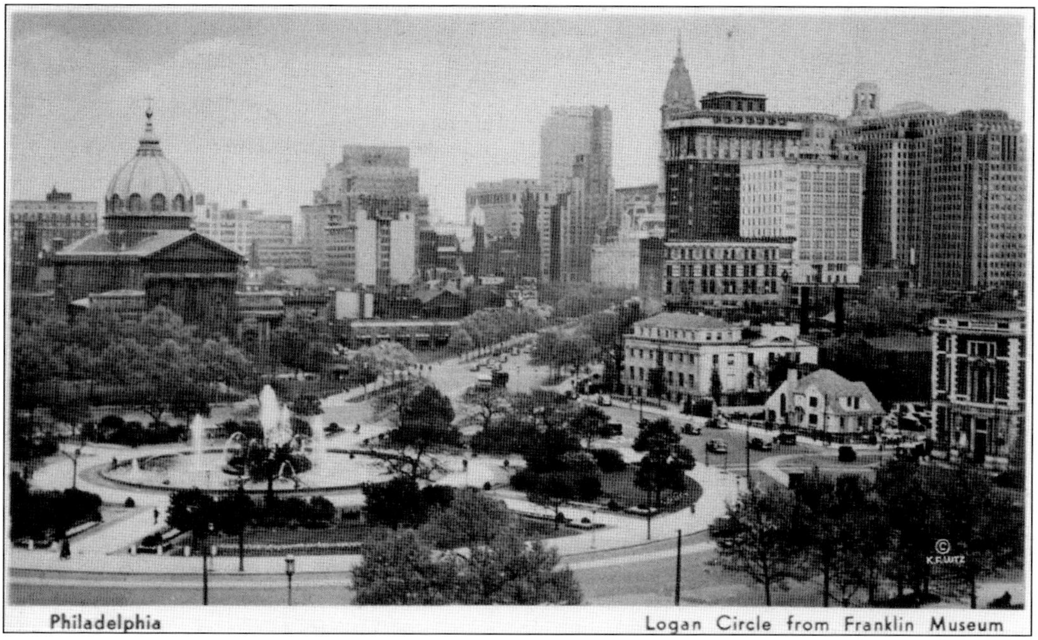

In addition to being the first eye hospital in the western hemisphere, Wills Eye Hospital started the country's first ophthalmology residency program. Its former building is at the center right of this 1938 card, taken more than 100 years after the hospital's opening in 1834, and six years after the hospital moved to Sixteenth and Spring Garden Streets. This spot was to have become a new home for the Philadelphia Orchestra, but the Depression shelved those plans. (K.F. Lutz, Philadelphia.)

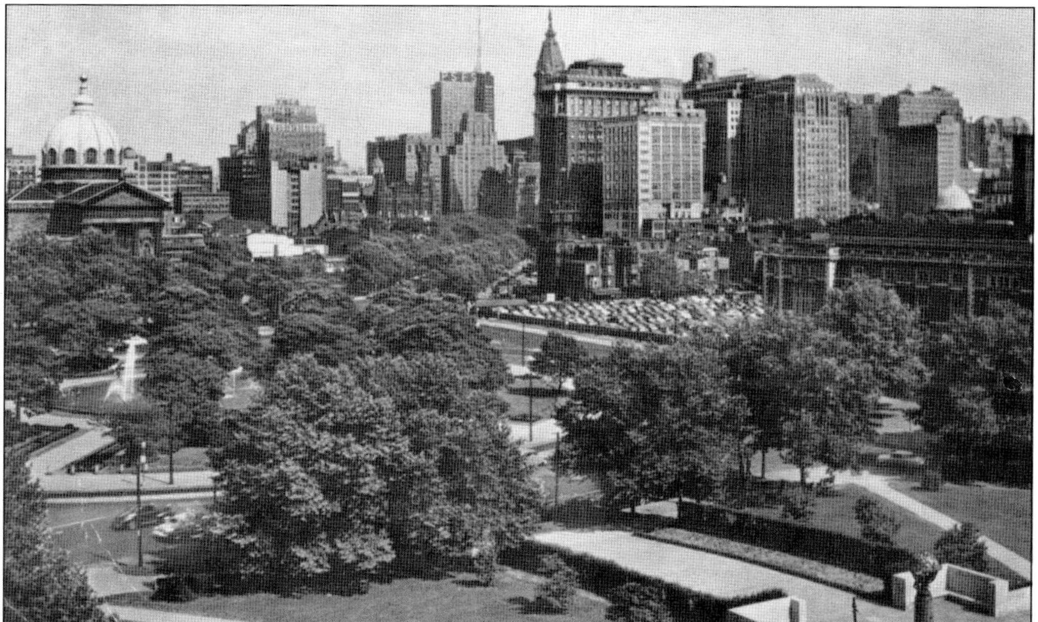

Here is the same scene some 20 years later; the old hospital building has been supplanted by a parking lot. The Four Seasons Hotel was built there in 1983. Wills Eye Hospital has relocated several times in Philadelphia and is now affiliated with the medical college of Thomas Jefferson University. It is still the nation's largest hospital devoted to eye care. (K.F. Lutz, Philadelphia.)

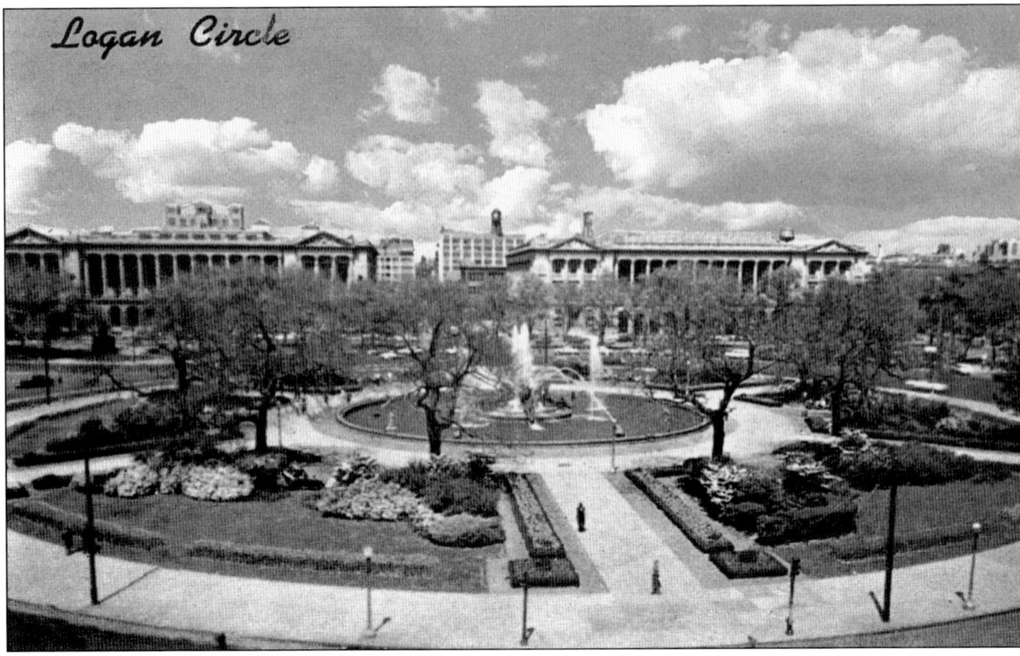

Among the most arresting edifices in Philadelphia are the Central Library of the Free Library of Philadelphia and the Family Courthouse, both opposite Logan Circle. The symmetry of these twin Beaux Arts palaces is perhaps the most sophisticated element of the entire Parkway. They were modeled after the lookalike buildings of the Hôtel de Crillon by the Place de la Concorde on the Champs-Élysées in Paris. (Art Color Card Distributors.)

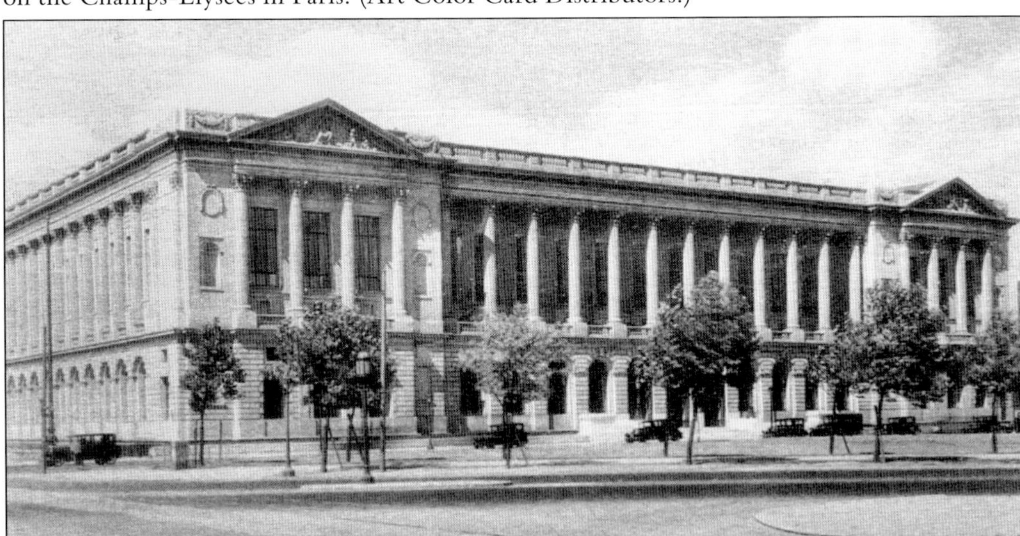

The Philadelphia Free Library system circulates over seven million books and other items annually. The main facility is the Central Library, which was one of the world's largest libraries when it opened on June 2, 1927. It had been planned since 1911, but various obstacles delayed construction. An expansion of this library has been discussed for years. Julian Francis Abele, the primary designer, was one the nation's first African American architects. (Ruth Miller, Art Adv. Service, Philadelphia.)

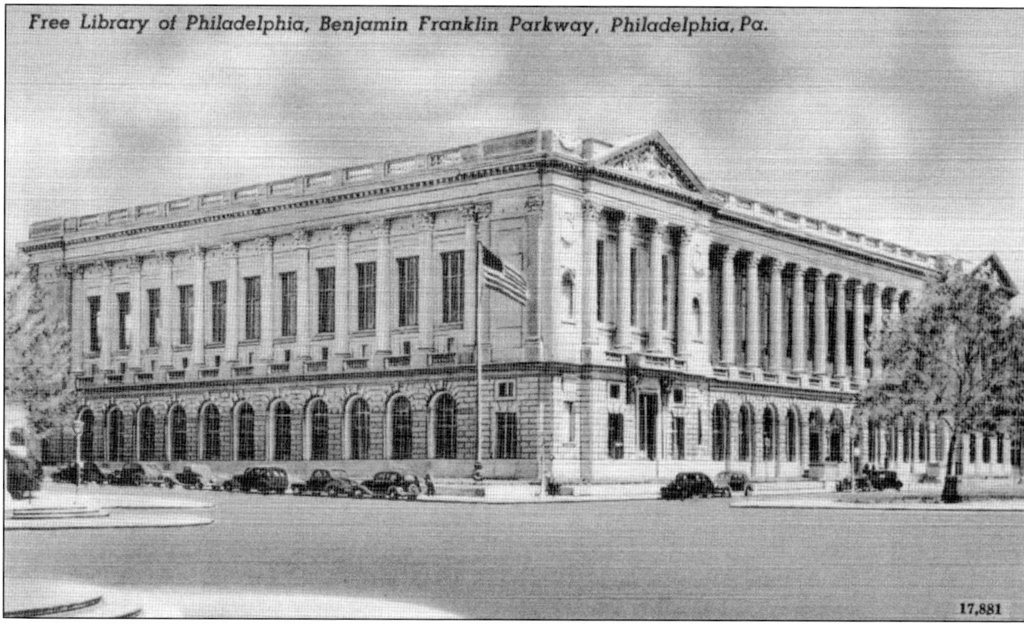

An open-air reading room was initially located on the Central Library's rooftop terrace. In 2008, that space became a green roof demonstration site as part of Mayor Michael Nutter's environmental initiatives for the city. The patio offers splendid views of Logan Circle and the adjoining area. Among other things, the Central Library has on display the raven that inspired Edgar Allen Poe's narrative poem "The Raven." It was owned and stuffed by Charles Dickens in 1841. (Colourpicture.)

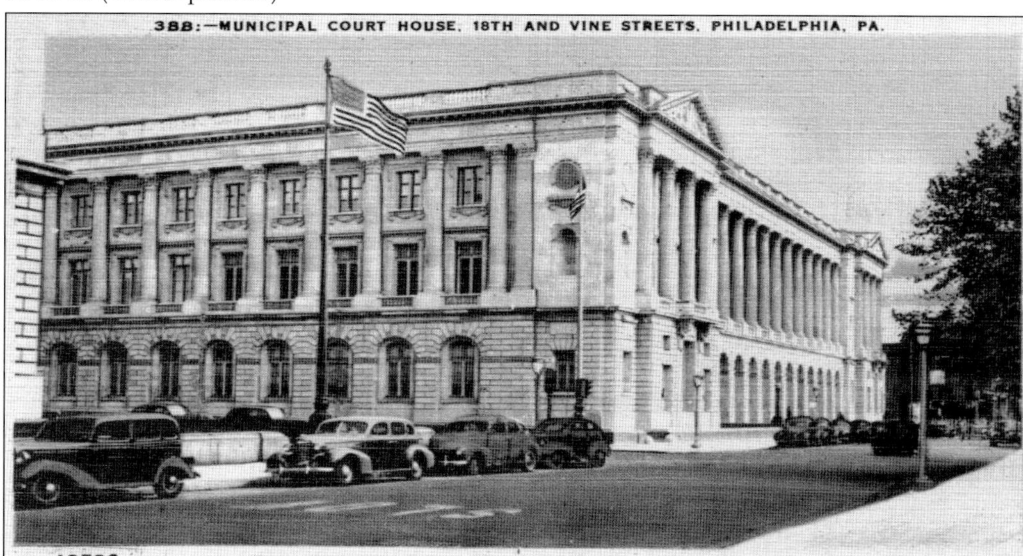

Drawn up by architect John T. Windrim, the Family Court building matches the Central Library and was completed in 1941 as the Philadelphia County Court building. It has been abandoned by the city because new family court facilities are opening nearby. If this edifice was enlarged, the matching look of the two limestone-faced structures would be ruined. Fortunately, a planned conversion into a luxury hotel will reposition the historic building into a new visitor destination along the Parkway. (Unmarked postcard; courtesy Gus Spector.)

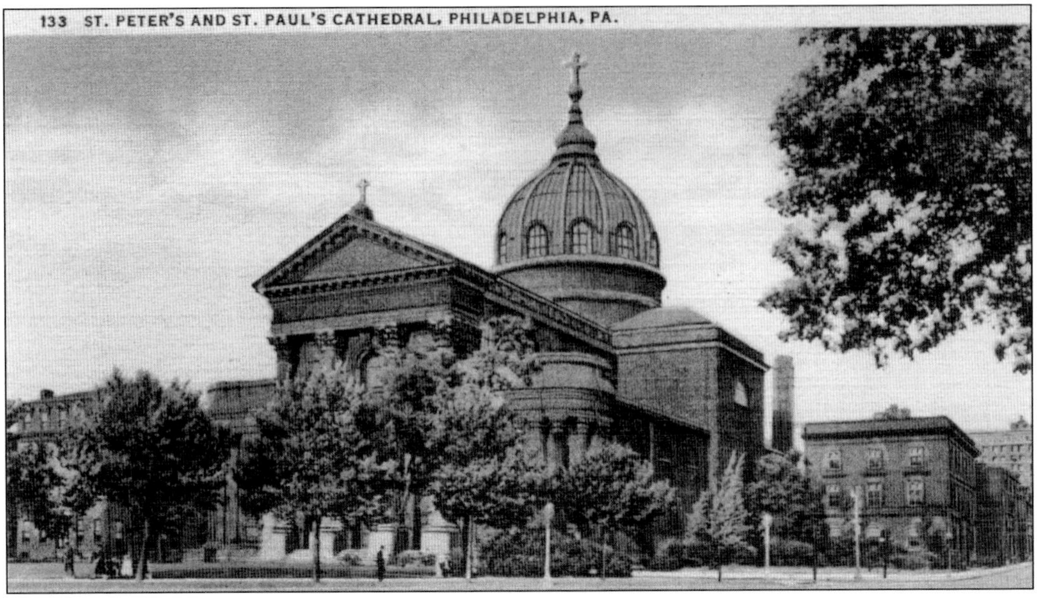

Philadelphia's Irish population was large enough by the 1830s to support the construction of a Catholic cathedral. The Basilica of Saints Peter and Paul was begun by Bishop Francis Patrick Kenrick in 1846, continued under Bishop John Nepomucene Neumann, and finished under Bishop James Frederick Wood. It actually witnessed the Great Central Sanitary Fair of Philadelphia; Abraham and Mary Todd Lincoln surely beheld the cathedral from the fairgrounds on Logan Square. (Lynn Boyer, C.T. Art-Colortone.)

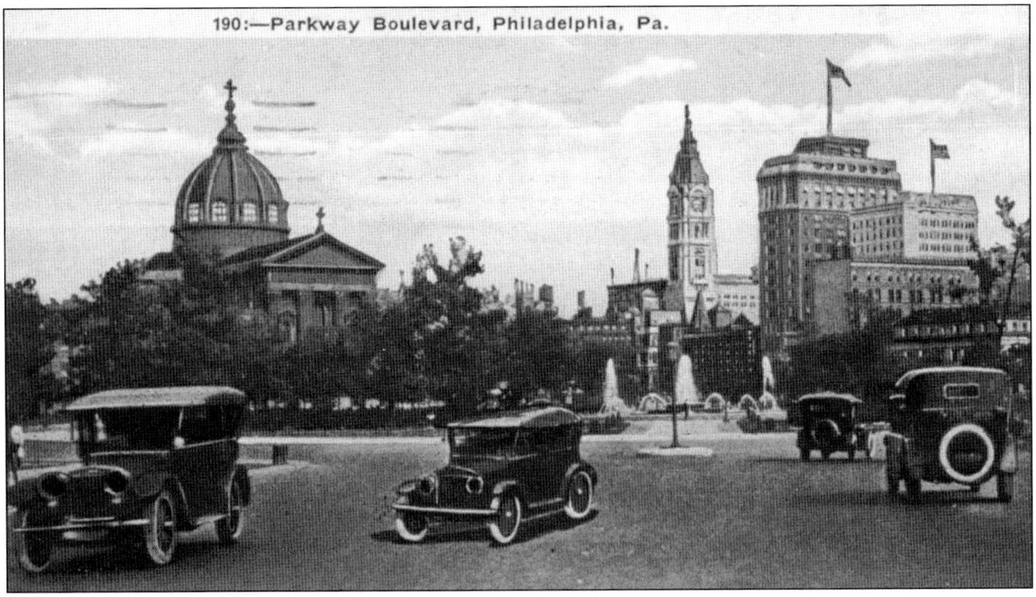

Dedicated on November 20, 1864, the cathedral is the seat of Catholic authority in Philadelphia, as well as the regional heart of Catholicism in southeastern Pennsylvania. The regal building is the oldest structure along the Parkway, and one of only two or three buildings that survived the Parkway's creation. (The Victorian-era carriage house on Cherry Street that now accommodates Mace's Crossing Pub is another survivor.) Logan Circle is packed with cars in this late-1920s scene. (P. Sander, Philadelphia.)

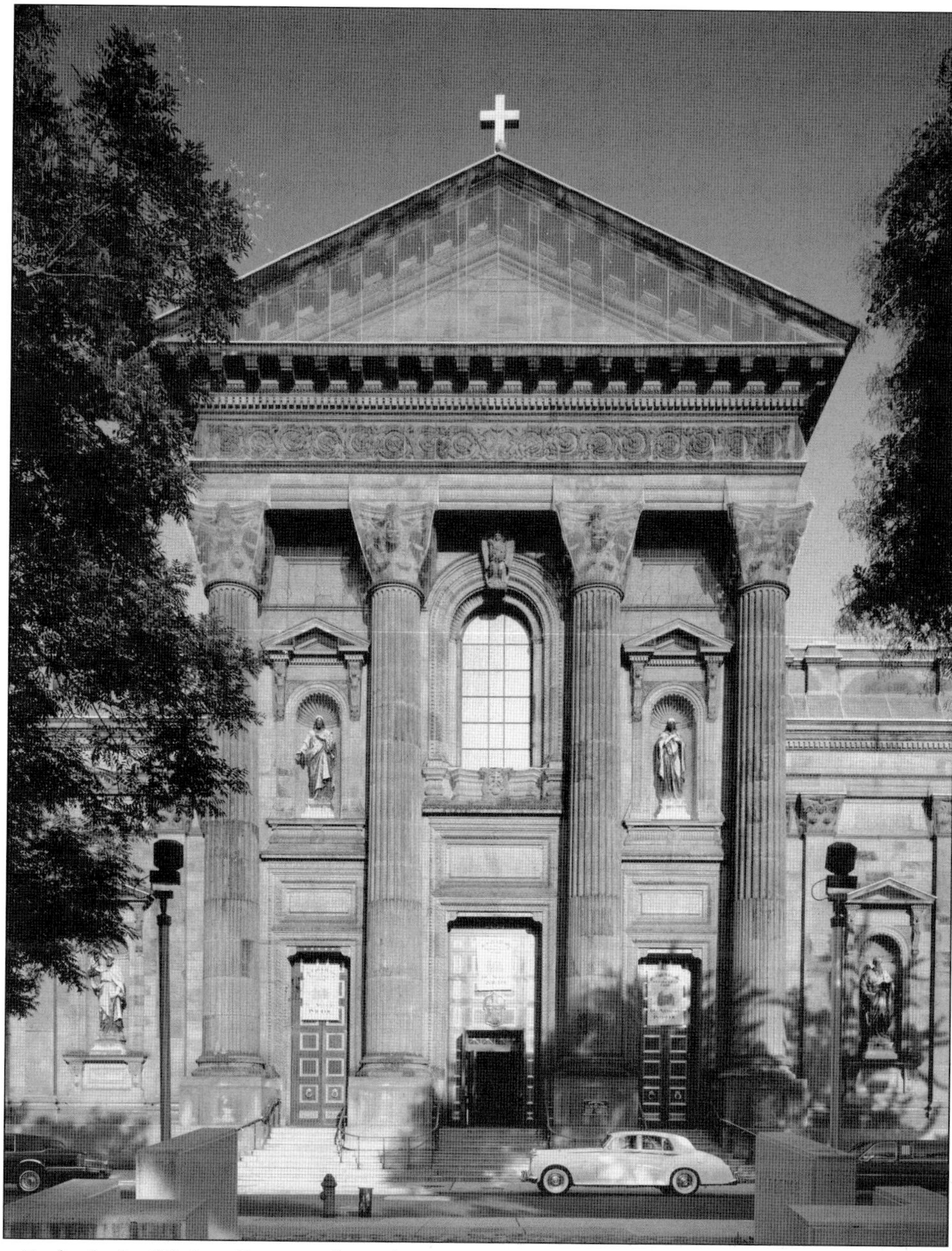

The Cathedral of Saints Peter and Paul was not only the largest cathedral in North America when completed, but it was also proclaimed as the nation's most sumptuous house of worship. Napoleon LeBrun and John Notman designed the brownstone structure, while Constantino Brumidi, the painter of the US Capitol's dome, decorated the interior. The cruciform-shaped building has a main altar and three side-aisle altars under a wide copper dome, reminiscent of Old World cathedrals. Architectural historian Theo B. White pronounced the cathedral "one of the grandest nineteenth-century statements in the vocabulary of the Italian Renaissance." Pope Paul VI designated it a basilica in 1976. Three years later, Pope John Paul II performed an outdoor mass at Logan Circle, immediately in front of the cathedral. (More on this papal visit in a later chapter.) (Library of Congress.)

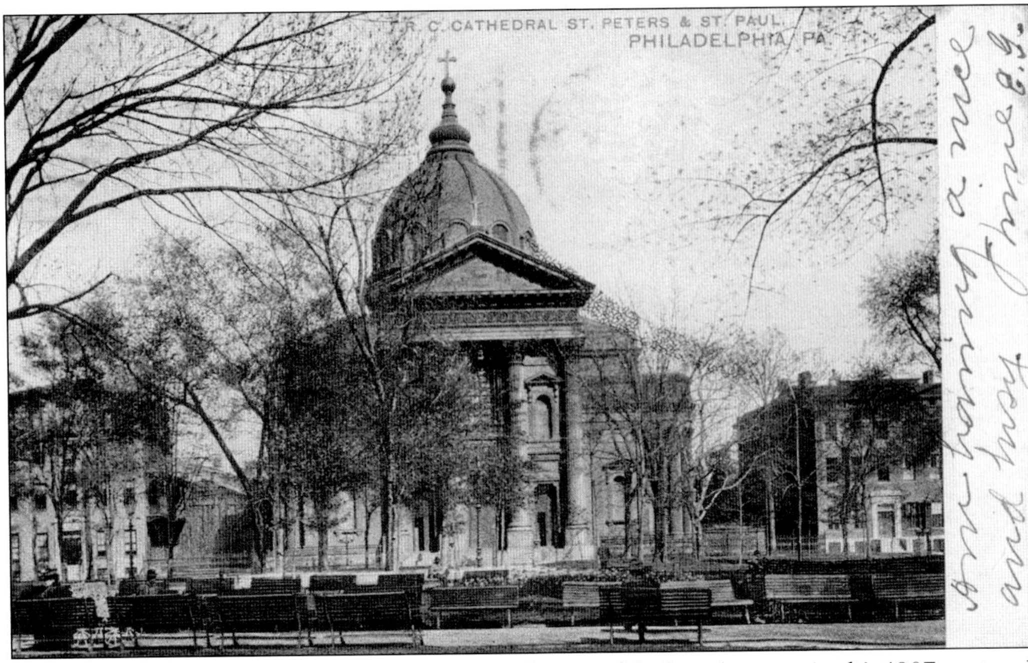

Sister Cities Plaza is across from the basilica, on the site of the benches seen in this 1907 postcard. A sister city, county, or state relationship is an official partnership between two communities, counties, or states in different countries. Philadelphia's Sister Cities include Douala, Cameroon; Florence, Italy; Inchon, Korea; Nizhni Novgorod, Russia; Tel Aviv, Israel; Tianjin, China; Torun, Poland; and Cárdenas, Cuba. (Metropolitan News.)

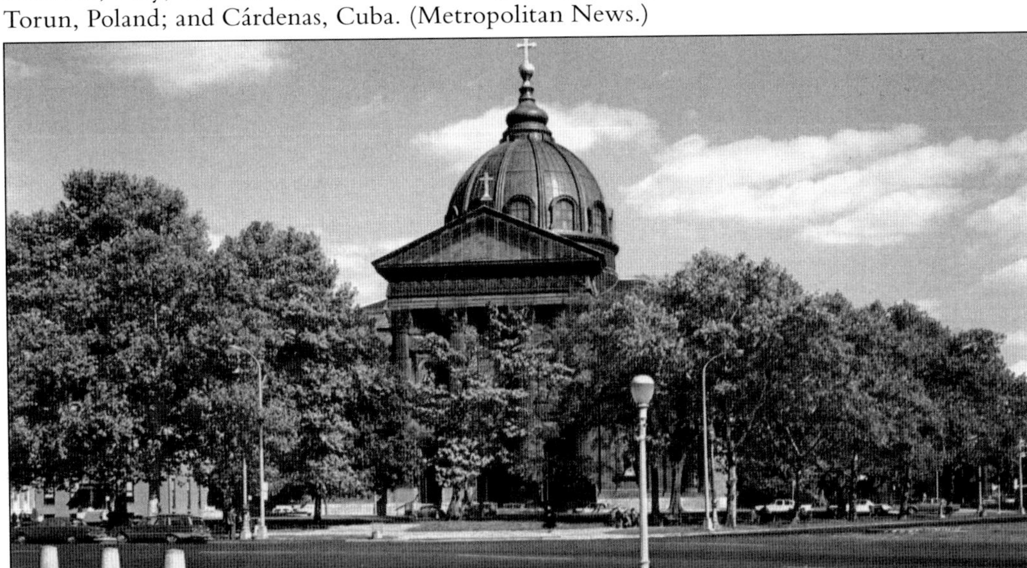

Logan Square's Sister Cities Plaza dates from 1976, the US bicentennial year. In 2012, the Center City District refurbished the 1.3-acre park to include a pavilion housing a café and visitors' center; a children's garden inspired by Philadelphia's Wissahickon Valley; and a kid's "sprayground," an interactive fountain embedded in bluestone. (David P. Willis & Company.)

Five

SANCTUARIES, STATUES, AND SCENES ALONG THE PARKWAY

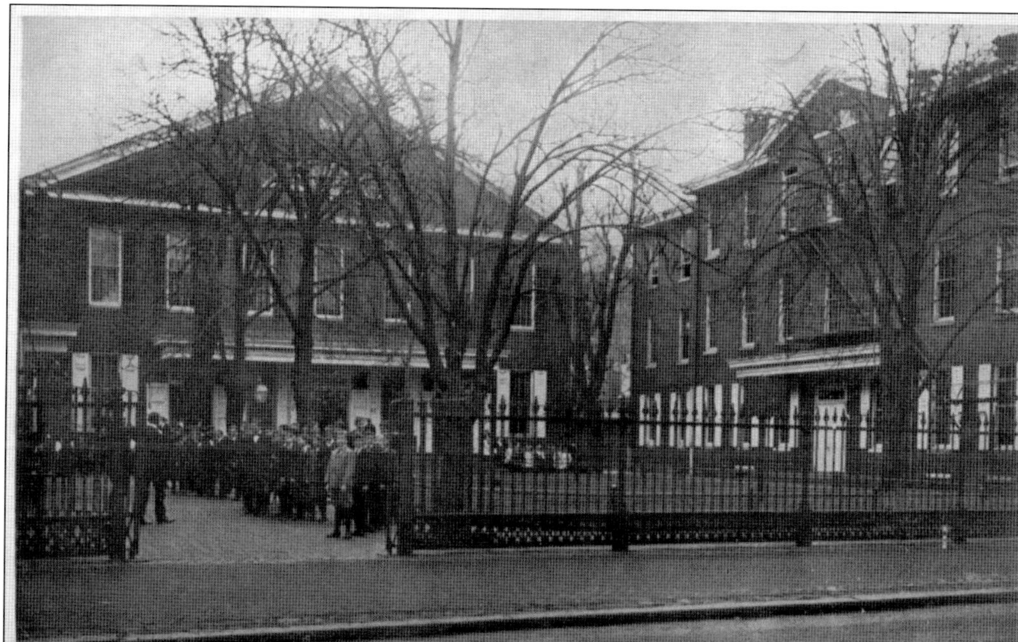

1141 Race Street Meeting House and School, Philadelphia, Pa.

Several longstanding religious houses are in the Parkway neighborhood besides the Cathedral Basilica. Race Street Friends Meetinghouse, at 1515 Cherry Street, was constructed in 1856–1857 by the Society of Friends for their annual meeting sessions. Now part of the Friends Center campus, this meetinghouse was at the forefront of women's involvement in Quakerism, the abolition of slavery, and the civil rights movement. (Philadelphia Post Card Company.)

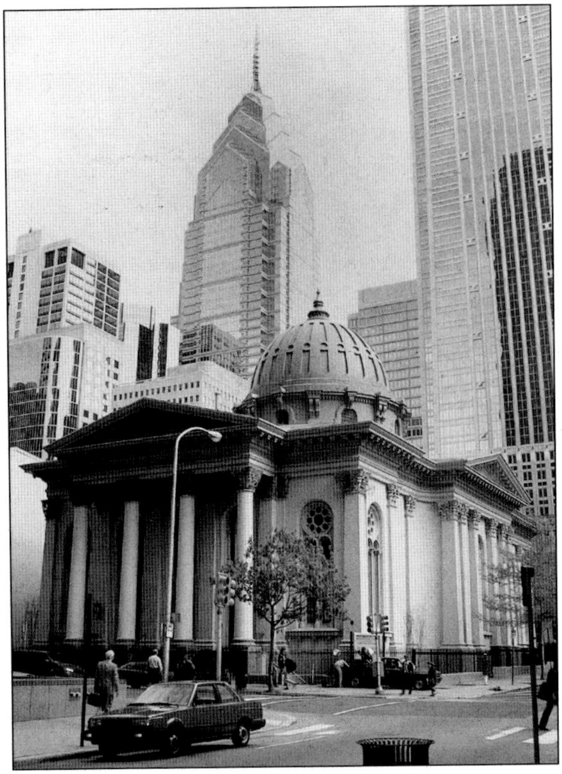

Arch Street Presbyterian Church, at 1724 Arch Street, was erected from 1853 to 1855 and has managed to thrive despite being girdled by skyscrapers. The church's sanctuary is an Italianate Revival tour de force, and its copper dome was influenced by St. Paul's Cathedral in London. This Presbyterian church is the spiritual home of Philadelphia's Welsh population, regardless of religious affiliation. (Corel Professional Photos.)

Designed by John Notman and dating from 1859, St. Clement's Episcopal Church, at Twentieth and Cherry Streets, was repositioned 40 feet west on July 19, 1929, to allow for the widening of Twentieth Street from the Parkway to Market Street. The 5,500-ton building was lifted onto steel beams, shifted on tracks, and placed on a new foundation. No evidence of this move is discernable today. This image is from *A Memorial on the Moving of St. Clement's Church* (c. 1929).

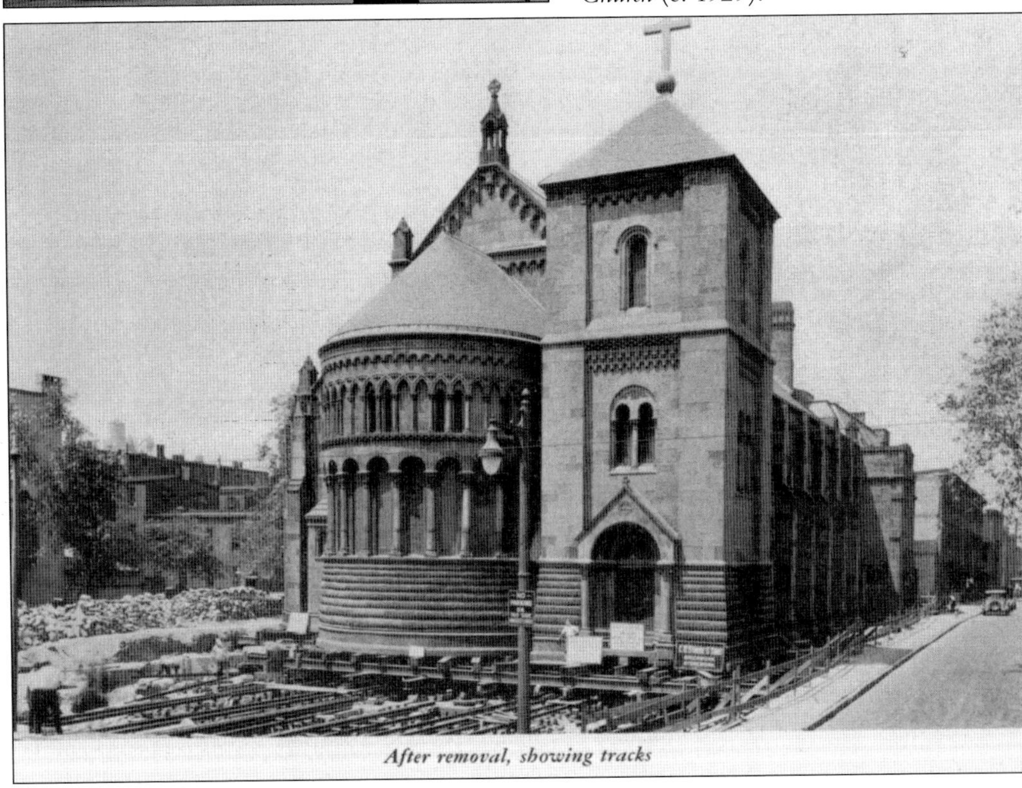

After removal, showing tracks

St. Francis Xavier Roman Catholic Church is another Parkway longtimer, though it is on the roadway's northern end, at Twenty-fourth and Green Streets. The parish began in 1839, but this stunning Romanesque church was raised in the 1890s to replace an older house of worship once located within modern-day Eakins Oval. Following a severe fire in 1906, St. Francis Xavier was rebuilt. In 2014, the church was the first site of Mass Mob Philly, an event in which some 680 people came to worship on Sunday, March 23, having been invited via social media. St. Francis Xavier's steeple is a prominent neighborhood landmark. (Photograph by author.)

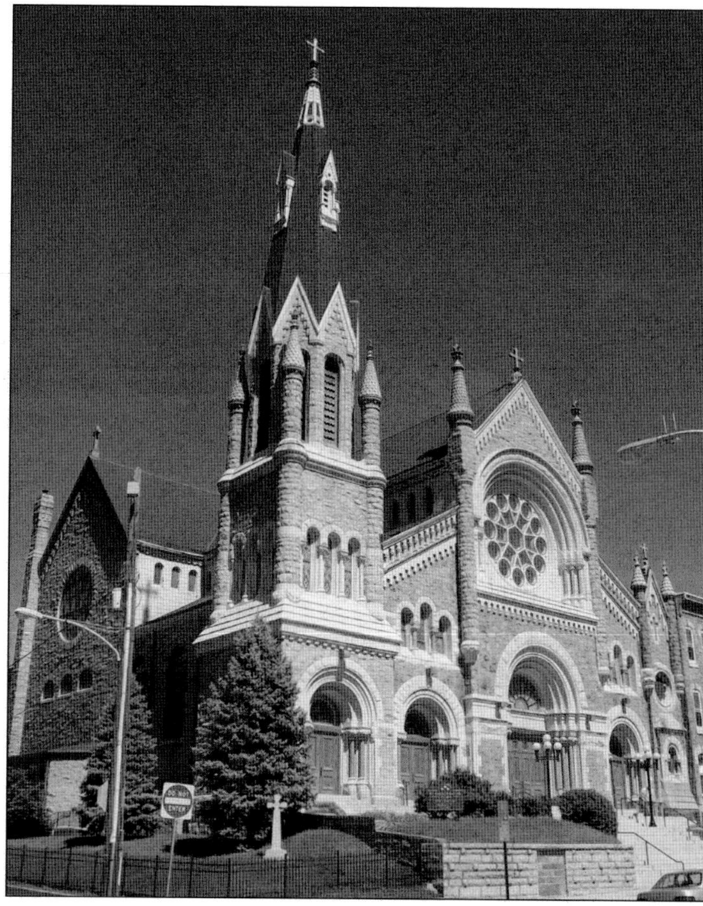

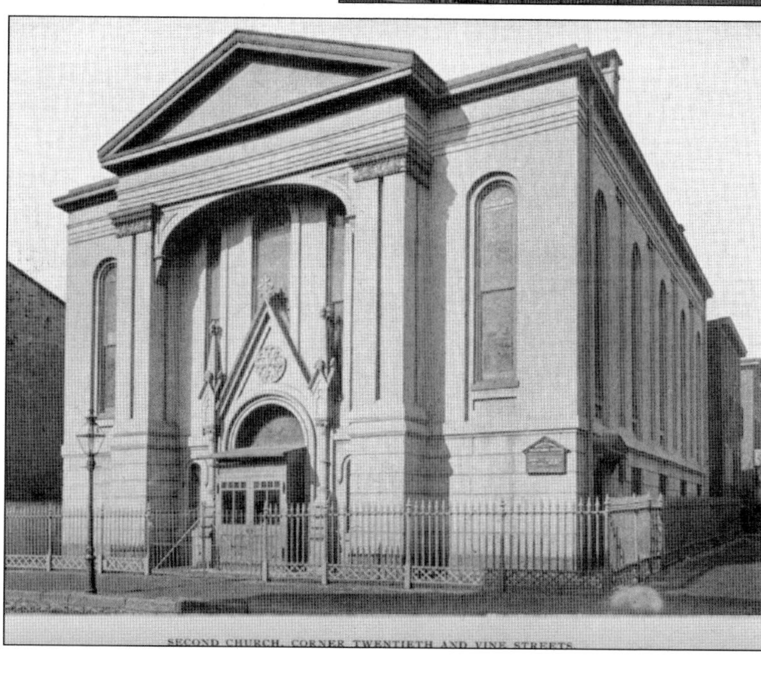

SECOND CHURCH, CORNER TWENTIETH AND VINE STREETS.

Second Reformed Presbyterian Church, at the northwest corner of Twentieth and Vine Streets, was one of hundreds of buildings condemned to create the Fairmount Parkway. It had been built for the Logan Square Presbyterian Church in 1849; Second Reformed purchased the property in 1875. Around 1910, the city bought it for Parkway demolition. This image is from *The Presbyterian Church in Philadelphia* (1895).

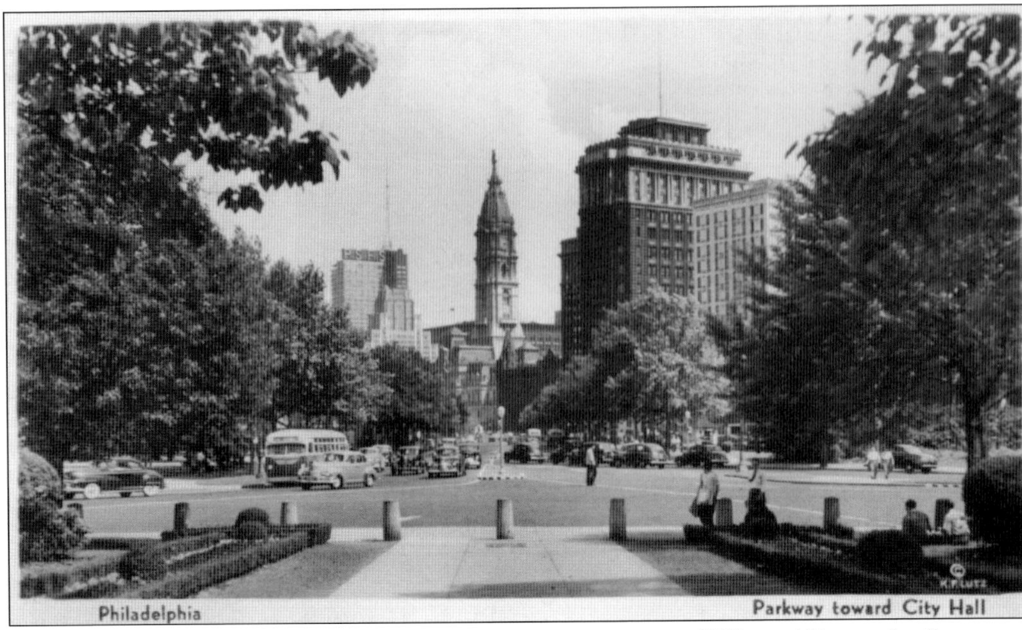

After World War I, the planting of "Tribute Trees" in memory of fallen soldiers and sailors swept the nation. Some 60 paulownias and red oaks were laid along the Parkway by the Civic Club of Philadelphia. A plaque in Logan Circle states that they were planted "as a tribute of honor and gratitude to the men who served their country in the Great War." Most were replaced about 1989. This 1940s postcard shows a somewhat congested scene. (K.F. Lutz, Philadelphia.)

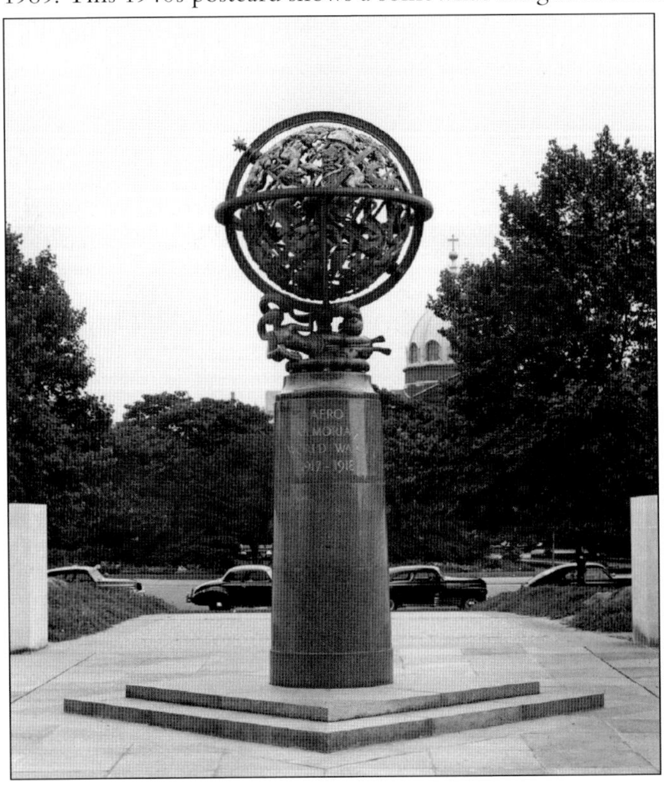

The Association for Public Art (formerly the Fairmount Park Art Association) is the nation's first private, nonprofit organization dedicated to integrating public art and urban planning. *Aero Memorial to World War I Aviators 1917–1918* is a work under its care. Situated in Aviator Park, within Logan Square, this gilded bronze by Paul Manship commemorates aviators who died during World War I. (The Library Company of Philadelphia.)

Close by is the *All Wars Memorial to Colored Soldiers and Sailors*, completed by J. Otto Schweizer and dedicated on May 30, 1934. The Commonwealth of Pennsylvania commissioned the bronze and granite memorial to recognize the patriotism of African American servicemen. Debate ensued regarding installing the work in Logan Square (as had been planned), so it was placed in a remote corner of Fairmount Park. In 1994, the sculpture was rightfully moved to its originally proposed location and rededicated. (Photograph by author.)

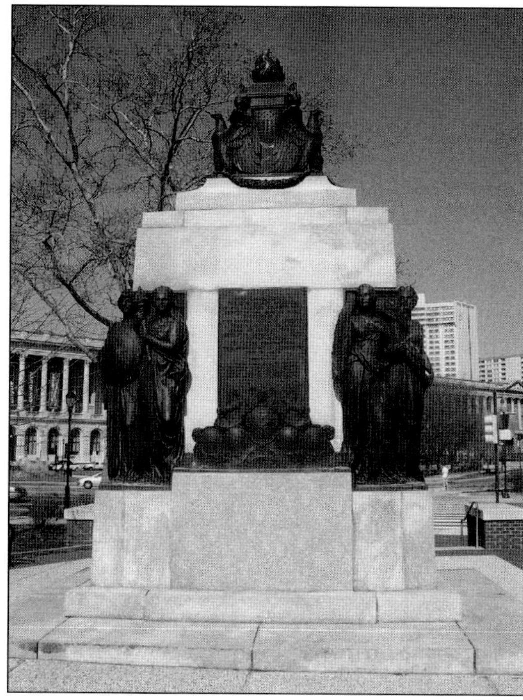

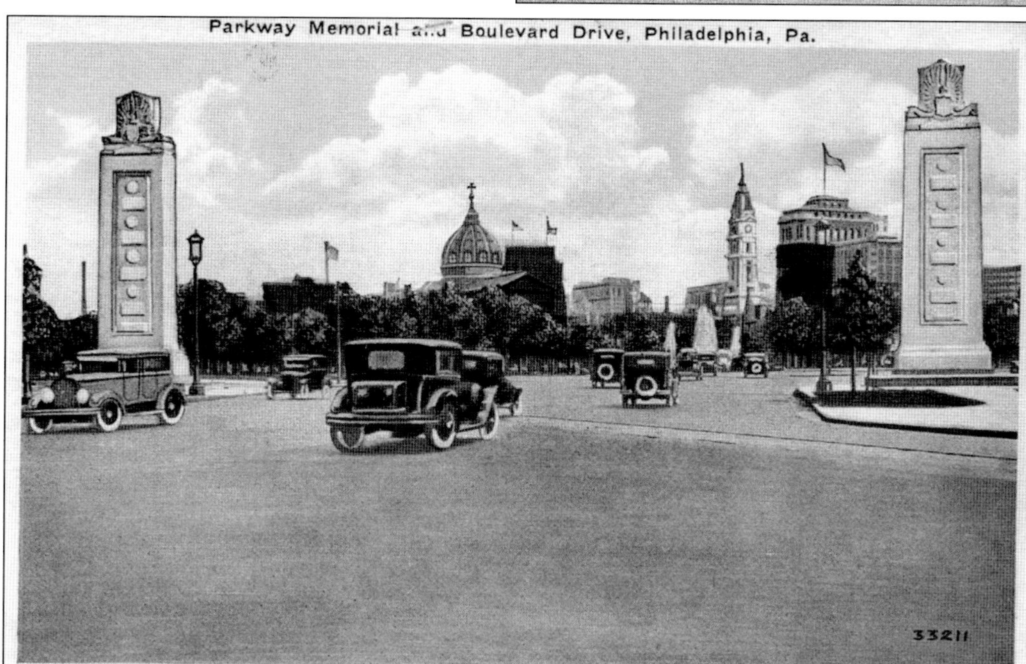

Philadelphia appropriated $88,000 for a Civil War memorial in 1918. The Civil War Soldiers and Sailors Memorial consists of two twin pylons of Tennessee marble, one depicting sailors and the other depicting soldiers. Initially set within Logan Square in 1927 as a formal gateway to the Parkway, the pylons were moved about 150 feet north in the 1950s due to construction of the Vine Street Expressway, which passes underneath the square's northern edge. (P. Sander, Philadelphia; courtesy Gus Spector.)

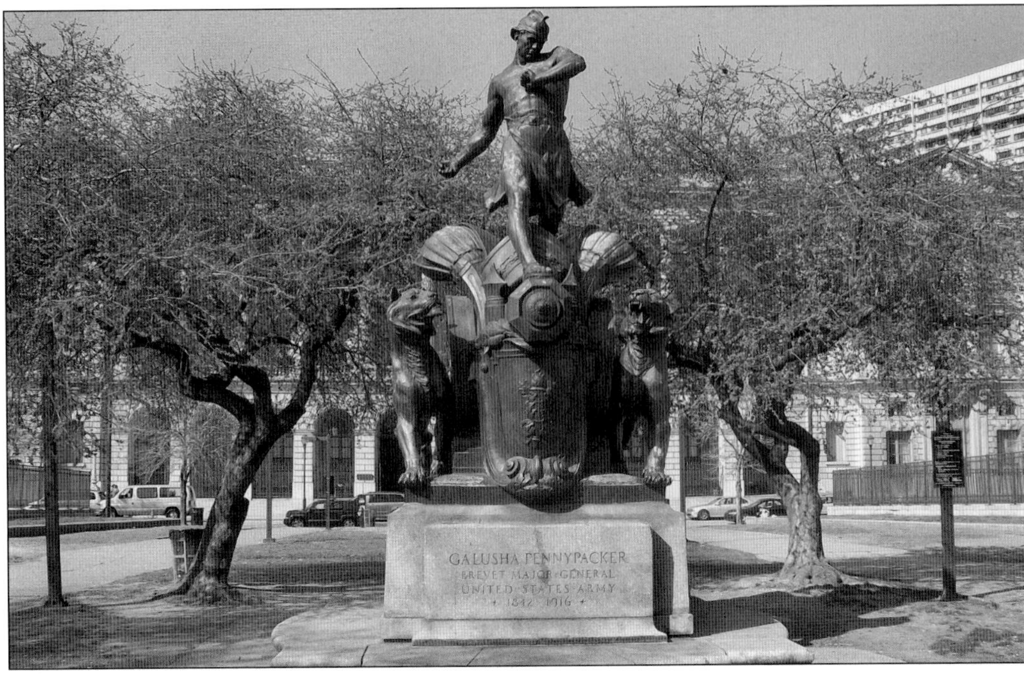

The Galusha Pennypacker statue, fronting the Family Courthouse, honors the youngest general officer in US history. At the onset of the Civil War, Galusha Pennypacker (1844–1916) embarked on a lengthy military career as a Union quartermaster sergeant at age 16. He was promoted to brigadier general when only 20 years old after being severely wounded. The Beaux Arts bronze memorial by sculptor Albert Laessle debuted on June 1, 1934. (Photograph by author.)

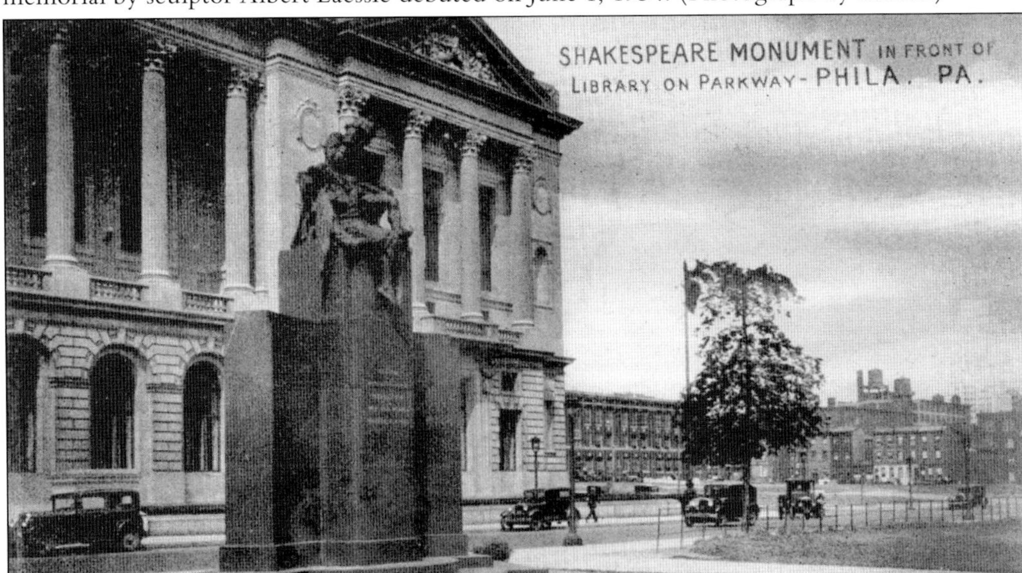

Created by Alexander Stirling Calder in 1926, the Shakespeare Memorial in front of the Central Library is one of the finest memorials to the "Bard of Avon." The sculpture, officially named *Hamlet and the Fool*, presents Tragedy (Hamlet) and Comedy (Touchstone, the fool) on a black marble pedestal that displays Shakespeare's memorable words: "All the world's a stage and all the men and women merely players." (Manhattan Post Card Company; courtesy Gus Spector.)

The stainless steel sculpture *Kopernik* (or *Copernicus*) was created in 1973 to commemorate the Polish astronomer on the 500th anniversary of his birth. A gift to the City of Philadelphia from local Polish American organizations, the abstract work by artist Talcott Dudley represents Earth's orbit around the sun. It sits next to the United Fund Building, an innovative structure finished in 1971 as the headquarters of United Way of Southeastern Pennsylvania. (Photograph by author.)

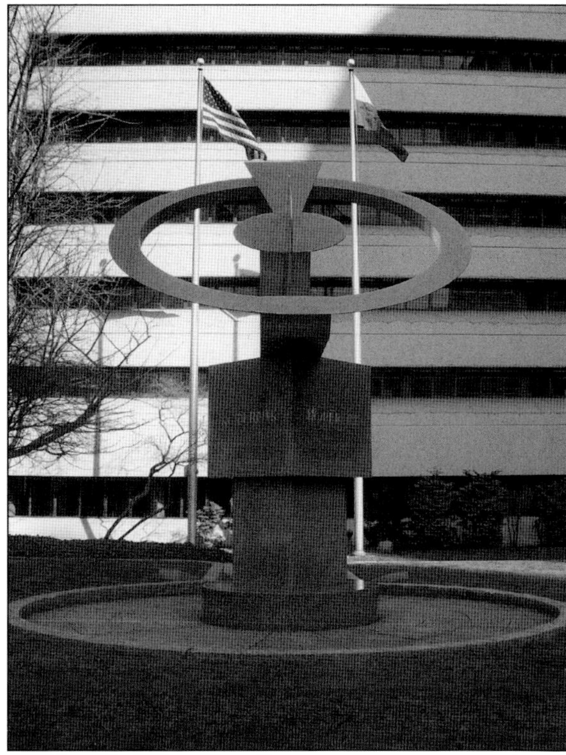

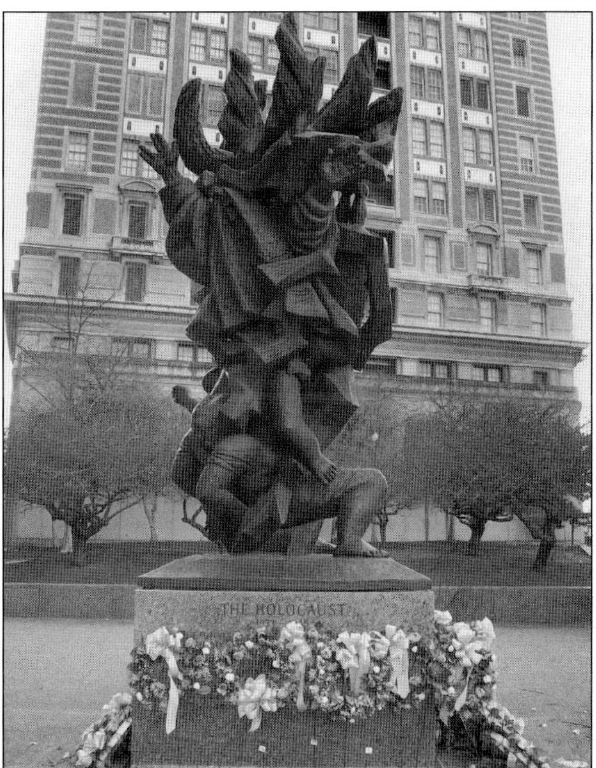

The Bell Parkway Building serves as a backdrop to the *Monument to the Six Million Jewish Martyrs*, reportedly the first Holocaust memorial in America. The Association of Jewish New Americans, in cooperation with the Federation of Jewish Agencies of Greater Philadelphia, presented the work to the city on April 26, 1964. Sculpted by Nathan Rapoport, it is commonly referred to as the Philadelphia Holocaust Memorial. (Photograph by author.)

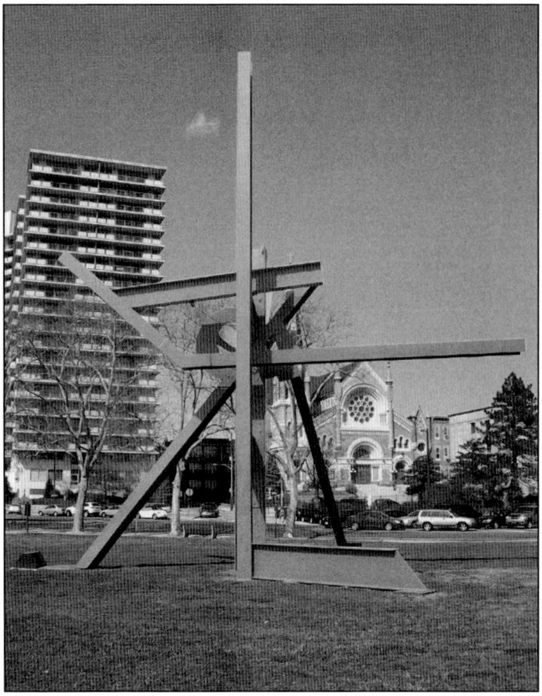

In 2007, the Fairmount Park Art Association (now the Association for Public Art) placed the 40-foot-tall abstract work *Iroquois* opposite St. Francis Xavier Church after its donation by Philadelphia art patron David N. Pincus. The red-painted steel piece, honoring Native Americans, is by Mark di Suvero, who said of *Iroquois*, "You have to walk in through the piece, you have to have it all the way around you and at that moment, you can feel what that sculpture can do." (Photograph by author.)

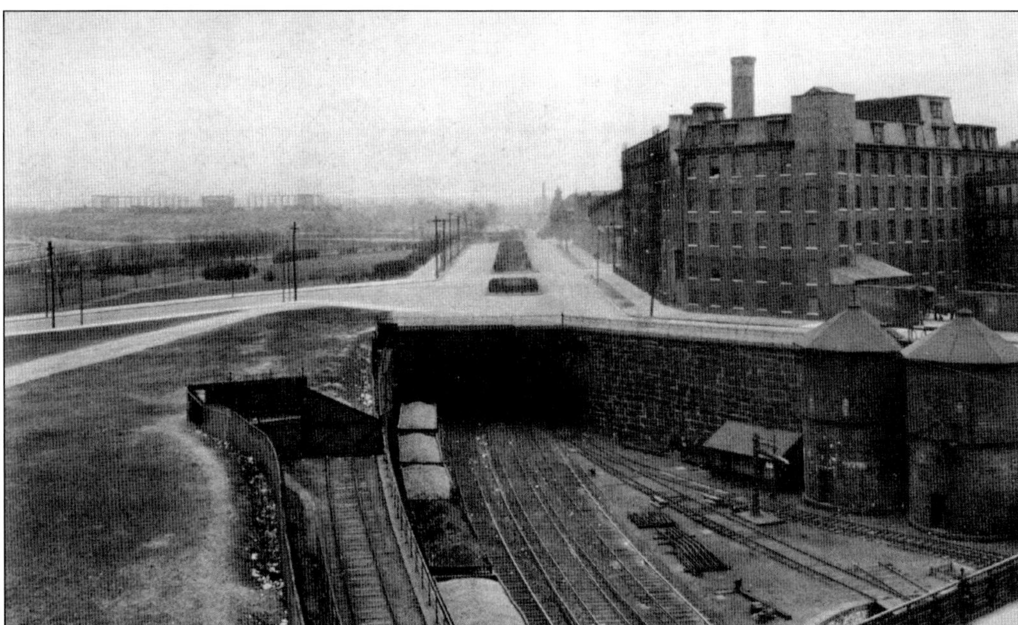

The Philadelphia Museum of Art is under construction on the horizon of this 1923 photograph of Pennsylvania Avenue (which had been incorporated as part of the Parkway early on) and the Pennsylvania Avenue Subway. The rail route was Philadelphia's first subway, excavated in the 1890s by the City of Philadelphia and the Reading Railroad to remove train traffic from surface streets. Part of the Reading's "City Branch" line, the long-abandoned subway is explored by urban adventurers and might soon become part of a subterranean rail park. This image is from John Frederick Lewis's *The Redemption of the Lower Schuylkill* (1924).

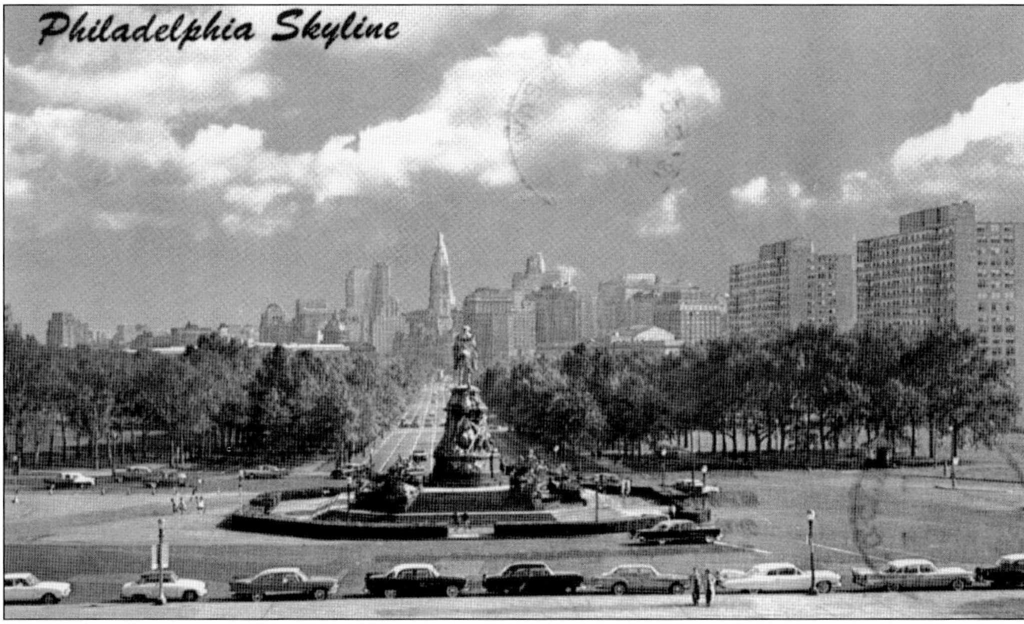

This 1950s panoramic postcard shows the most emblematic scene of Philadelphia. The city's skyline has changed much over the years, but the view up the Ben Franklin Parkway is basically the same. Yet one thing is missing here: Eakins Oval, the prodigious traffic loop added in 1967. The oval was named after celebrated Philadelphia realist painter and fine arts teacher Thomas Eakins (1844–1916). Furthermore, the many Tribute Trees emphasize the Parkway's role as a wedge of parkland connecting calm and green Fairmount Park to harsh and gray downtown Philadelphia. (Art Color Card Distributors.)

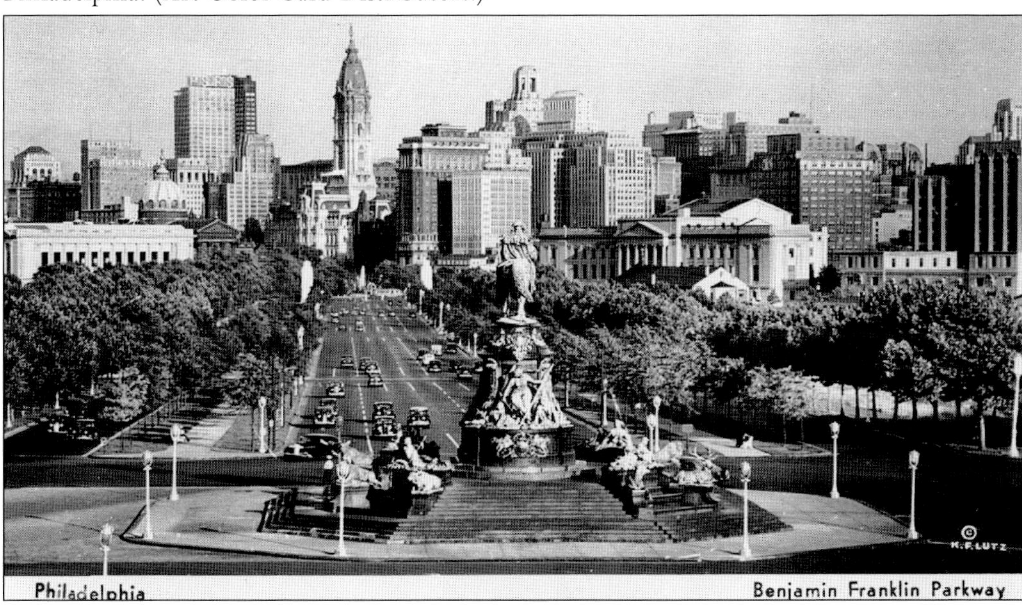

There had been talk of erecting a heroic monument to George Washington in Philadelphia since about 1810, but it was not until 1897 that the city's Washington Monument was unveiled. Encircled by fountains and standing 44 feet high, this ornate statue was once the largest equestrian memorial in America. It remains one of the greatest equestrian monuments in the world. (K.F. Lutz, Philadelphia.)

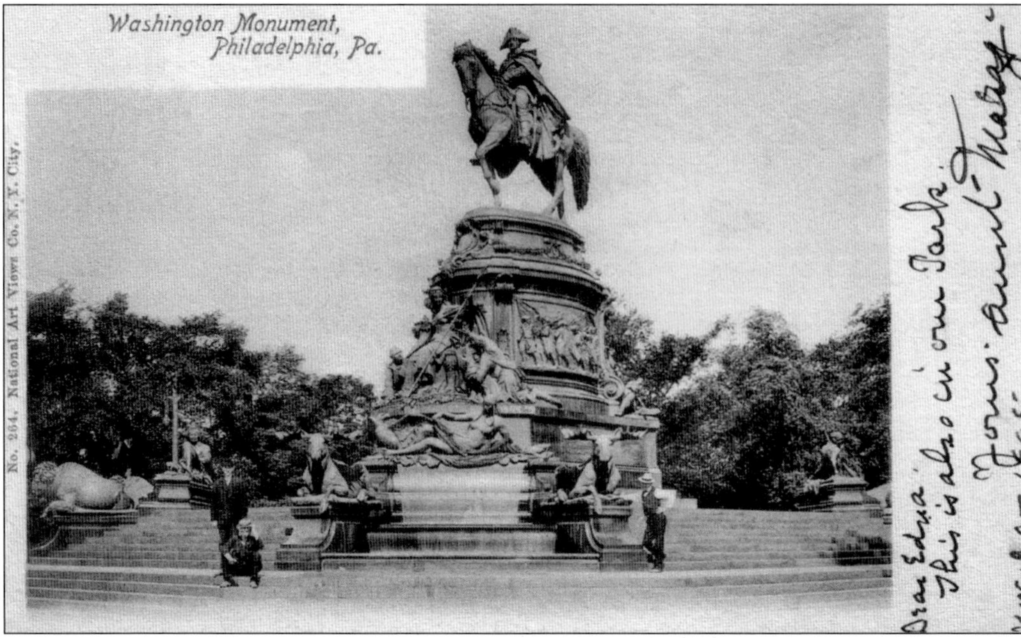

Philadelphia's Washington Monument was created for $250,000 by Rudolf Siemering, a German sculptor who had a distinguished career for his baroque-style work. The State Society of the Cincinnati of Pennsylvania formally donated the bronze and granite memorial to the city on May 15, 1897. It was placed at the Green Street entrance to Fairmount Park, about a block north of its modern-day setting, where the work was moved in 1928. (National Art Views Company.)

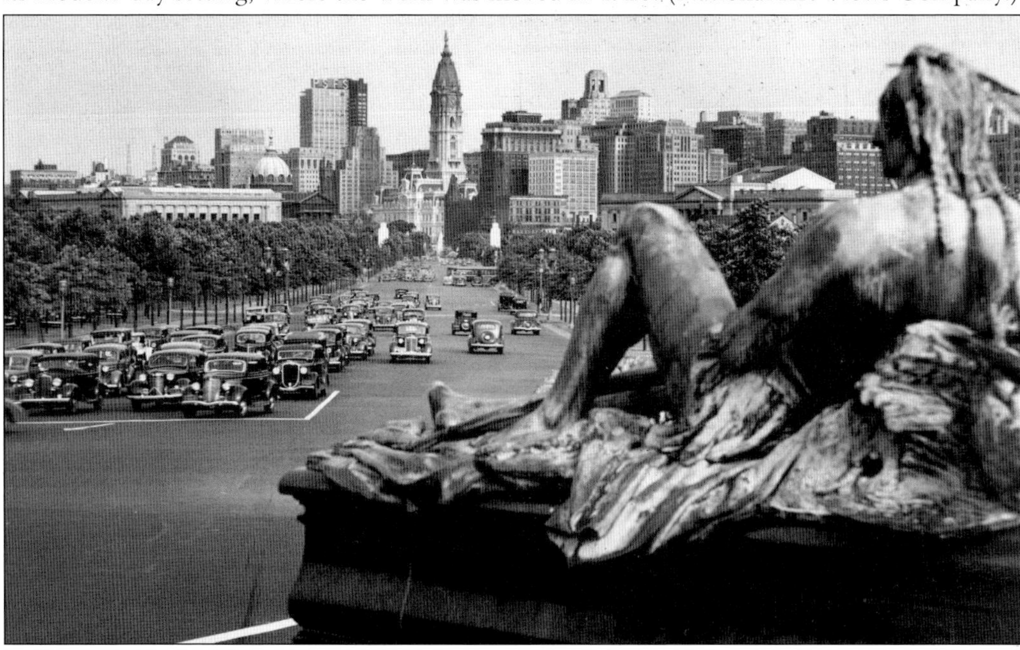

The 1897 debut of the Washington Monument was accompanied by a tremendous military parade and a procession of 10,000 bicyclists. Pres. William McKinley was the keynote speaker and pulled the unveiling rope. In this 1930s vista, a Native American figure surveys the relentless flow of traffic on the Parkway. (The Library Company of Philadelphia.)

Six

Logan Square/Circle
West Side

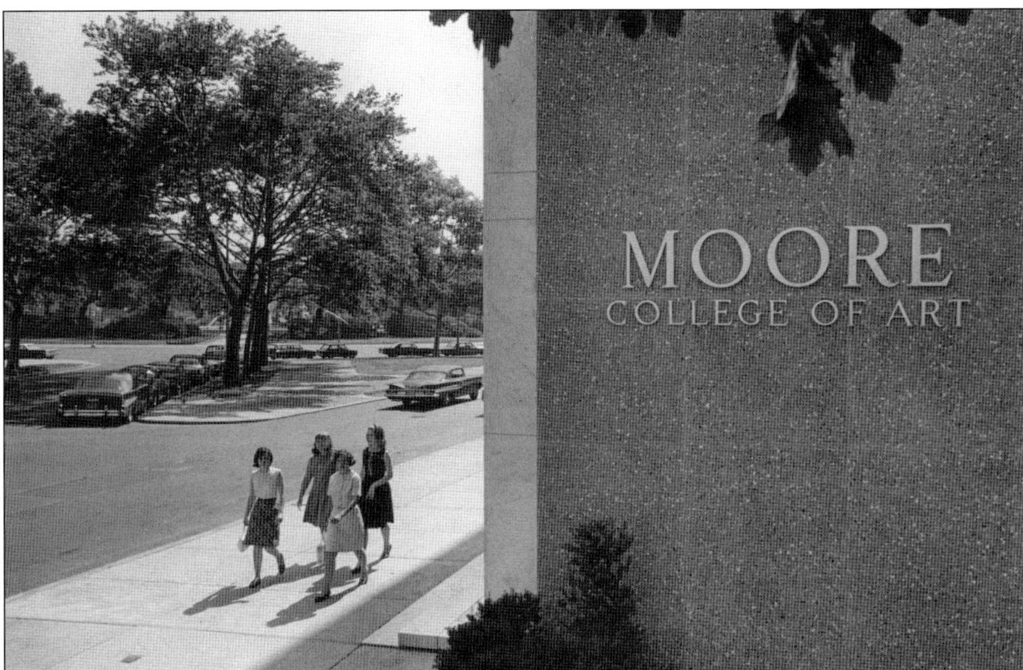

Moore College of Art and Design is the first women's art college in the United States. Founder Sarah Worthington Peter established the school in 1848 to offer women education leading to careers and financial independence. Its first major, textile design, prepared women to work in trades of the Industrial Revolution. This 1960 photograph shows students walking by the school at Twentieth and Race Streets. (Moore College.)

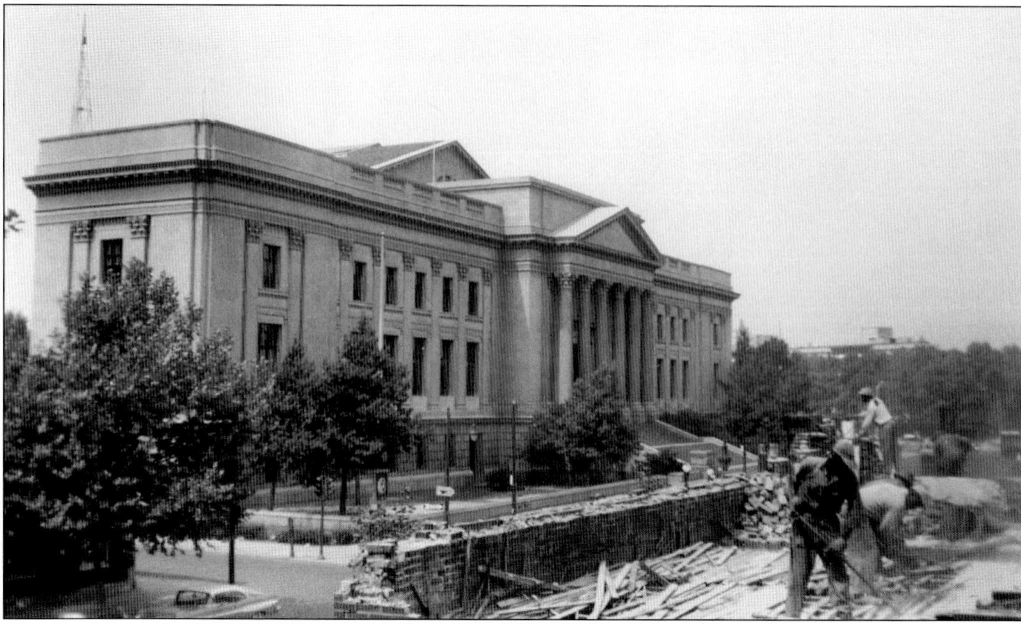

Many women who have become leaders in their fields have graduated from Moore College, including painter Alice Neel, interior designer Karen Daroff, fashion designers Adrienne Vittadini and Karen Harman, and photographer Sharon Wohlmuth. In this 1950s photograph, workmen are demolishing a structure in Logan Square to make way for the present-day Moore school. The Franklin Institute Science Museum looks on. (Moore College.)

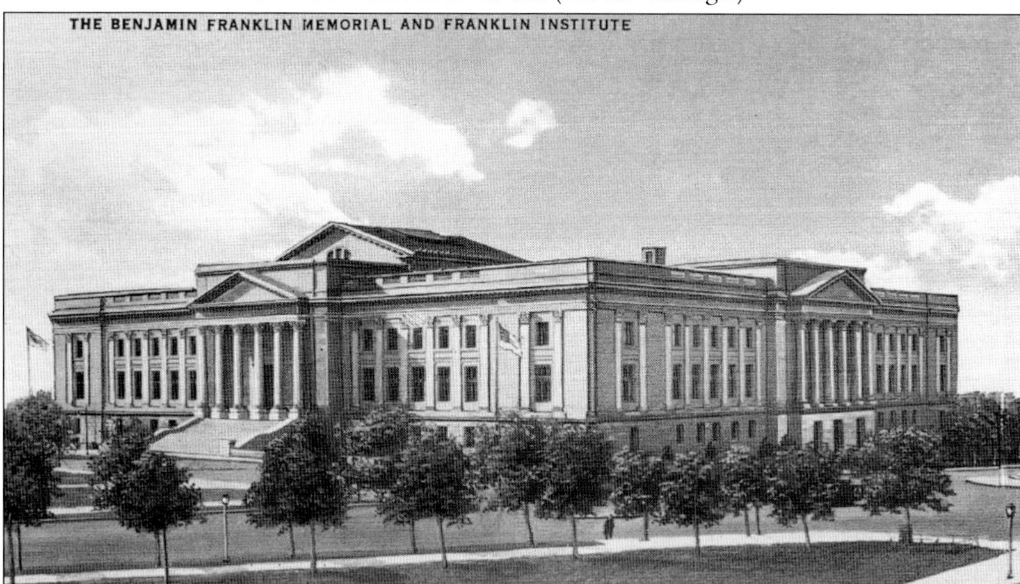

Founded in 1824 as the nation's first institute of applied sciences and mechanical arts, the Franklin Institute joined with the Poor Richard Club of Philadelphia around 1930 to develop both a contemporary science museum and national memorial to Benjamin Franklin. This lovely tinted card highlights the resulting building, which opened on January 1, 1934, at Twentieth Street and the Parkway. The Franklin Institute is the most visited museum in Pennsylvania. (Ruth Miller, Philadelphia.)

The Franklin Institute's Memorial Hall was designed by John T. Windrim, who modeled the great rotunda after the Pantheon in Rome. Its domed ceiling is self-supporting and weighs 1,600 tons, and the floor, walls, and columns are made of rare marbles from Portugal, Italy, and France. Memorial Hall houses many of Ben Franklin's belongings. This prospective drawing is from the early 1930s. (Author's collection.)

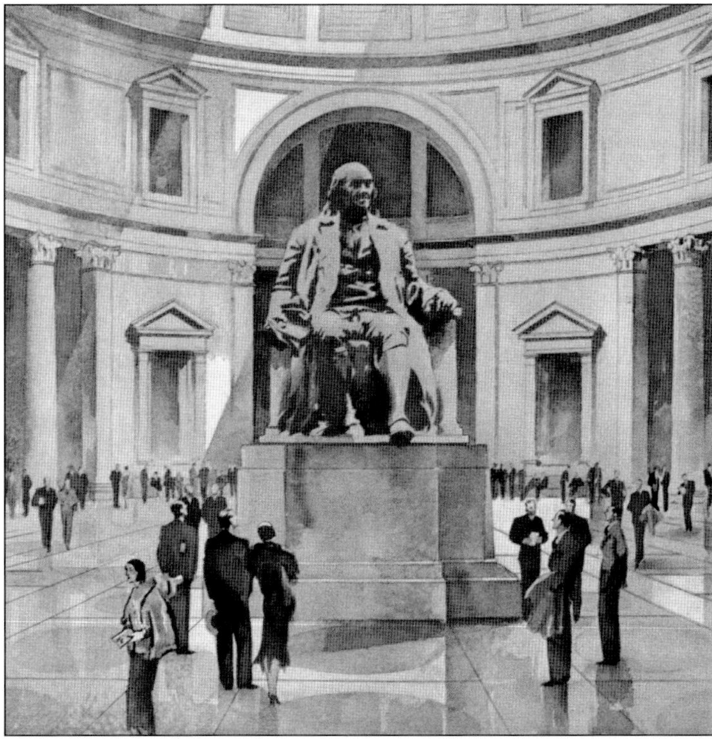

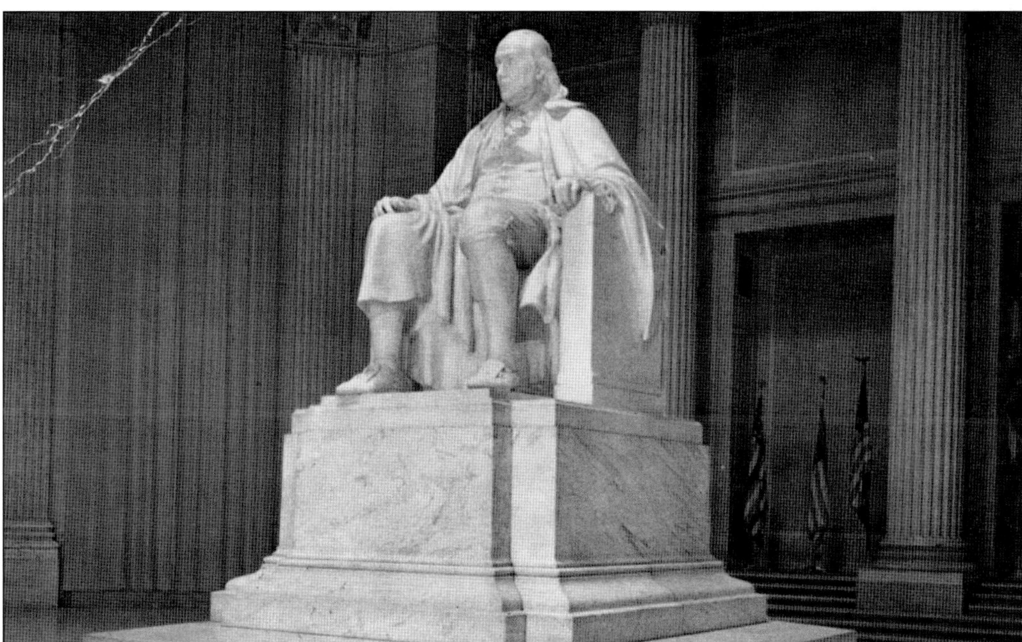

In 1972, Congress designated Memorial Hall as the national memorial to the American genius whose name it bears. The marble statue of Benjamin Franklin, dedicated in 1938, was devised by sculptor James Earle Fraser. Weighing 30 tons, the work sits on a 92-ton pedestal of white Seravezza marble. It was rededicated as the Benjamin Franklin National Memorial in 1976. Incidentally, the renaming of the Parkway in 1937 had nothing to do with the Franklin Institute. (Colourpicture.)

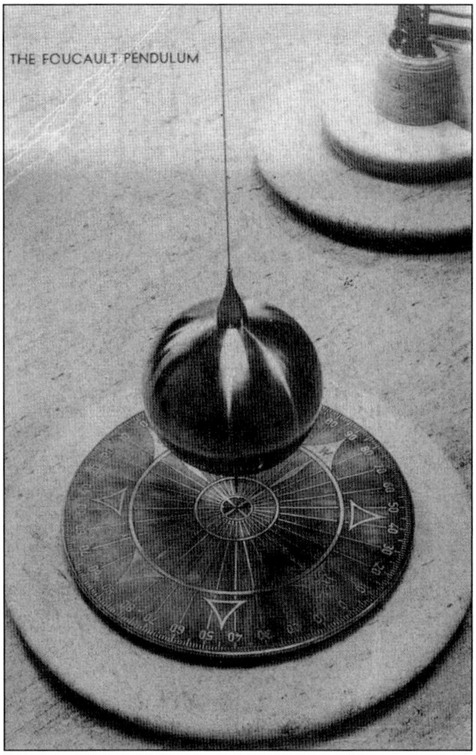

Since being installed on February 15, 1934, the Foucault Pendulum has been swinging at the Franklin Institute Science Museum as a visual representation of Earth's rotation. Generations of youngsters have watched from the Pendulum staircase as the bob slowly sways from side to side. This is a 1930s postcard; the pendulum base is different these days. (Ruth Miller, Art Adv. Service, Philadelphia; courtesy Gus Spector.)

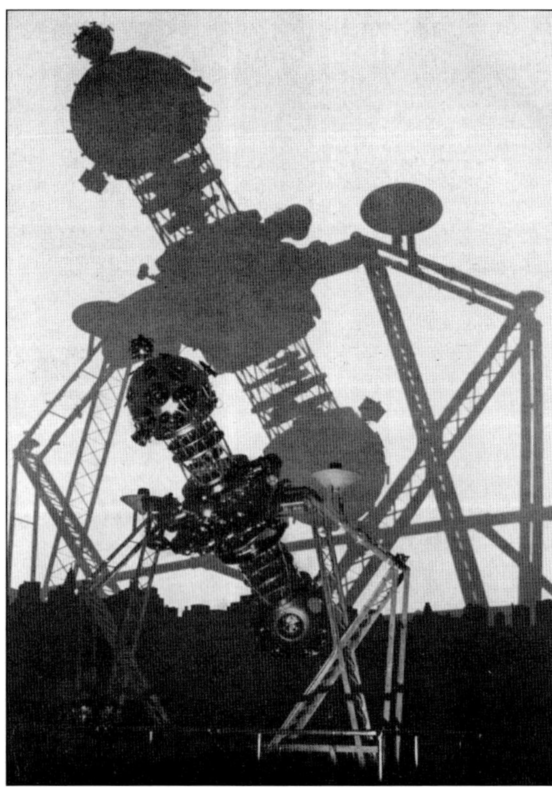

Philanthropist Samuel Fels, of "Fels-Naptha" soap fame, donated the Fels Planetarium at the Franklin Institute in 1933. Many Philadelphians remember the planetarium's "Giant Ant" optical projector, which could project the Milky Way galaxy onto the hemispheric ceiling as it appeared from anyplace in the world at anytime. Nowadays, a digital projection system offers the same "Sky Tonight" views of decades ago. This image is from *The Planetarium: History, Construction, Operation* (Sky Publishing Company, 1943).

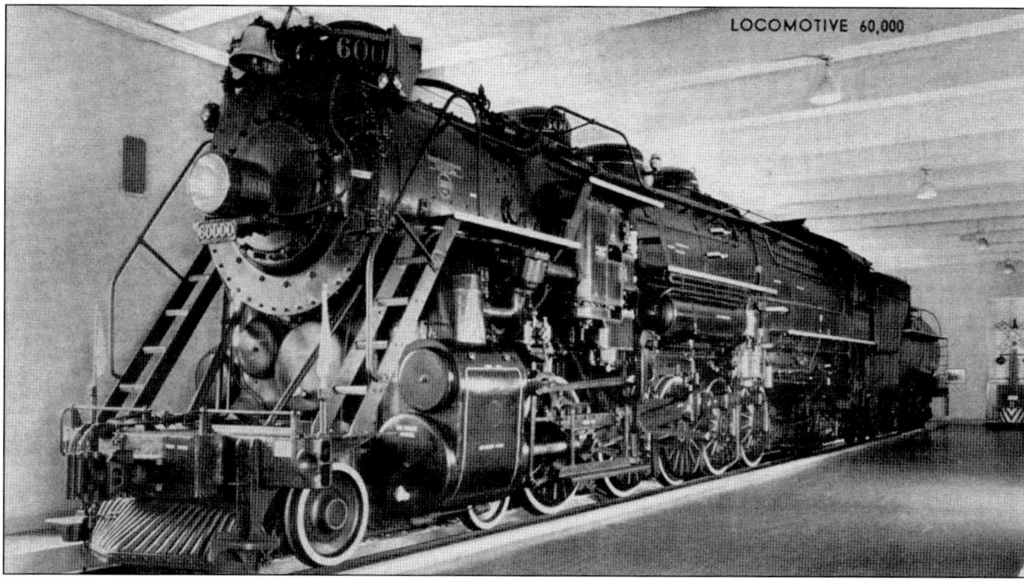

Baldwin No. 60,000 was designed to be the best steam locomotive that Baldwin Locomotive Company ever assembled. Weighing about 350 tons, including tender, this experimental model employed new steam technologies to ascertain the gain in efficiency of using high-pressure steam and high ratios of expansion. As it turned out, Baldwin 60,000 was deemed too heavy and too complicated in actual operation. (Ruth Miller, Art Adv. Service, Philadelphia; courtesy Gus Spector.)

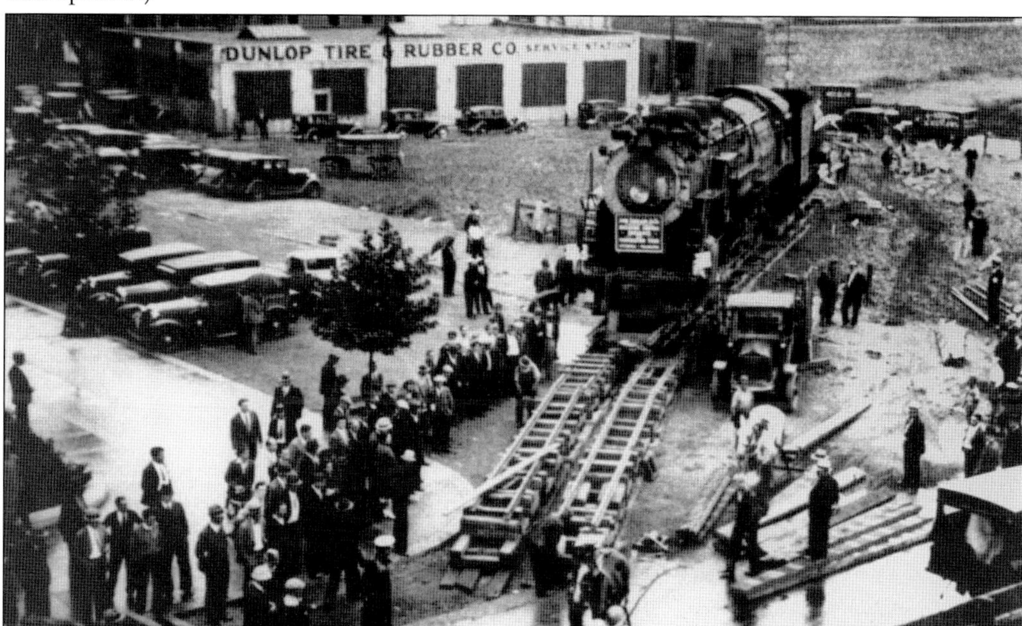

Baldwin sold No. 60,000 to the Franklin Institute for $1 in 1933. Over several days that September, it was dragged to the museum atop city streets around the Parkway. Mules did the pulling, as this photograph attests. Today, the old locomotive moves back and forth 15 feet—via electric motor—several times daily. Visitors of all ages have enjoyed the brief ride from inside the cab for decades. (Historical and Interpretive Collections, Franklin Institute.)

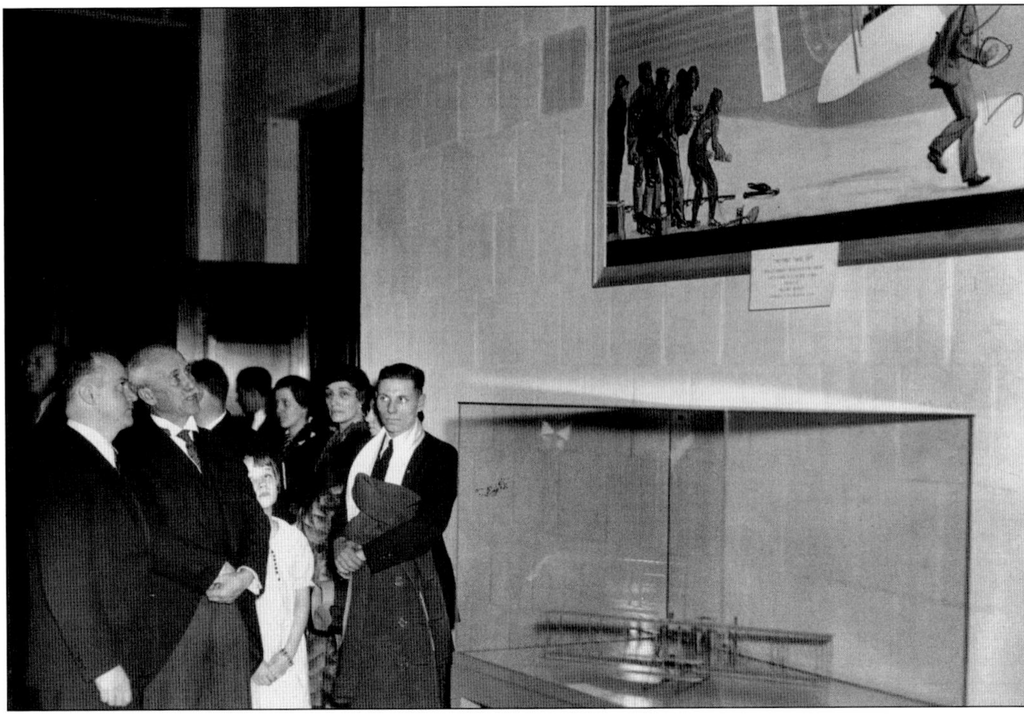

Orville Wright was a guest of honor at the dedication of the Franklin Institute's Hall of Aviation on December 17, 1933—exactly 30 years after the Wright brothers' first flight at Kitty Hawk. Wright bequeathed his collection of aviation devices to the Franklin Institute because it was the first scientific organization to give the Wrights credit for achieving sustained powered flight. The institute thus possesses the world's largest collection of Wright brothers artifacts. (Acme Newspictures, Inc.)

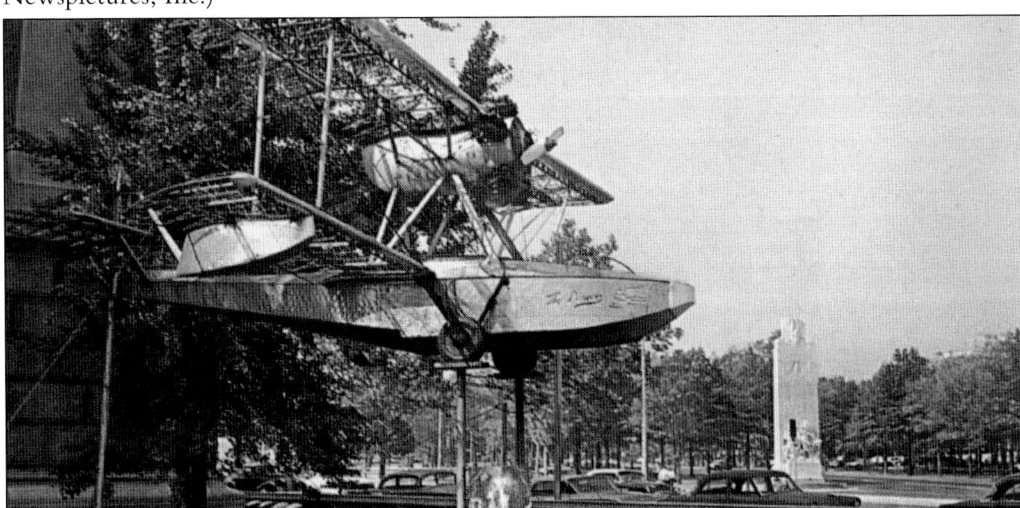

In 1931–1932, Philadelphia's Budd Company fabricated the world's first stainless steel airplane to demonstrate the practicability and reliability of shot welding. This seaplane, called the *Pioneer*, is a permanent outdoor exhibit outside the Franklin Institute at Twentieth Street and the Parkway. (Joseph F. Morsello, Philadelphia.)

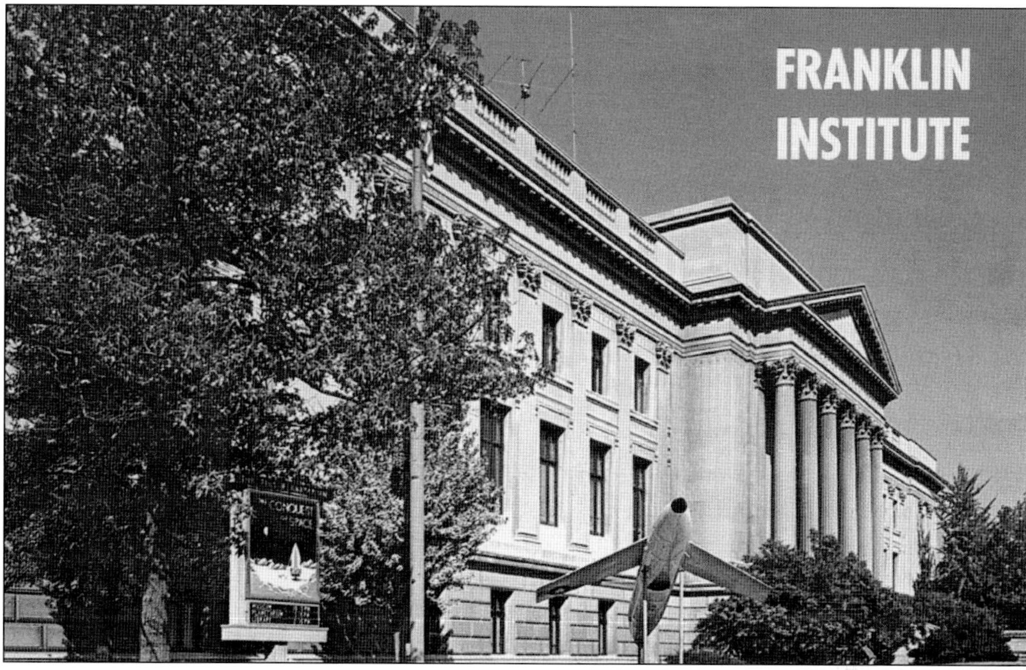

This card was postmarked in 1964. According to the sign on the left, the institute was evidently presenting an exhibit called "The Conquest of Space" when the image was taken. The jet plane displayed alongside Twentieth Street is no longer there. One sentimental attraction still at the Franklin Institute is the giant—220 times normal size—walk-through human heart, experienced by countless visitors since January 29, 1954. (Art Color Card Distributors.)

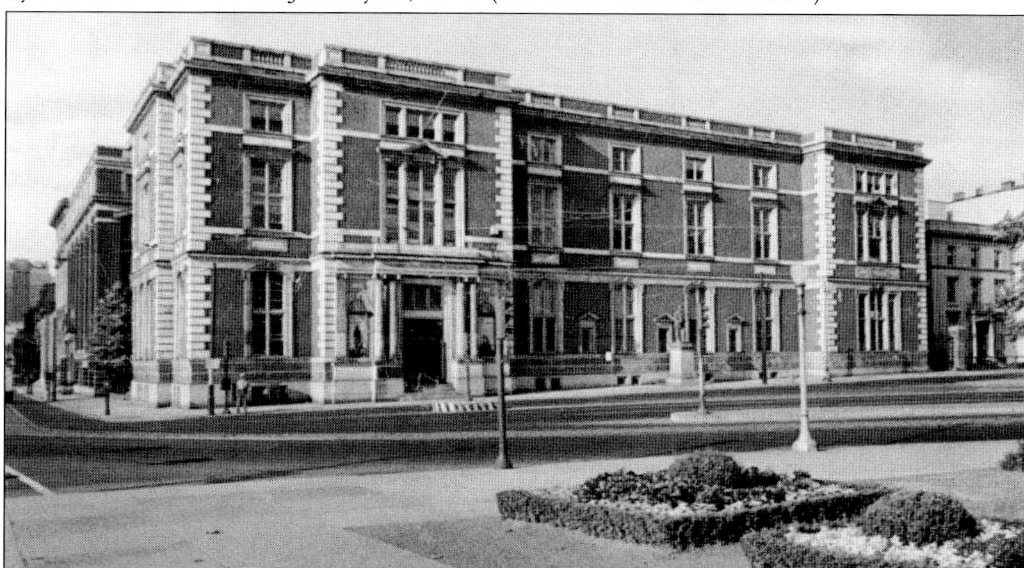

Organized in 1812 when Philadelphia was the nation's cultural, commercial, and scientific center, the Academy of Natural Sciences is the oldest natural sciences academy and natural history museum in the country. It occupied several locations until moving to Nineteenth and Race Streets in 1876. The choice of a site facing Logan Square was fortuitous, since a "Museum Mile" in that neighborhood had not been contemplated back then. (United News Company.)

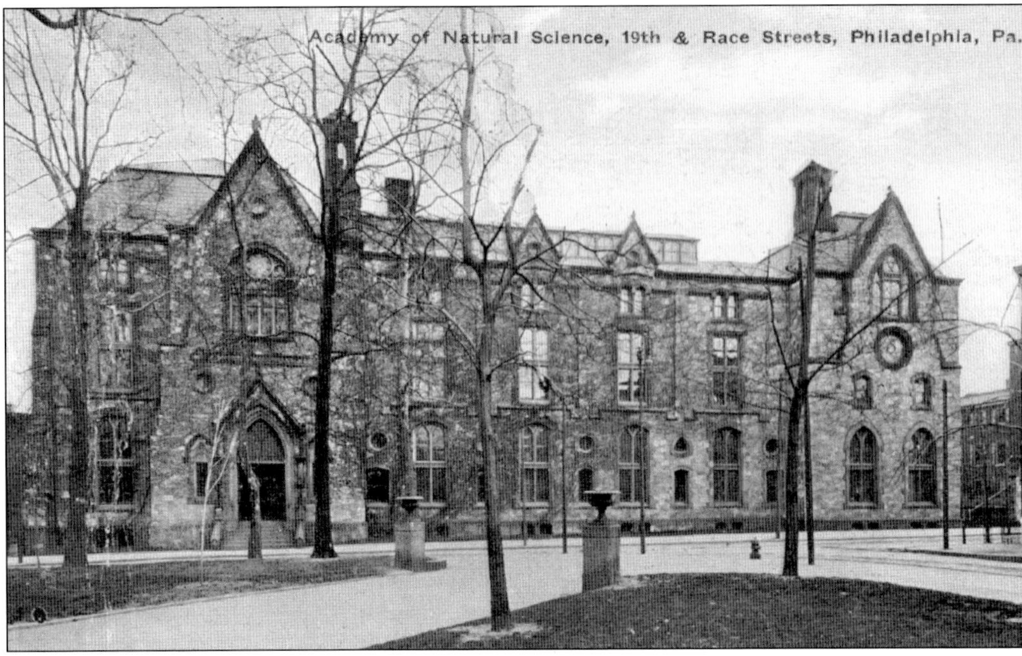

Constructed in the then-popular Gothic architectural style, the Academy of Natural Sciences was considered outdated by the early 1900s. The academy decided to modernize the facility for its centennial anniversary in 1912, adding red brick and marble trim to the facade. This is the building's original appearance. (Souvenir Post Card Company.)

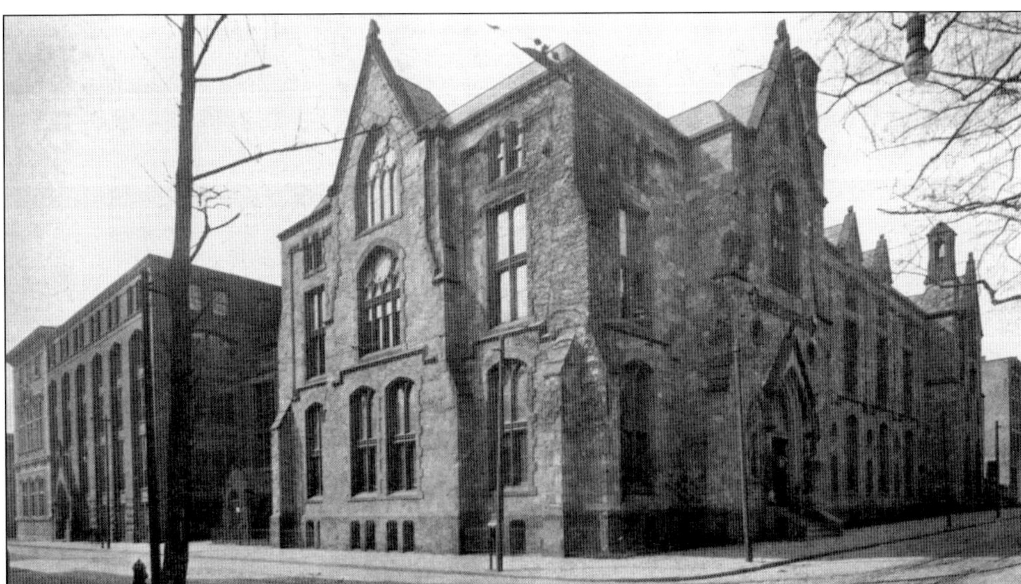

The Academy of Natural Sciences is one of the few places that have type specimens—the specimens that actually define a species—on public display. Plus, the academy was the first American institution to recognize the importance of Charles Darwin's ideas on evolution; Darwin was elected to membership in 1860. This image, showing the building's earlier look, is from *A Short History of the Academy of Natural Sciences* (1906). (Author's collection.)

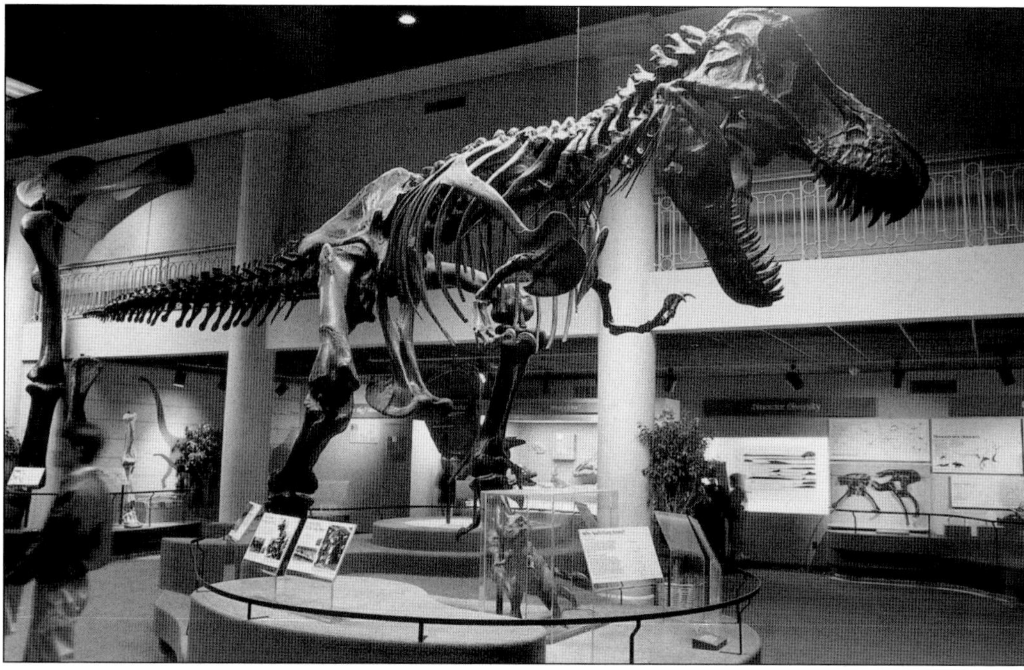

In 1868, the academy was the first museum anywhere to display a mounted dinosaur skeleton. Curator Joseph Leidy's studies of this fossil, the *Hadrosaurus foulkii*, established him as the father of paleontology and made the academy the preeminent institution in that field in the 1800s. *Hadrosaurus foulkii* was found in 1858 in Haddonfield, New Jersey, by Philadelphian William Parker Foulke. To commemorate the academy's 175th anniversary in 1987, a bronze sculpture of two dinosaurs was installed in front of the building. (Corel Professional Photos.)

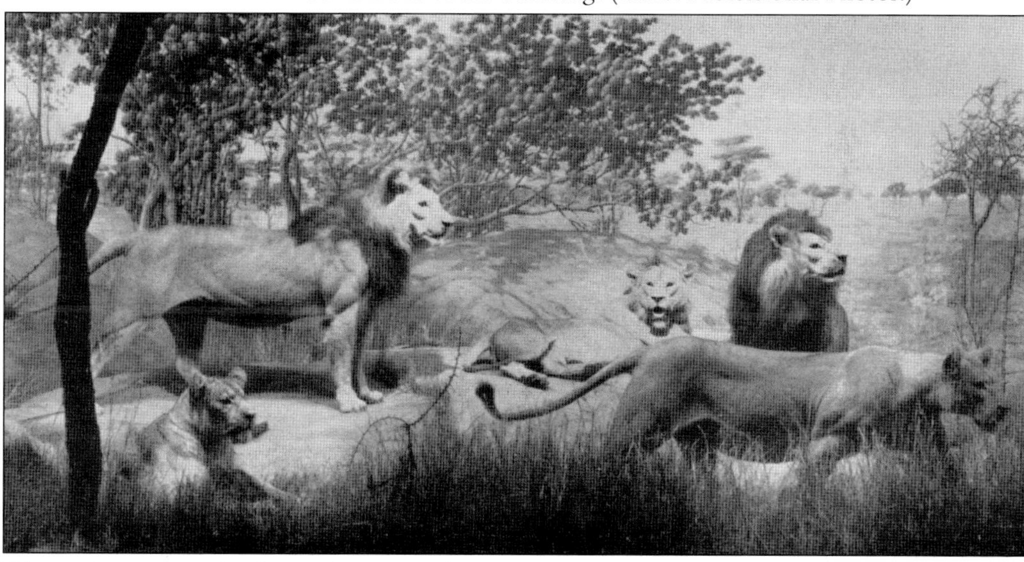

The academy organized expeditions to the American West, the Arctic wilderness, Africa, and Asia in which explorers brought back new types of plants and animals. Game animals were also acquired in the 1920s and 1930s, when they were still plentiful and relatively unfamiliar to Americans. As such, the academy was one of the first museums to create full-sized dioramas of wildlife habitats. This image is from a 1940s guide to the museum, as is the following one.

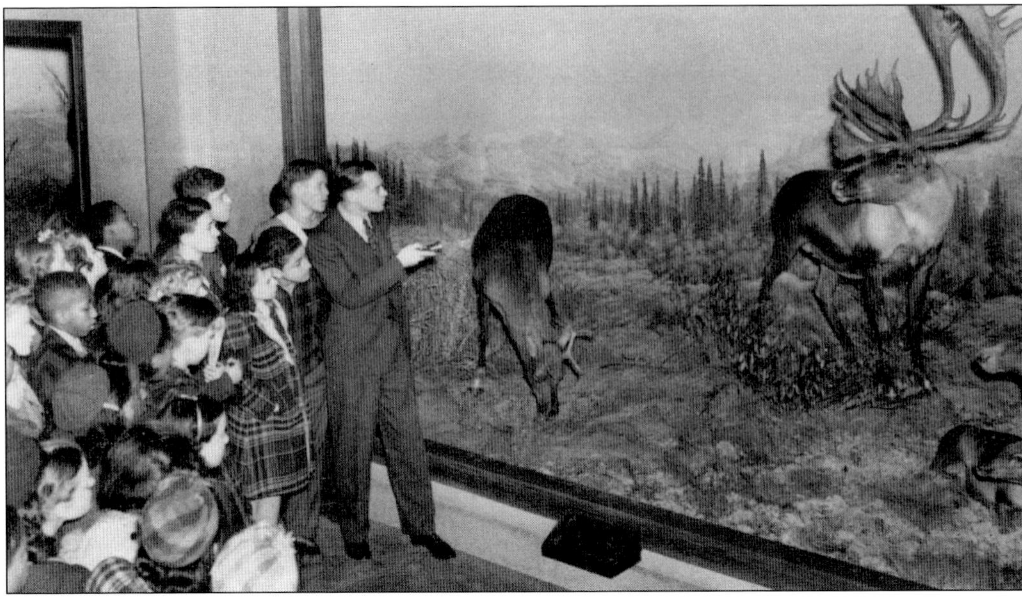

These dioramas are memorable to Philadelphians who saw them as children, and they remain popular to this day. The academy has also accumulated one of the world's most substantial groupings of both extinct and extant plants and animals. Furthermore, its collection of natural history artwork ranks among the oldest and best in the country.

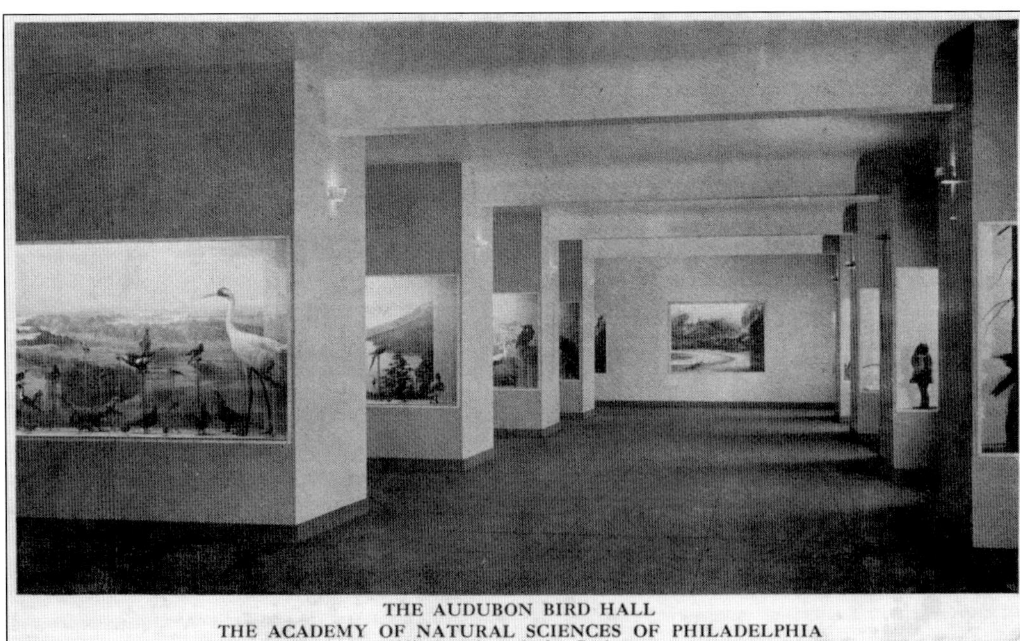

Known today as the Academy of Natural Sciences of Drexel University, the institution is a worldwide leader in biodiversity and environmental research. The Audubon Bird Hall is featured in this vintage card. (Academy of Natural Sciences.)

Seven

North and South of the Ben Franklin Parkway

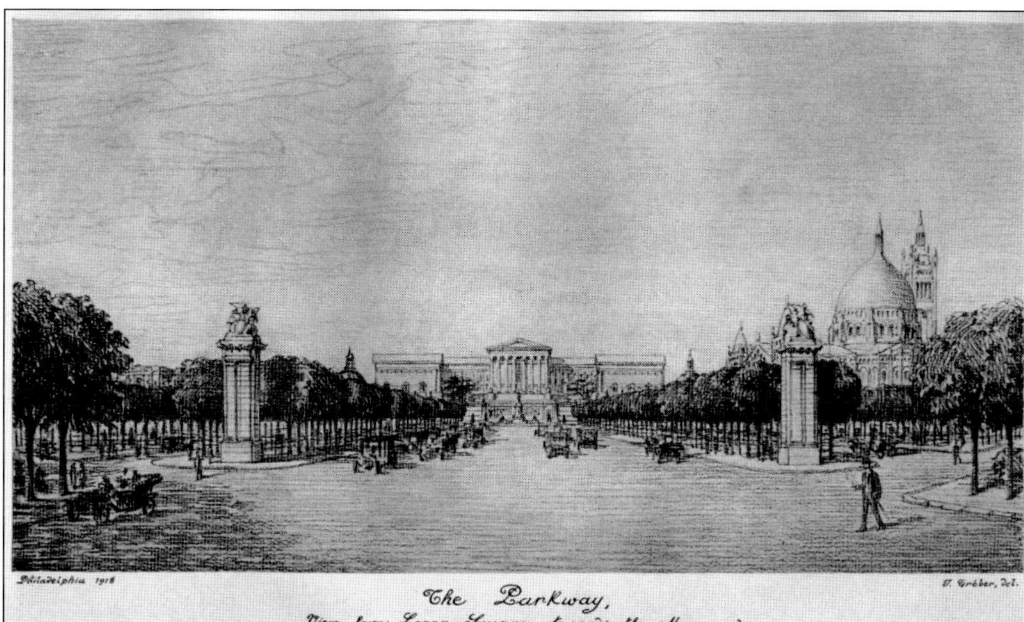

This 1918 prospect of the Benjamin Franklin Parkway from Logan Square is by Jacques Gréber. At that time, the Philadelphia Museum of Art was located at Memorial Hall in West Fairmount Park and was known as the Pennsylvania Museum and School of Industrial Art. The never-built Episcopal cathedral appears on the right, and the twin pylons of the Civil War Soldiers and Sailors Memorial are on either side of the street. (Author's collection.)

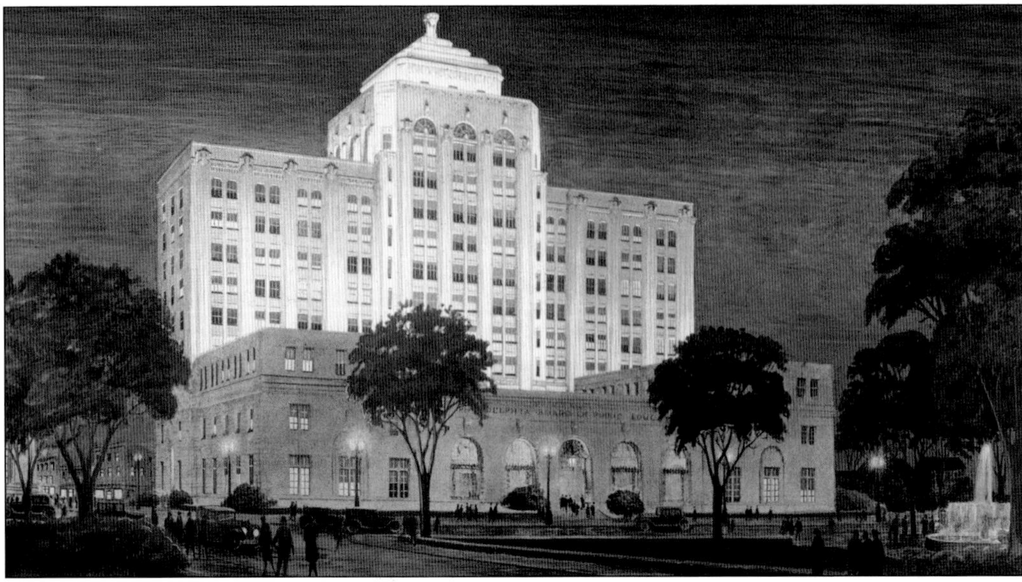

The former Philadelphia Board of Public Education Administration Building is at 230–250 North Twenty-first Street, west of the Franklin Institute on the Parkway's south side. Erected in 1931–1932, the classical/art deco edifice was the design of Irwin T. Catharine. He was the architect of many Philadelphia public schools and was the son of the chair of the board of public education. (The Library Company of Philadelphia.)

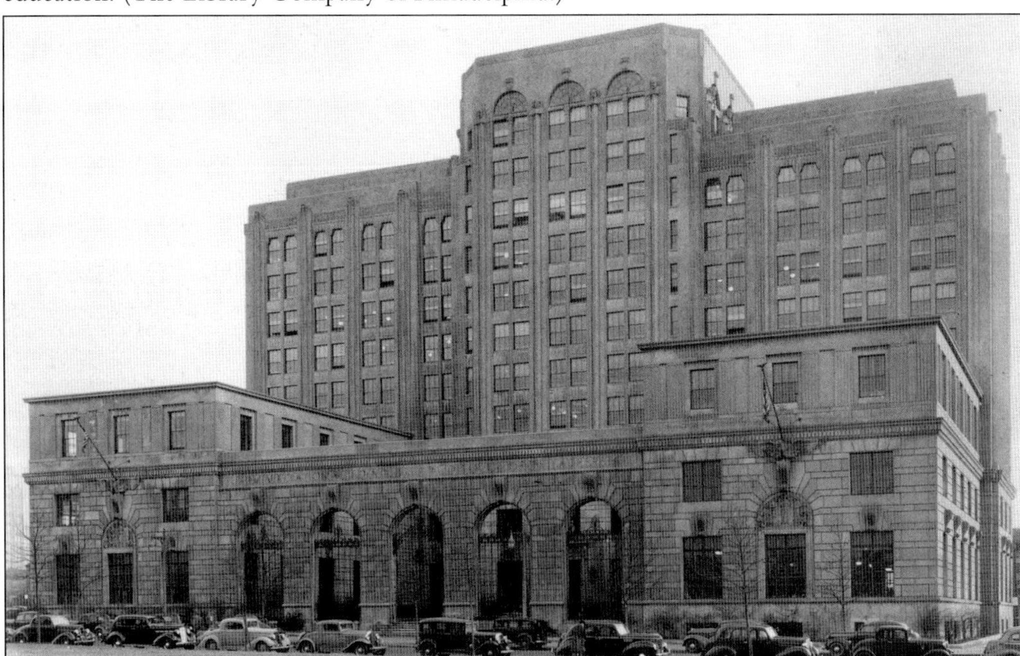

The original proposal for the Administration Building called for a 21-floor tower, but this height was denied due to the building's proximity to the Parkway. The structure served as headquarters of the School District of Philadelphia until it was sold and converted into condominiums in 2005. It had been added to the National Register of Historic Places in 1983. (The Library Company of Philadelphia.)

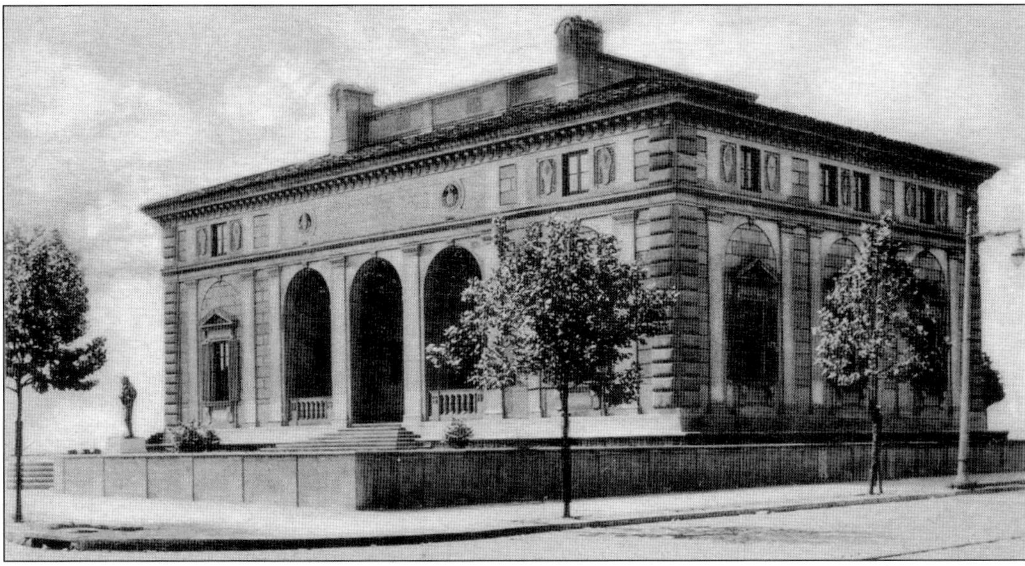

The Bruce S. Marks Scout Resource Center, at Twenty-second and Winter Streets, was next to the Board of Education Administration Building. The Beaux Arts structure was built and opened in 1930 after city leaders invited the Philadelphia Boy Scout Council to move its operations to the Parkway. The Scouts vacated the building—the nation's first designed for the Boy Scouts of America—in 2013. (Unmarked postcard; courtesy Gus Spector.)

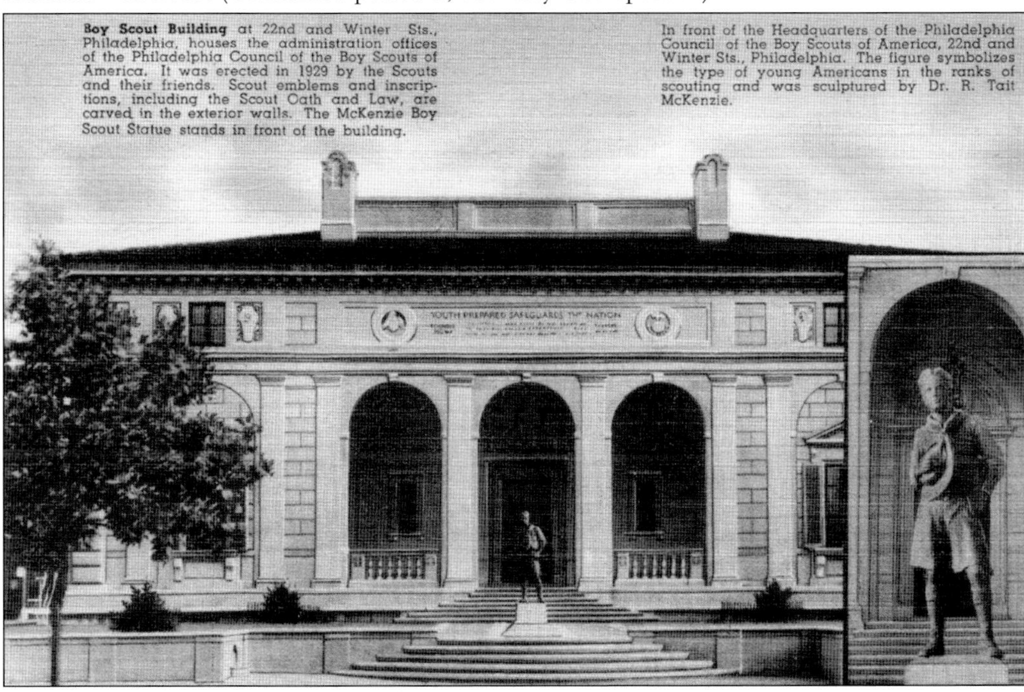

A life-size bronze statue named *The Ideal Scout* stood in front of the Boy Scout building until 2013. Known also as "The Boy Scout," the work was sculpted in 1937 by R. Tait McKenzie, who based it on a series of statuettes he cast in 1914 for the benefit of the first Boy Scout chapter in Philadelphia. Replicas of *The Ideal Scout* can be found all around the United States. (Colourpicture, Cambridge; courtesy Gus Spector.)

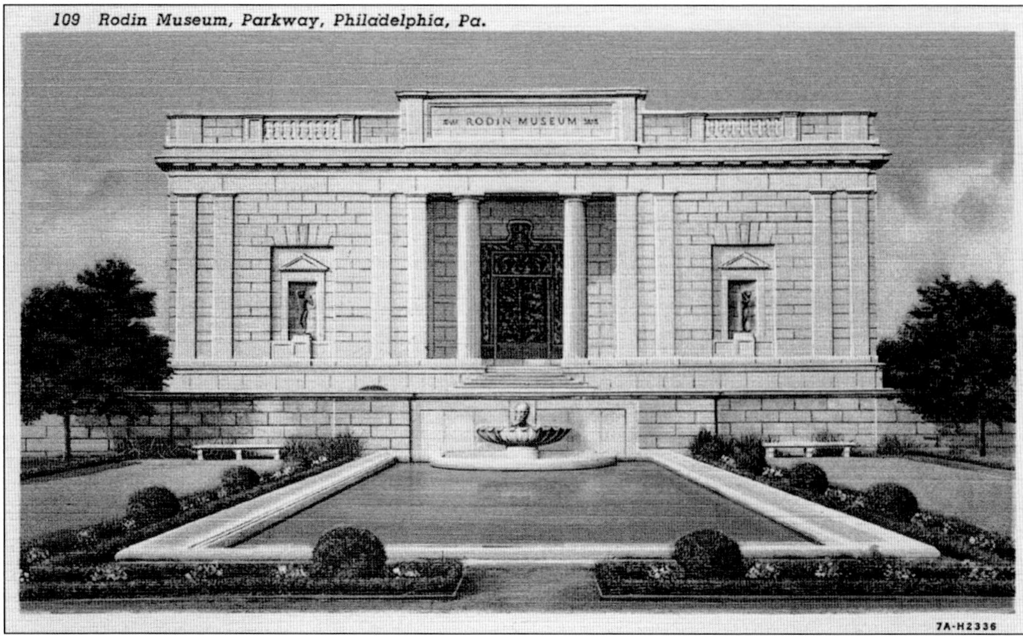

The largest public collection—outside Paris—of sculptures by François-Auguste-René Rodin (1840–1917) resides at the Rodin Museum in Philadelphia. With its charming French garden, the Rodin is one of only a few galleries anywhere dedicated to a single artist, and it is one reason why Philadelphia is often spoken of as "the American Paris." Standing on a site once used by the Knickerbocker Ice Company, the museum was designed by Paul Crét and Jacques Gréber in conjunction with their work on the Parkway. (C.T. Art-Colortone.)

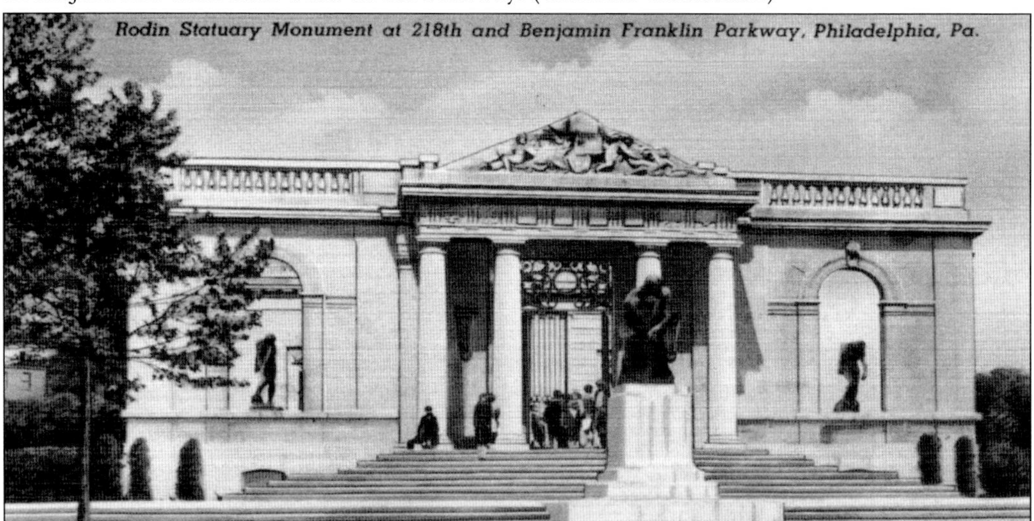

Philanthropist Jules Mastbaum's enthusiasm for the eminent French artist led him to acquire a tremendous array of Rodin's bronze casts, plaster studies, drawings, and other artifacts. He gave the collection to the City of Philadelphia just before he died in 1926. The gallery, copied from the Musée Rodin in Paris, opened in 1929. This postcard highlights the museum's entrance portal, known as the "Meudon Gate," which is modeled after the facade of Château d'Issy, a French manor outside of Paris. ("218th" in the caption should read "21st.") (Colourpicture.)

The Rodin Museum represents every phase of Auguste Rodin's illustrious career. Among many masterpieces, its exhibit rooms contain *The Age of Bronze* (1875–1876), *Eternal Springtime* (1884), *The Burghers of Calais* (1884), and *The Kiss* (1886). Since 1939, the gallery has been administered by the Philadelphia Museum of Art, which is just a short stroll away past Von Colln Memorial Field, a neighborhood baseball park. The Rodin and its grounds underwent an extensive renovation from 2010 to 2012. (Photograph by author.)

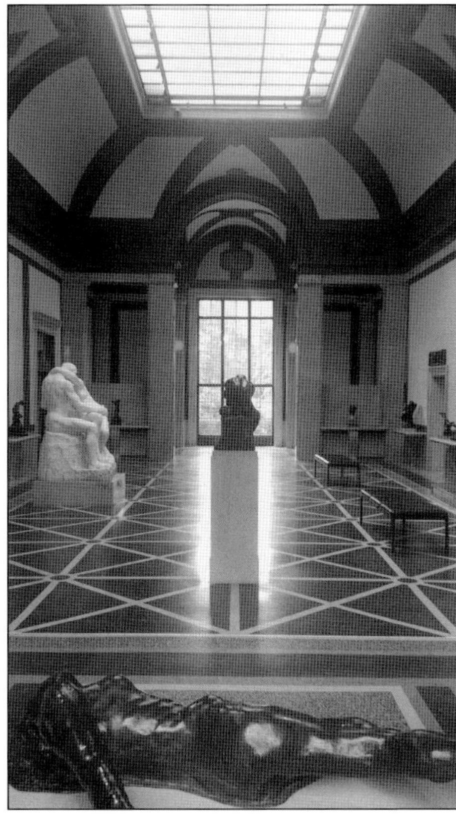

The Thinker, which became the universal symbol of Auguste Rodin, welcomes visitors along the Parkway. A number of casts of it exist worldwide, including a small-scale version inside the Rodin Museum. At the front entrance is *The Gates of Hell*, a stunning sculptural group of over 200 figures in the throes of despair and pain. Inspired by Dante's *Divine Comedy*, Rodin labored on this composition for nearly 37 years. (Frank Burd, Philadelphia Post Card Company.)

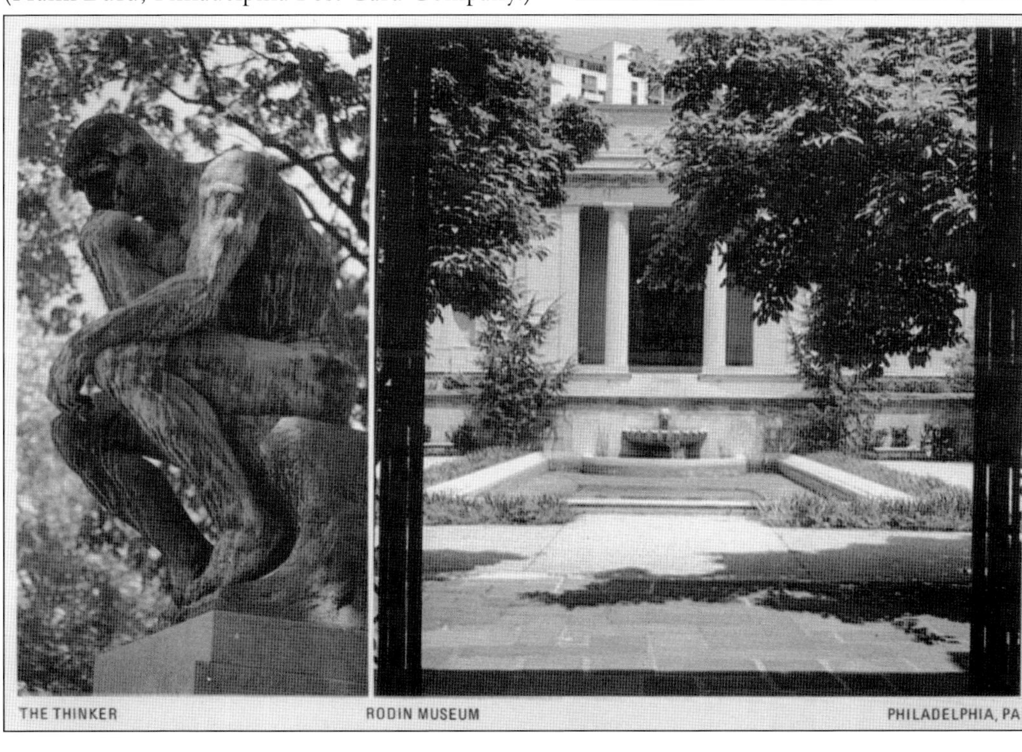

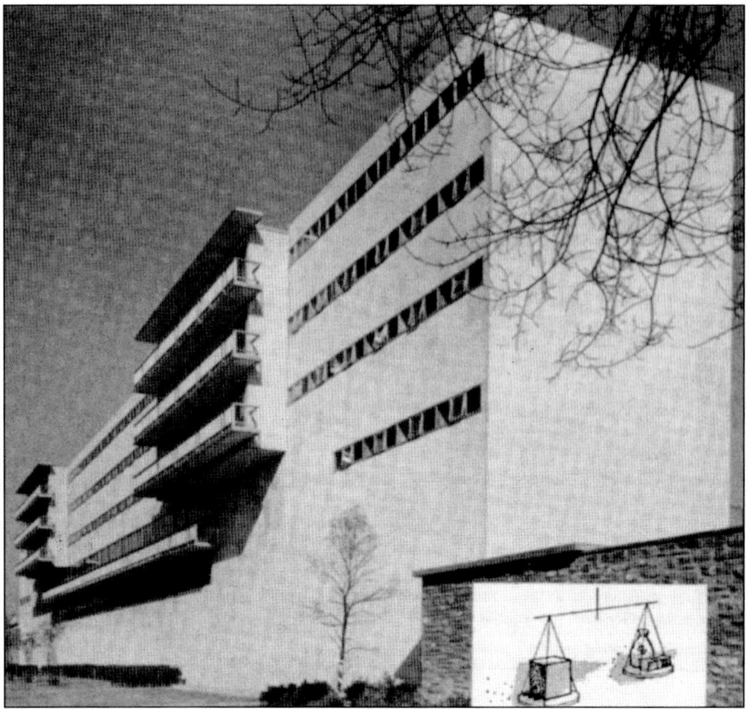

For inexplicable reasons, Philadelphia's leaders decided to build what was essentially a prison right on the Parkway. The Youth Study Center, a juvenile detention facility, opened on May 12, 1952. This image, from an advertisement in a 1953 *Architectural Record*, states that reinforced concrete was selected for the structure since it allowed for economical construction. This may be why the center looked so inhospitable and shoddy years later.

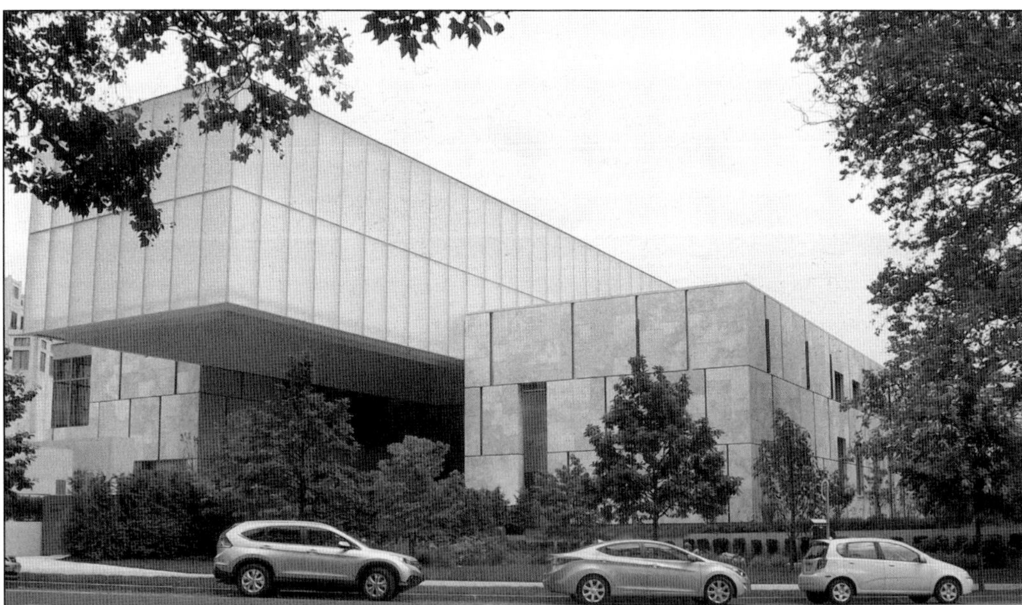

The Parkway continues to evolve. The ill-sited Youth Study Center has been razed, and its location has been home to the Barnes Foundation since 2012. This modish museum houses an amazing collection of masterworks by Renoir, Cézanne, Matisse, Rousseau, Picasso, and other French artists. The paintings, sculptures, and decorative pieces were relocated from the Barnes compound in Merion, Pennsylvania, following a lengthy court battle. (Photograph by author.)

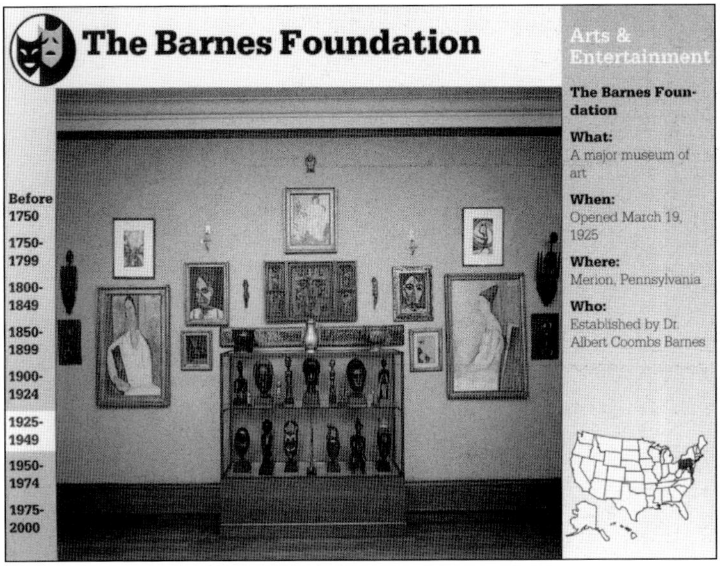

Philadelphian Albert Barnes graduated from the University of Pennsylvania Medical School and codeveloped a popular antiseptic called Argyrol. He purchased 12 acres of property in Merion and built a private house gallery and art school in the 1920s. There, he accumulated one of the world's largest collections of impressionist and postimpressionist art. This is a 1990s "Grolier Story of America" card of the original Barnes facility.

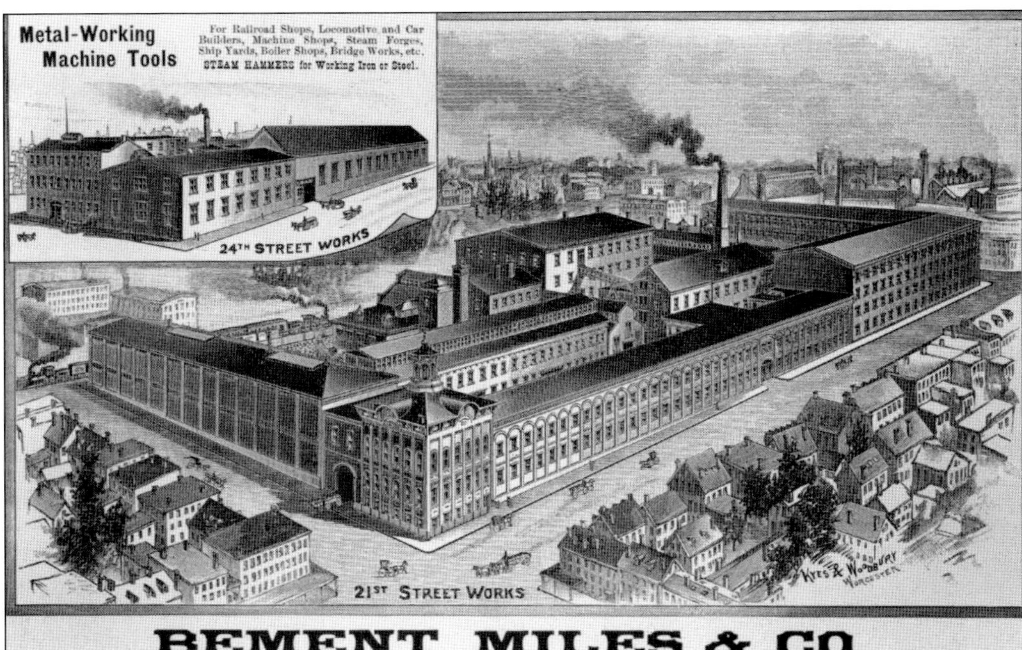

Some of Philadelphia's greatest manufacturing concerns were once based in or near the Parkway's footprint. These heavy industries were often related to the railroad industry, including the renowned Baldwin Locomotive Works. Bement, Miles & Company occupied ground now partially inhabited by the Barnes Foundation. Until the 1920s, over 1,000 men worked at Bement, producing machine tools and hydraulic machinery for locomotive and railcar builders, boiler shops, and the like. (Author's collection.)

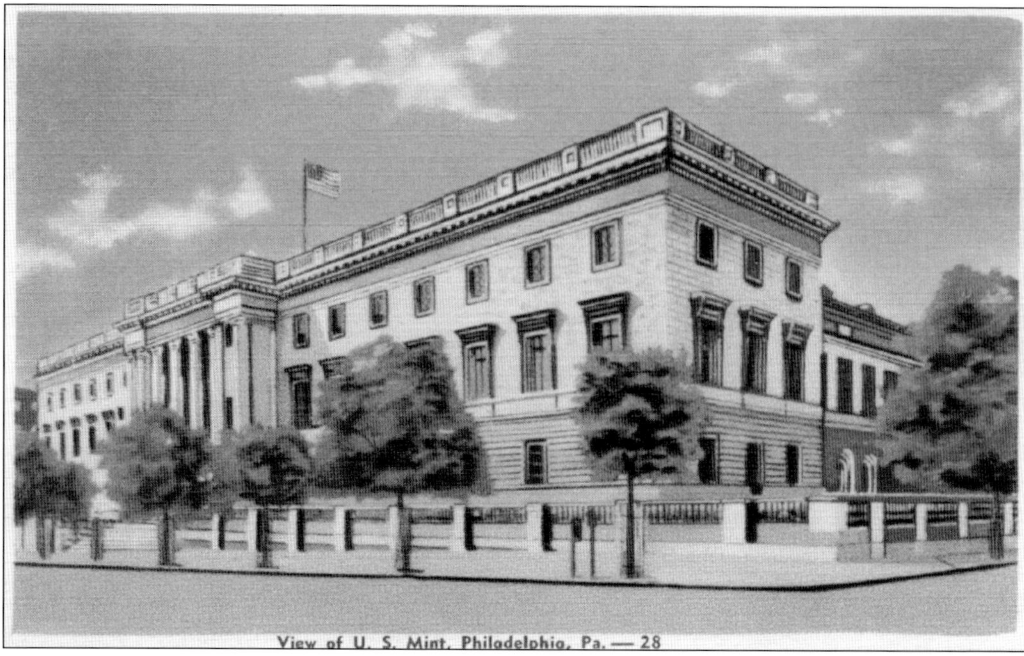

This handsome edifice was the third US Mint erected in Philadelphia. When opened in 1901, it was the biggest and best-equipped mint in the world, producing 501 million US coins and 90 million coins for foreign countries in one year alone. The granite and marble structure, with its Roman temple facade, stands on Spring Garden Street between Sixteenth and Seventeenth Streets, not far from the Parkway. It now houses the Community College of Philadelphia. (Dexter Press, Pearl River, New York.)

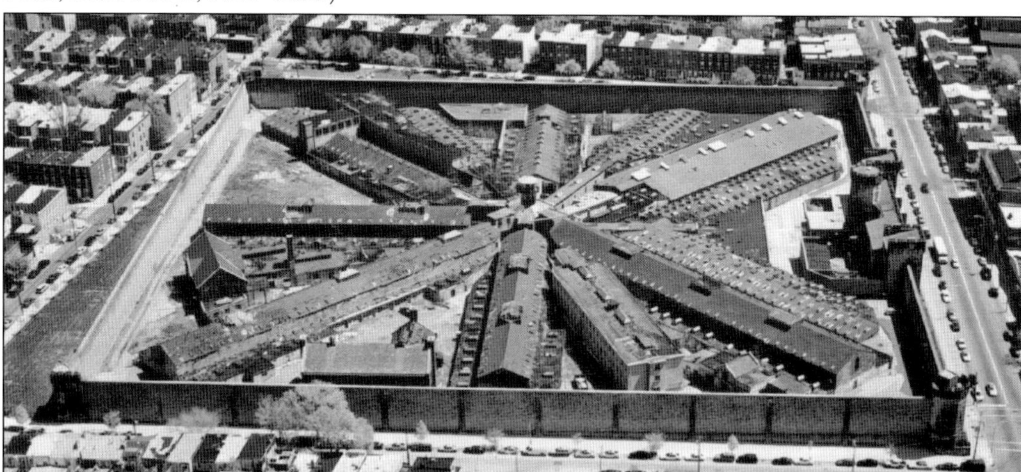

Eastern State Penitentiary is considered a Parkway institution despite being blocks away on Fairmount Avenue. Shunning corporal punishment, the penitentiary followed a Quaker-inspired system of prisoner isolation. Convicts were led to their cells blindfolded and would hopefully become penitent if left to think about their wrongful behavior. Prominent visitors such as Charles Dickens did not agree with this policy. Architect John Haviland designed the massive fortress, which including a menacing Gothic Revival facade. Some 300 prisons around the globe were built according to Haviland's plan. The most expensive building in America when opened in 1829, "Eastern State Penn" is now a tourist attraction rivaling San Francisco's Alcatraz. (Library of Congress.)

Eight

Lodging, Living, and Living It Up on Philly's Museum Mile

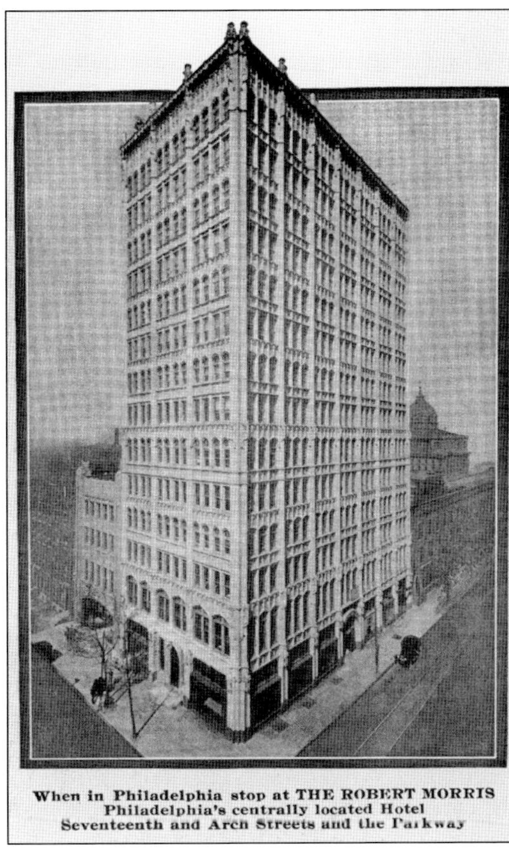

The Robert Morris Hotel was originally built at Seventeenth and Arch Streets as the Wesley Building. Commissioned as office space by the United Methodist Church, the first six floors were built in 1914–1915. The remaining eight floors were added in 1921–1922, when it became the Morris Hotel. The archetypal Gothic Revival building then became a boardinghouse before again being converted into an office building. (Unmarked postcard.)

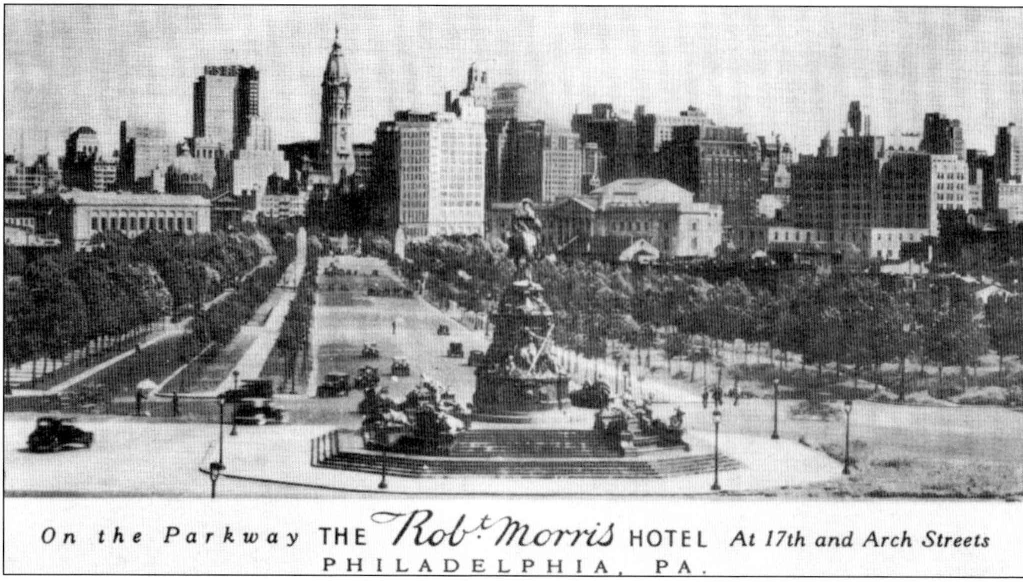

There was talk about refurbishing the Wesley/Morris building back into a hotel, but, in 2012, it became the Arch Luxury Apartments. This 1920s postcard has the Morris Hotel (the bright structure at center right) too close to the Ben Franklin Parkway; it was probably drawn into this photograph during its 1921–1922 enlargement. The building was added to the National Register of Historic Places in 1984. (Maryland Litho.)

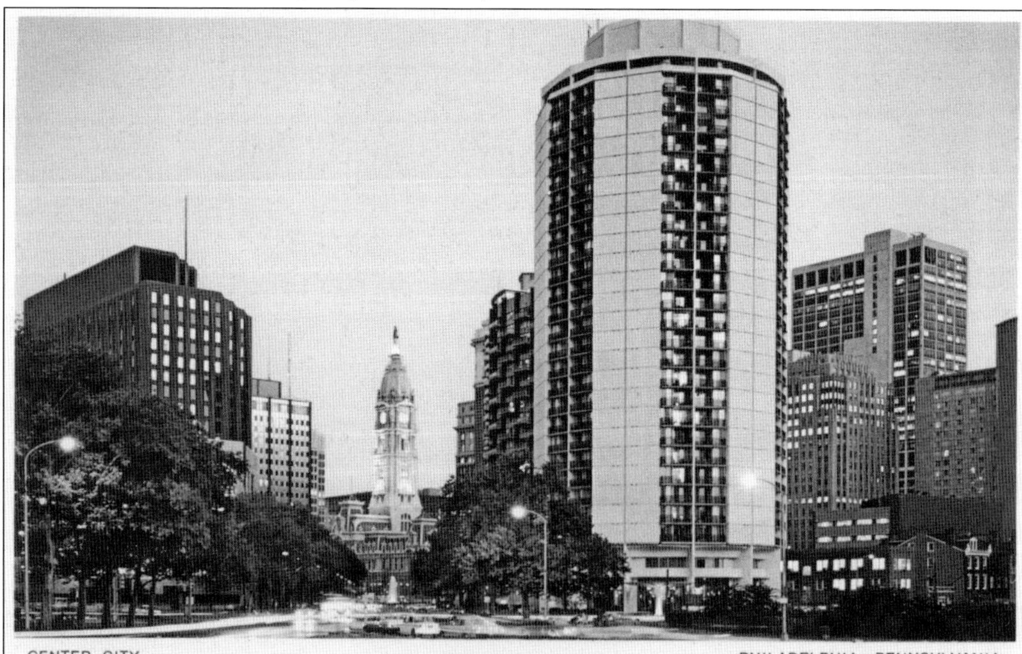

Embassy Suites Hotel is the dominant building in this 1970s postcard. This distinctive structure at Eighteenth Street and the Parkway has endured a trying existence since opening in 1966 as the Plaza Apartments. By 1980, it had become the Plaza Hotel, then turned into the Palace Hotel, and then become a Radisson Suites Hotel. In 1991, the cylindrical high-rise was shuttered after the mortgage holder foreclosed and kicked out dozens of guests. (Philadelphia Post Card Company.)

The 21-story Sheraton Penn Center Hotel was located at 1725 Pennsylvania (now John F. Kennedy) Boulevard. Built in 1956–1957, this international-style inn became the Philadelphia Centre Hotel in 1981, but closed five years later and was then torn down. The lot remained vacant until 2005, when construction began on the Comcast Center. Occupying the rear portion of the site, the Comcast Building is one of the tallest skyscrapers between New York and Chicago. (Lusterchrome.)

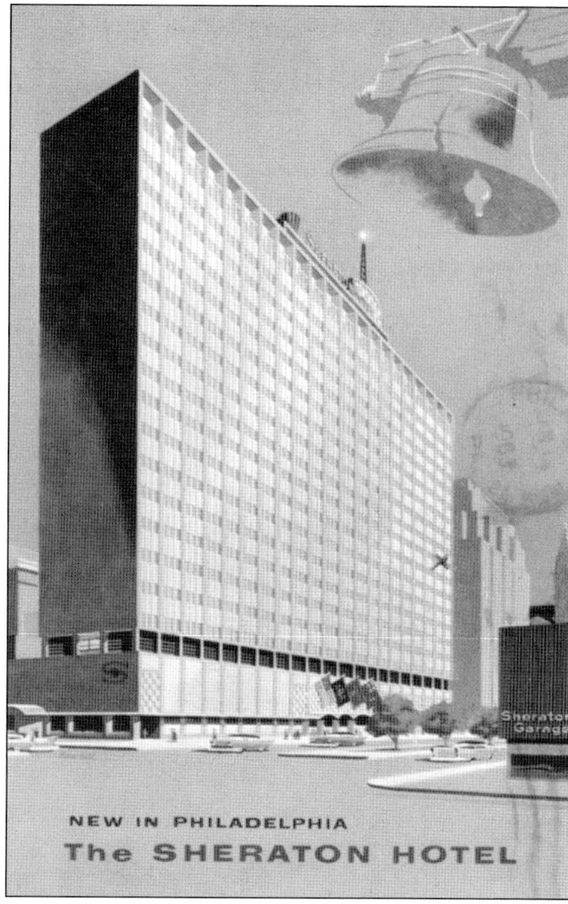

The Y-shaped Franklin Motor Inn, now a Best Western Hotel, was built in the late 1950s on the block between Twenty-first and Twenty-second Streets, between Spring Garden and Hamilton Streets and Pennsylvania Avenue. The parcel was previously occupied by a warehouse complex for Gimbels Department Store; a cotton and woolen factory, in the late 1800s; and a railcar manufactory, in the mid-1800s. It is currently slated to become home to a Whole Foods Market, with high-end apartments above. (Unmarked postcard.)

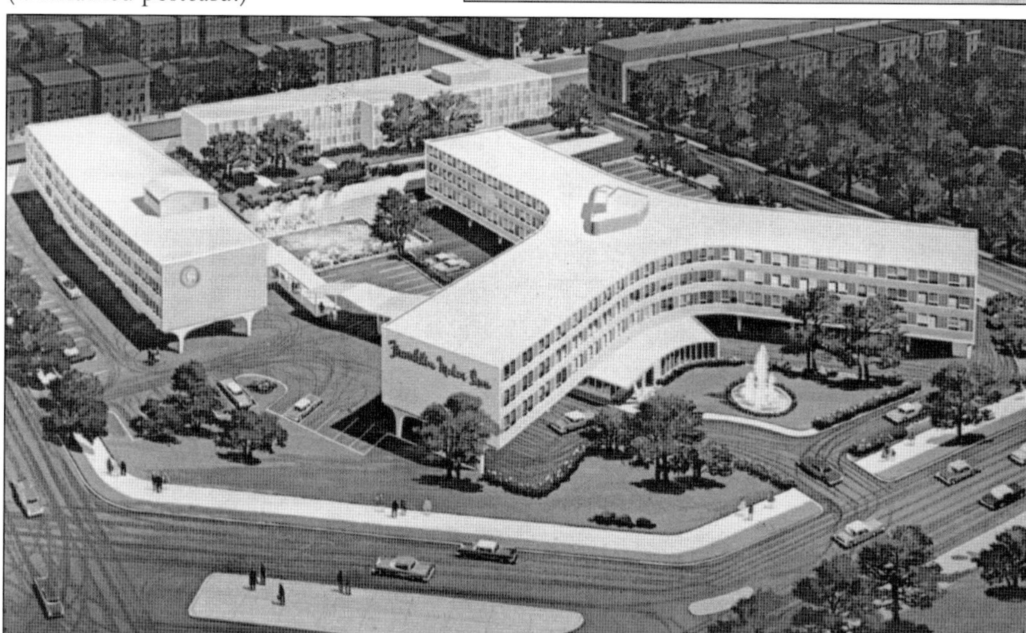

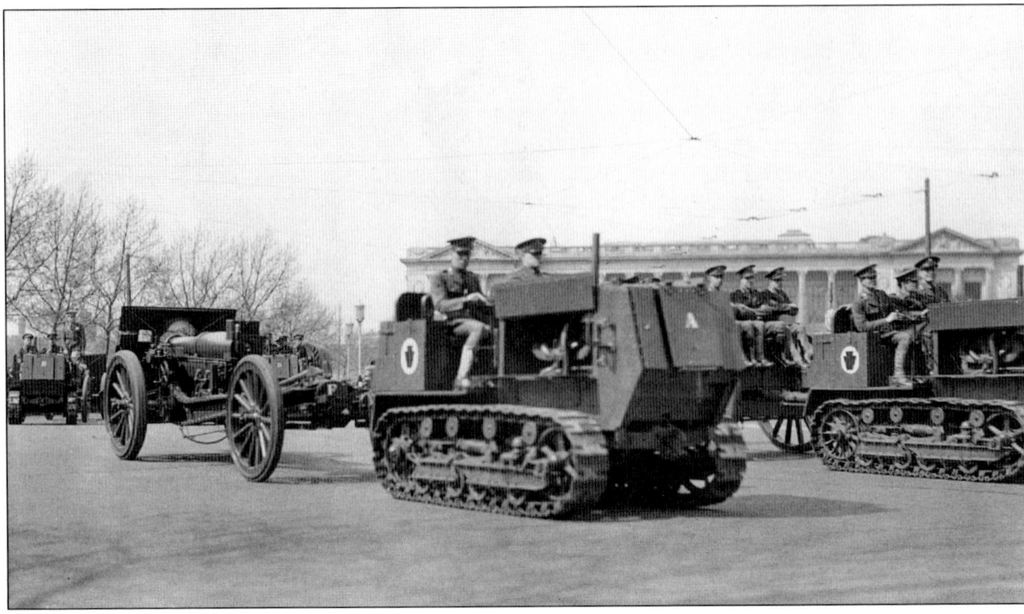

Numerous pageants and processions have been held along the Parkway through the years. Today's drivers speeding on the vaunted avenue would be surprised to learn that tracked military vehicles once paraded over it. In 1935, members of the 108th Field Artillery (Pennsylvania National Guard) operated artillery tractors pulling 155-millimeter howitzers on the Parkway. (The Library Company of Philadelphia.)

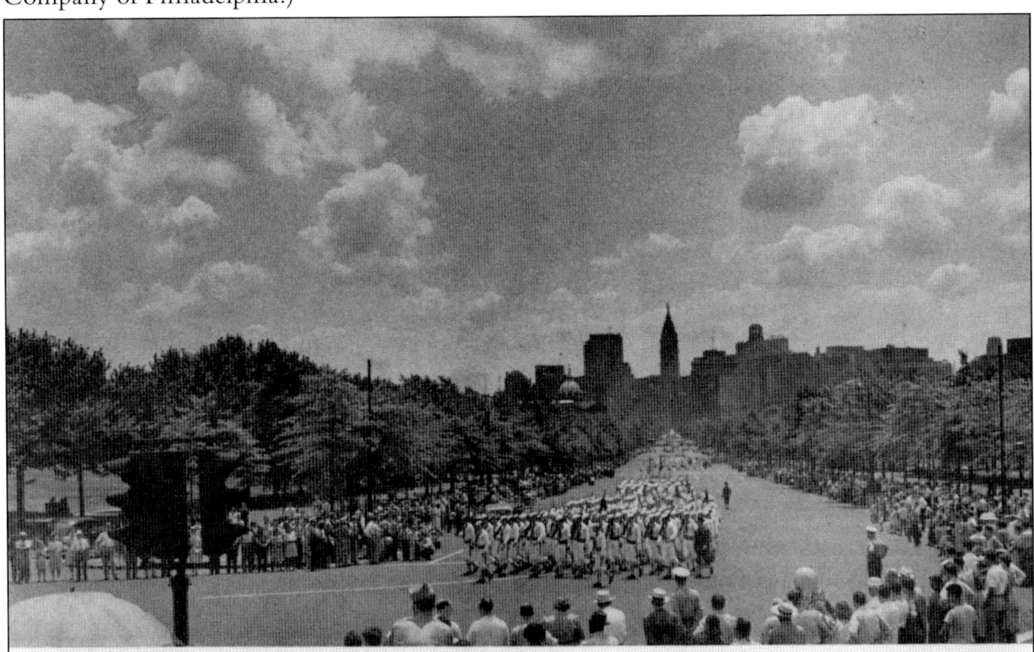

Here, members of the Army's 82nd Airborne Division march toward the Philadelphia Museum of Art on July 4, 1946. Some 5,000 soldiers participated in a World War II victory commemoration along the Parkway and in Fairmount Park. The parade included flyovers of military aircraft and a sizeable fireworks display that night. This image is from *Fairmount Park, Philadelphia* (1946).

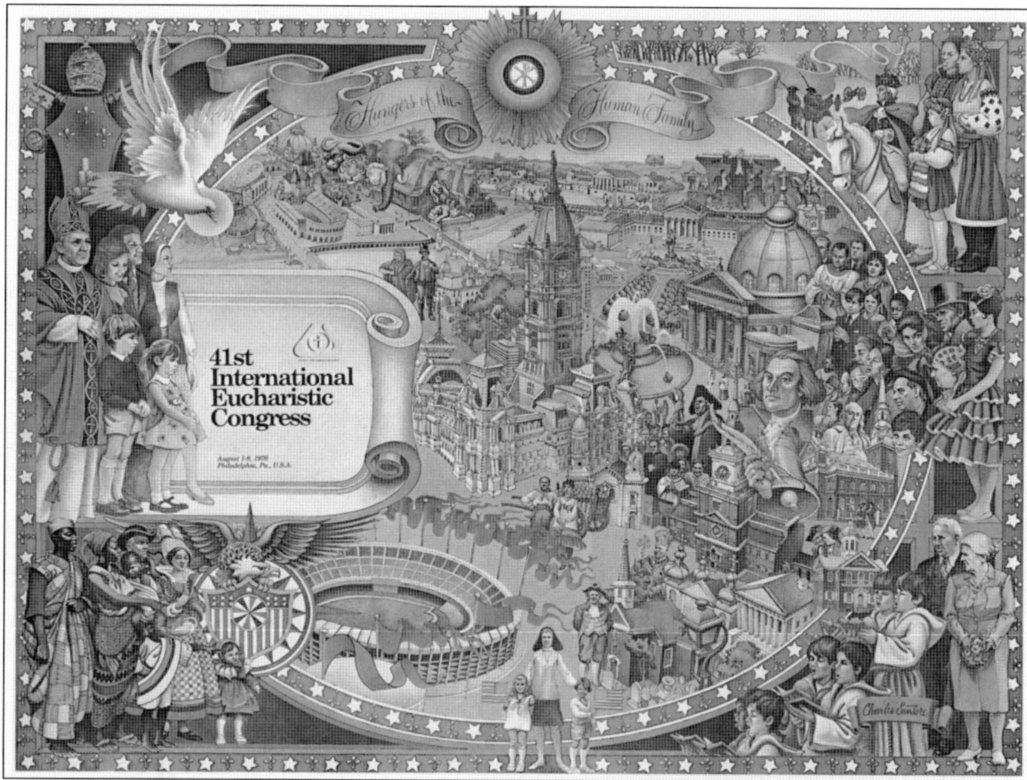

The 41st International Eucharistic Congress was held in Philadelphia on August 1–8, 1976, and concluded with a procession up the Parkway toward the museum. This interfaith ecumenical gathering of church leaders and scholars was one of the largest religious meetings in US history. Mother Teresa and Dorothy Day appeared on the same stage to discuss the topic of women and the liturgy. This image is from *41st International Eucharistic Congress, Philadelphia, Pennsylvania* (1976).

You are cordially invited
to participate in the Mass
celebrated by
His Holiness
Pope John Paul II
Wednesday, October 3, 1979 at 4:00 P.M.
Logan Circle, Philadelphia, PA

ADMIT ONE

In 1979, Pope John Paul II became the first active pontiff to ever visit Philadelphia. The now-saint performed an open-air Catholic mass at Logan Circle on Wednesday, October 3, 1979, from a platform erected over Swann Memorial Fountain. This is an invitation to the special papal mass, which was part of John Paul's first North American tour. Pope Francis, is scheduled to visit Philadelphia in 2015. (Author's collection.)

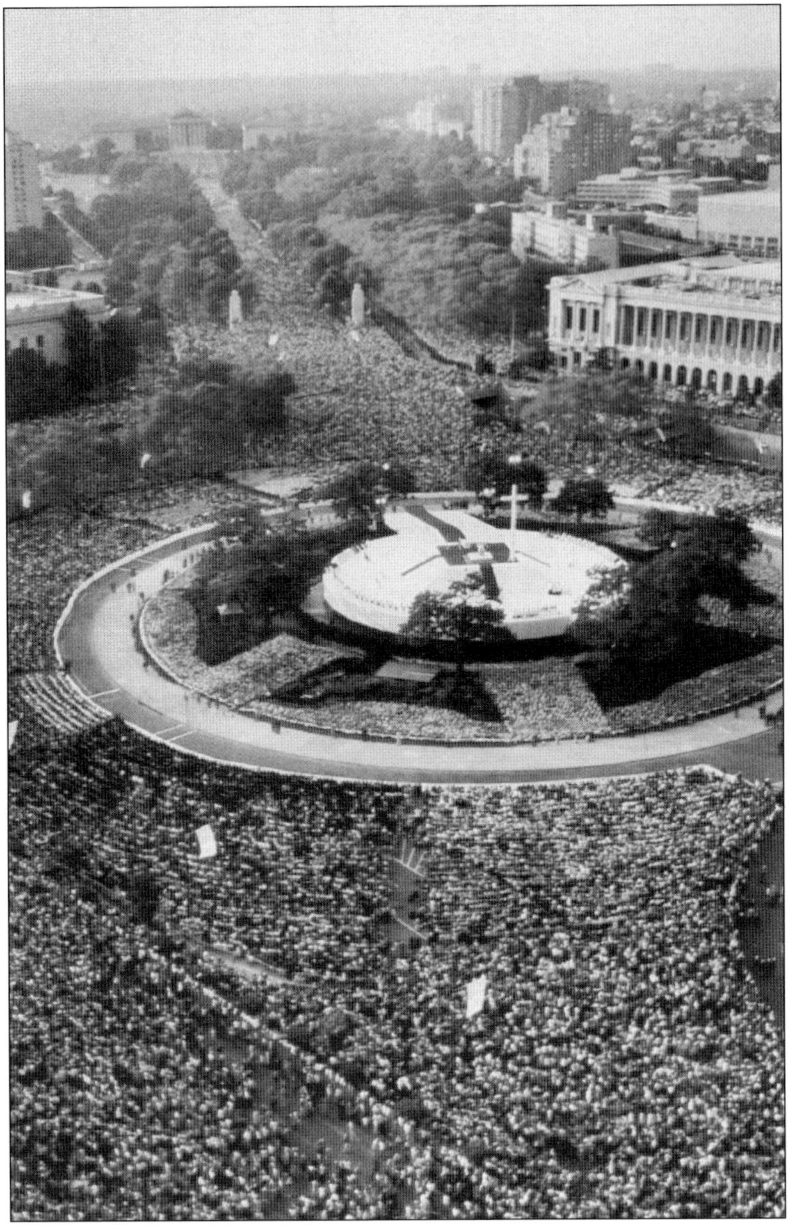

The Cathedral of Saints Peter and Paul served as an excellent backdrop to the outdoor mass in 1979; an estimated one million spectators crowded the Parkway to witness this once-in-a-lifetime event. Indeed, the 21-hour papal visit was one of Philadelphia's finest days. Pope John Paul II had come to the city three years earlier for the International Eucharistic Congress as the relatively anonymous Cardinal Karol Wojtyla. His 1979 stopover prompted the largest media and security mobilization in Philadelphia history. The following day, October 4, the Pope visited the National Shrine of St. John Neumann at St. Peter the Apostle Church, in the Northern Liberties neighborhood of Philadelphia. John Nepomucene Neumann (1811–1860) was the first Catholic male saint in the New World and the third American citizen canonized. As Bishop of Philadelphia, he was involved with the construction of the Cathedral Basilica. (Coral-Lee, Cordova, California.)

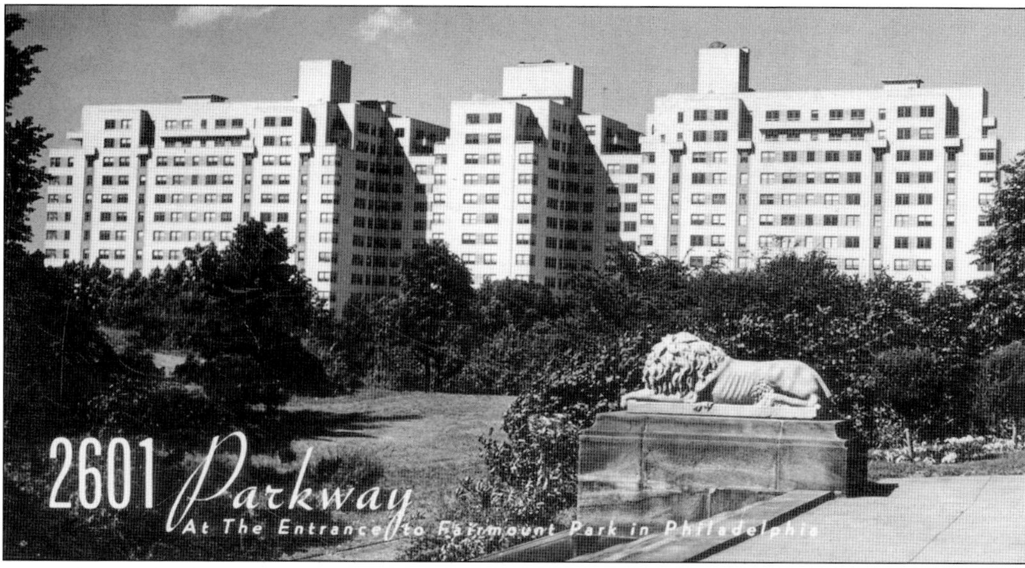

One of several residential high-rises in Philadelphia's Logan Square section, 2601 Parkway was the city's biggest apartment building when completed in 1940. Designed by Paul Crét "At the Entrance to Fairmount Park," its nearly 500 units have since been converted to condominiums. The complex offers breathtaking views of the art museum, the Schuylkill River, and the Parkway itself. Despite its name, 2601 Parkway is actually located along Pennsylvania Avenue. (Unmarked postcard; courtesy Gus Spector.)

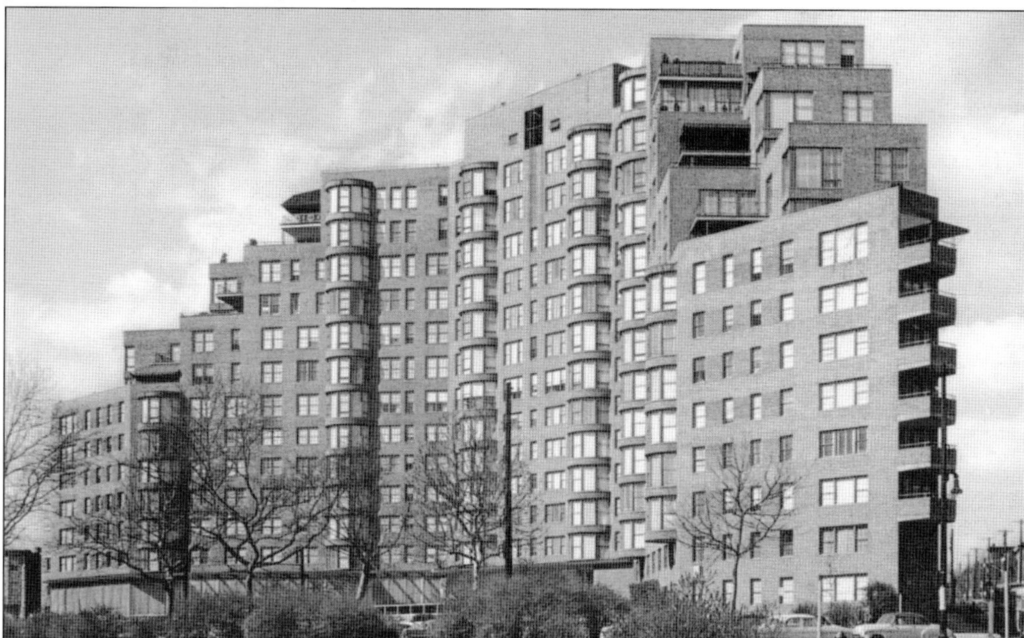
The 14-story Parkway House, with its communal roof deck, was built in a modernist yet conservative scheme after a design by the firm of Roth & Fleisher. Dating from the 1950s, Parkway House overlooks the Parkway from 2201 Pennsylvania Avenue. This was the first major Philadelphia building designed by a woman, Elizabeth Fleisher. (K.F. Lutz, Philadelphia; courtesy Gus Spector.)

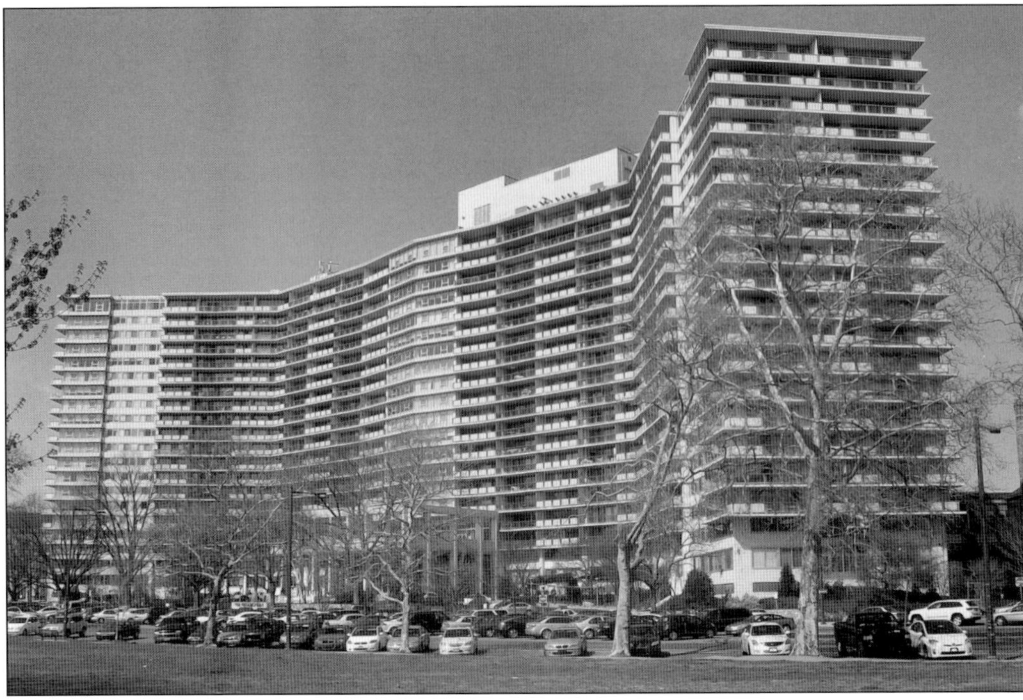

Looming over the Ben Franklin Parkway at 2401 Pennsylvania Avenue is the 776-unit Philadelphian. This 20-story condominium was reportedly the world's largest apartment house when erected in the late 1960s. The Philadelphian is often cited as the most impressive address in town, offering a diversity in floor plans from modest studios to opulent three-bedroom residences. (Photograph by author.)

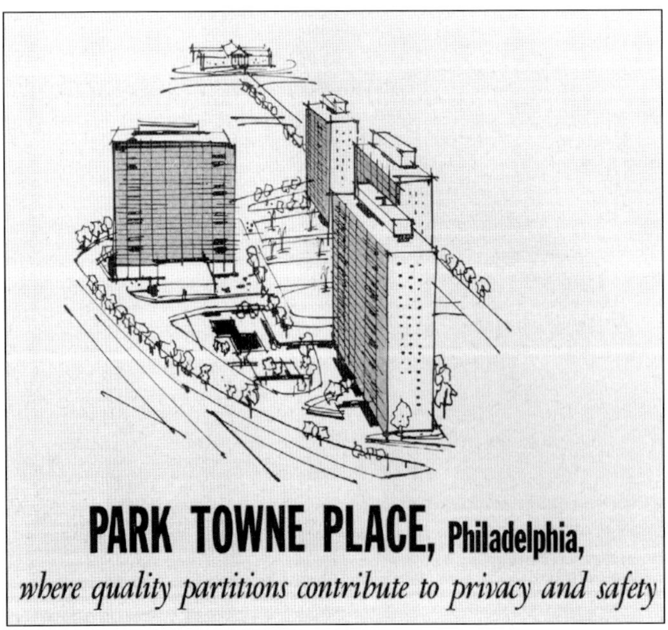

Park Towne Place Apartments have faced the Parkway, to the north, and the Vine Street Expressway, to the south, since 1959. The four 19-story towers were built within Philadelphia's North Triangle Redevelopment Area, a zone that contained the last Victorian-era buildings removed alongside the Parkway. This suburban-like complex was one of the nation's major urban renewal projects of the 1950s. A multimillion -dollar renovation is in the works to return Park Towne to where it was in Philadelphia's rental market when it opened. (Author's collection.)

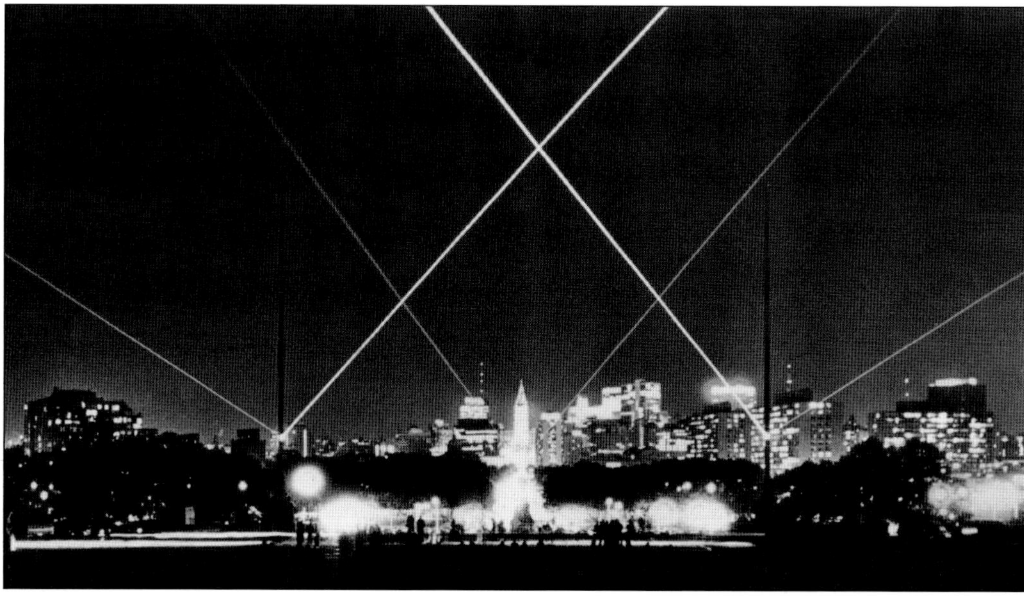

Park Towne served as the control room for *Open Air*, a light show that lit up the Parkway for three weeks in fall 2012. However, this was not the first time for such a decorative light installation. In May 1973, the Philadelphia Museum commissioned artist Rockne Krebs to install a temporary laser sculpture called *Sky Bridge Green*. Using two argon lasers at the museum's east portico, Krebs sent beams of green light shimmering high above the Parkway. (Author's collection.)

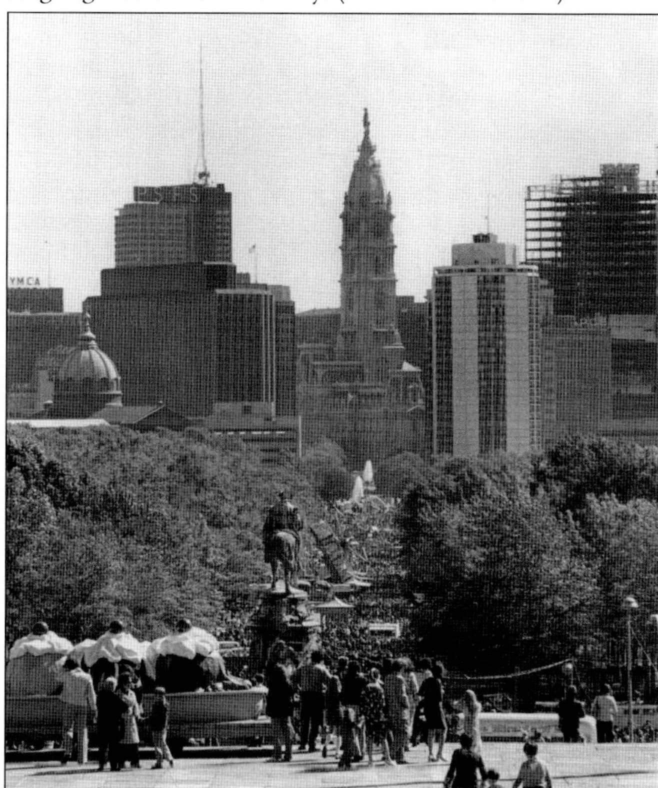

Super Sunday was a street festival held every fall in the 1970s, 1980s, and 1990s to benefit the Parkway's cultural institutions. Philadelphians could enjoy the last days of summer with food, games, and rides. Unfortunately, the fair encountered competition from other local events, and the last Super Sunday took place in 1998. In this 1973 image, the Parkway is jammed with people as the statues of William Penn and George Washington observe from either direction. (Unmarked postcard, courtesy Gus Spector.)

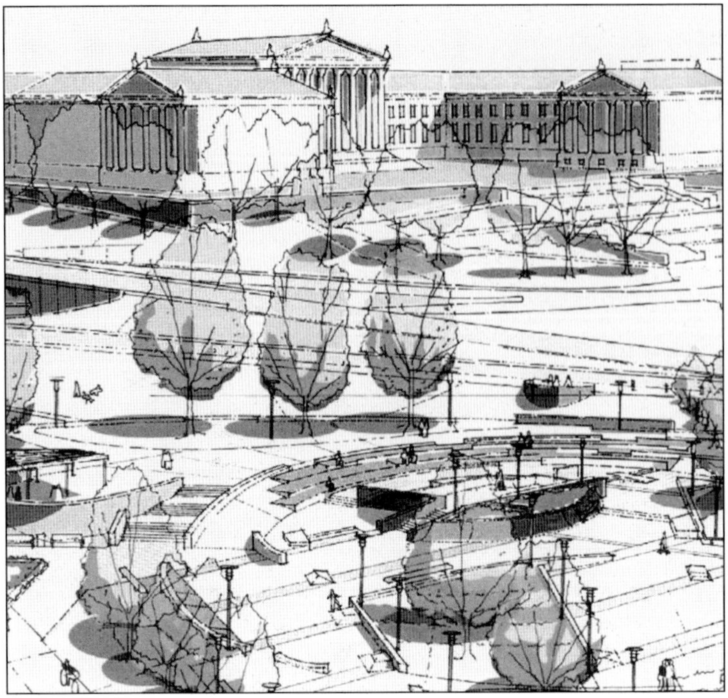

Franklin's Paine Skatepark Fund raised $4.5 million to build skateboarding sites around the city following the loss of Love Park as a skate park. Paine's Park opened on May 22, 2013, as the largest public skate park in North America. Directly across from the Philadelphia Museum of Art, the 2.5-acre mixed-use plaza creates new links between the Parkway and the heavily used Schuylkill River Trail. (Courtesy Friday Architects/ Planners, Inc.)

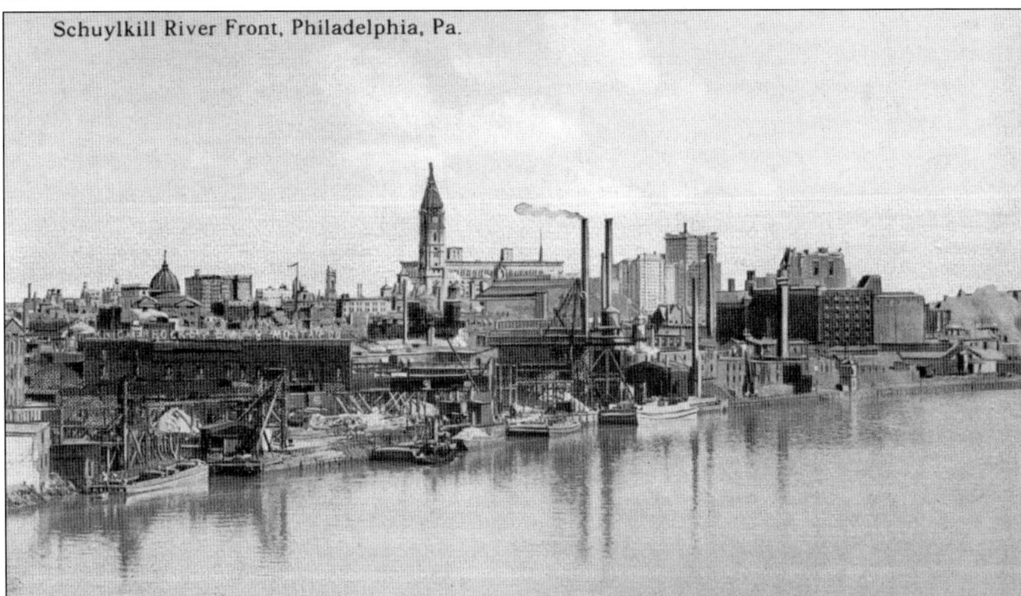

Paine's Park was once home to a diverse group of cotton mills, coal yards, gasworks, lumberyards, and even a city dump. These ramshackle enterprises were finally eliminated when the Parkway was constructed. An active set of CSX railroad tracks, put in by the Baltimore & Ohio Railroad, still carry freight trains by the site. The tracks enter the 2,540-foot Fairmount Park Tunnel under Eakins Oval and proceed beneath the art museum steps before paralleling and joining the Reading Railroad's Pennsylvania Avenue Subway and continuing northwards after exiting the tunnel at Twenty-seventh Street. This is the busiest rail freight tunnel in Philadelphia. City Hall Tower stands tall in this 1920s postcard. (Unmarked postcard.)

Nine

Around the Philadelphia Museum of Art

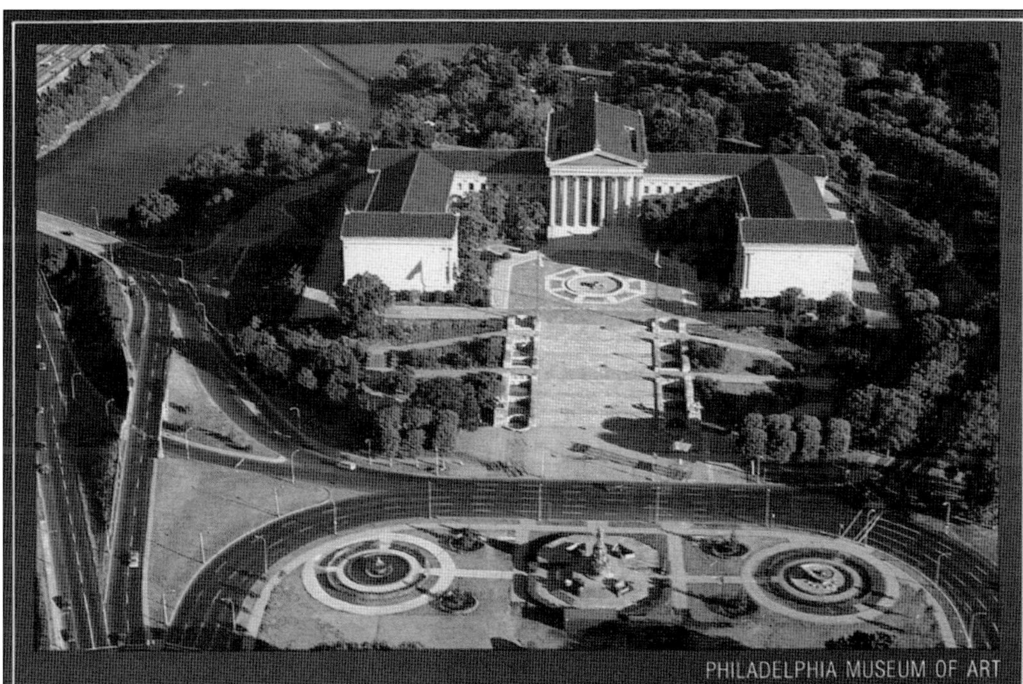

The Philadelphia Museum of Art is among the five most prestigious art museums in the world, as well as one of the largest museums in the United States. The striking Greek Revival edifice, hailed as the "Pantheon on the Parkway," was finished in 1928 after 12 years of planning and construction. Painter Henry McCarter derided it as "a wonderful Greek garage," which would be a clever compliment today. (Frank Burd, Philadelphia.)

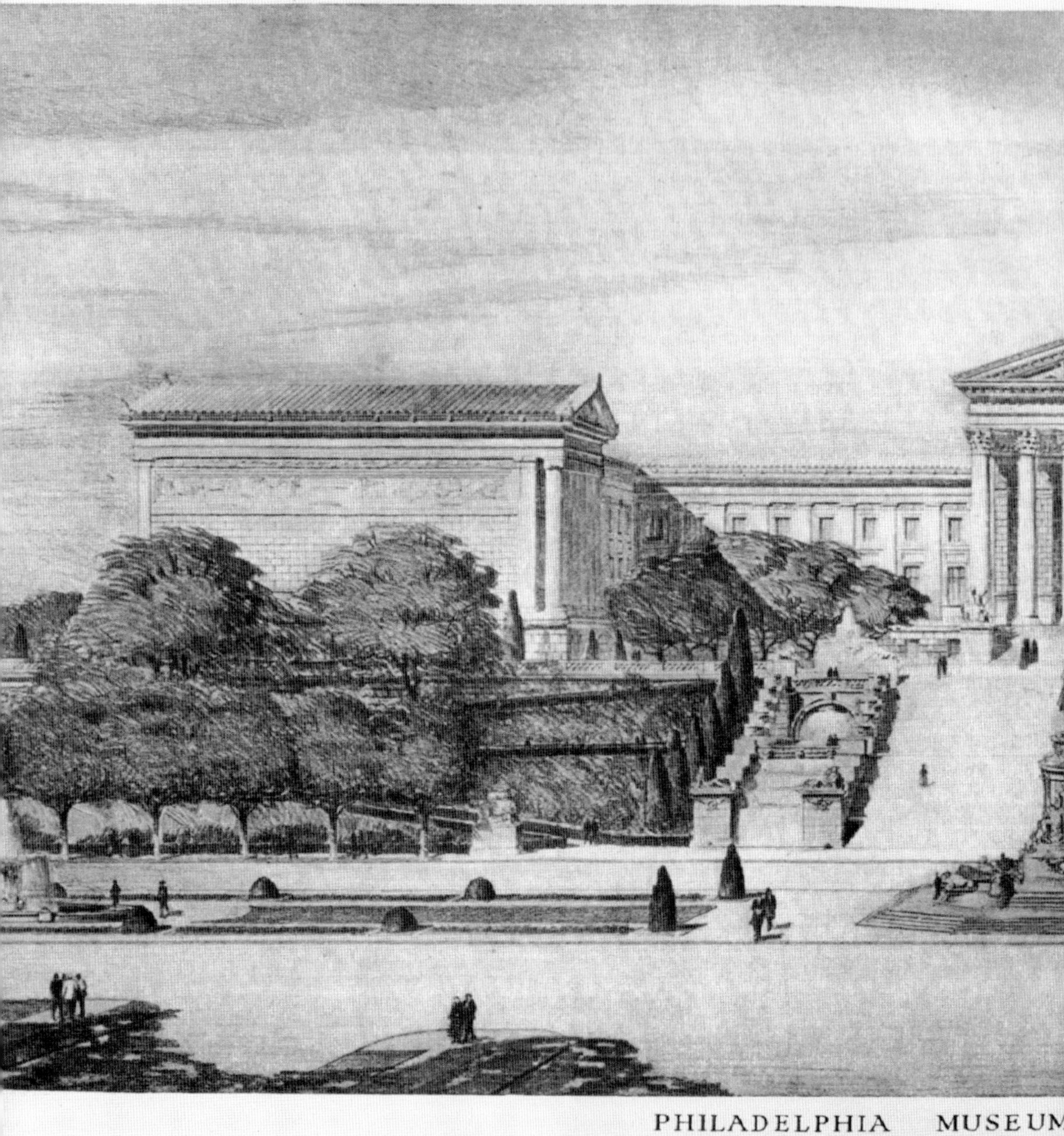

This drawing displays the Philadelphia Museum of Art essentially as it was built, but years before its completion. The museum has been based at Memorial Hall in West Fairmount Park since opening on May 10, 1877, and was first known as the Pennsylvania Museum and School of Industrial Art. Its founding was a consequence of the fine arts exhibition of the 1876 Centennial

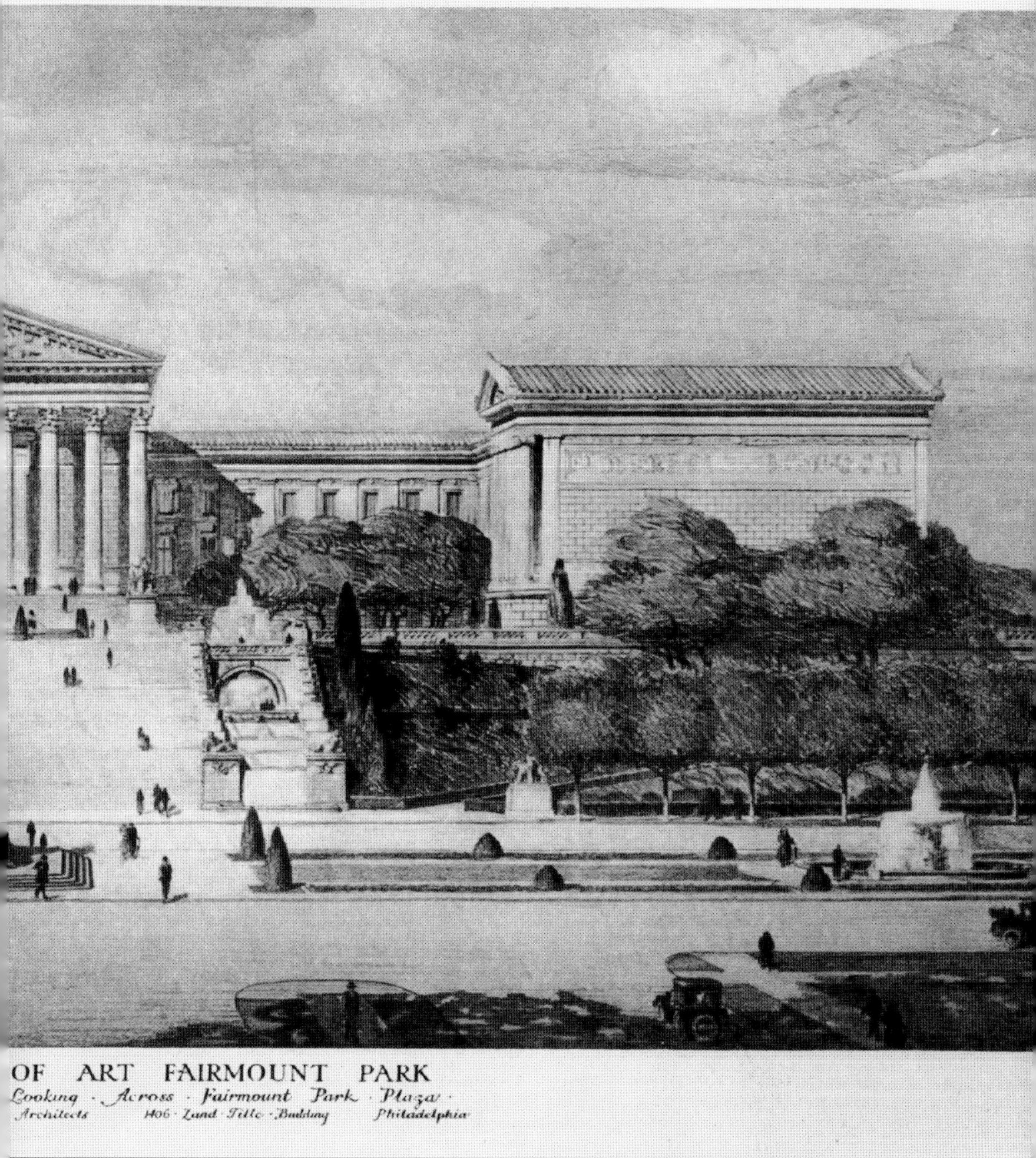

International Exposition, so the museum has always regarded 1877 as its inauguration. A benefactor later bequeathed $50,000 to the museum to change its name to the Philadelphia Museum of Art, which it did in 1938. This image and the following one are from *The Fairmount Parkway* (1919).

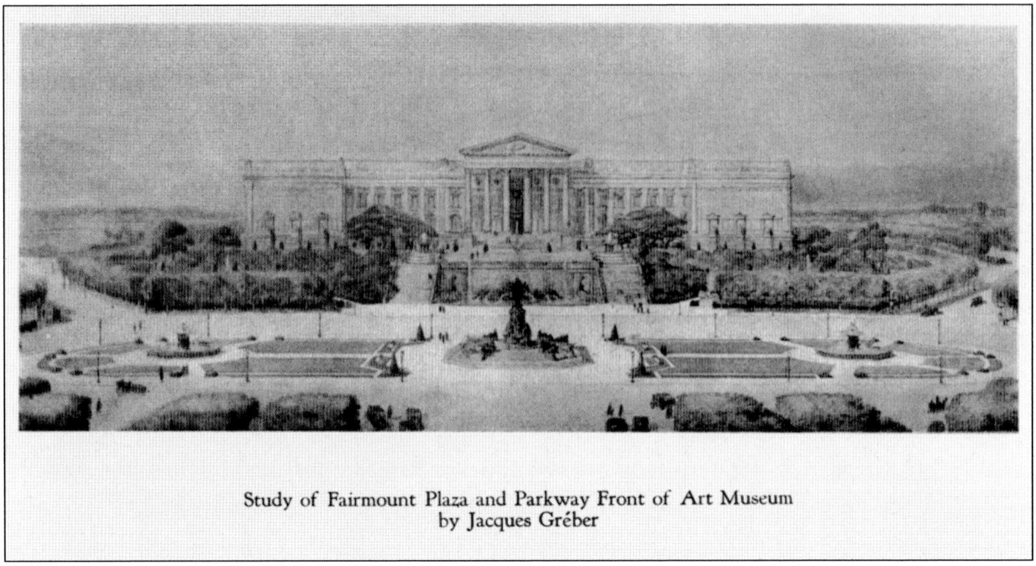

Jacques Gréber envisioned that the museum would be built at a lower elevation and that its front portico would have six columns rather than eight. He also pictured Fairmount Plaza as an ornate place with the Washington Monument positioned between two fountains. In future years, vehicular traffic would jam the street facing the museum, forcing pedestrians crossing there to make a "dash for art."

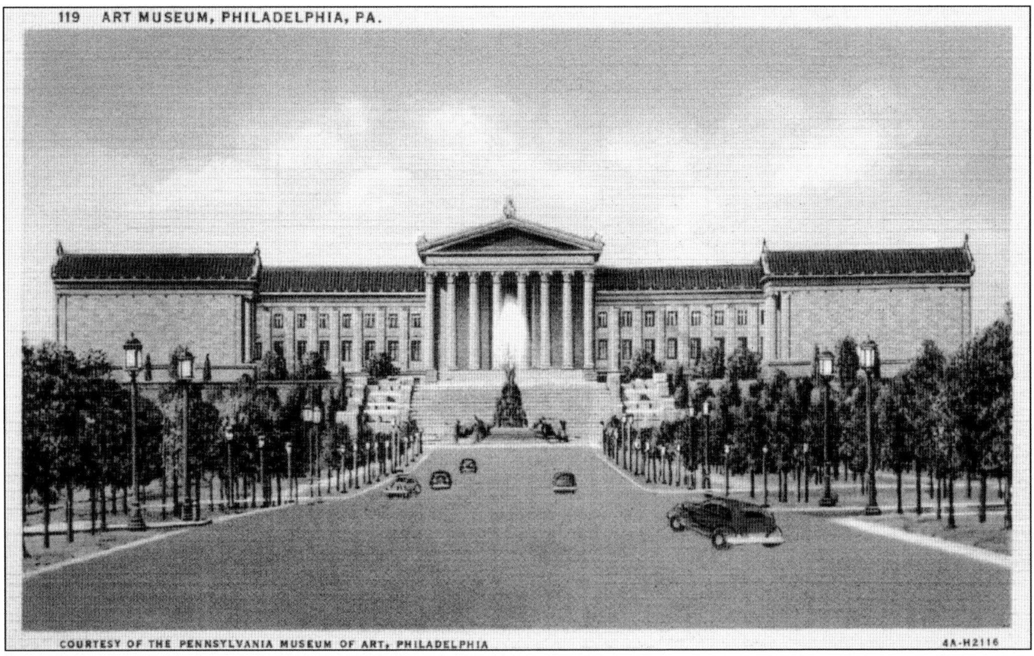

Julian Francis Abele, of Horace Trumbauer's architectural office, was a chief designer of the Philadelphia Museum of Art. He was adept at turning out French chateaus, Georgian townhouses, and classically inspired libraries, such as the Central Library of Philadelphia. A Pennsylvania historical marker noting his contribution to the architectural profession stands in front of the museum. (Lynn Boyer, C.T. Art-Colortone.)

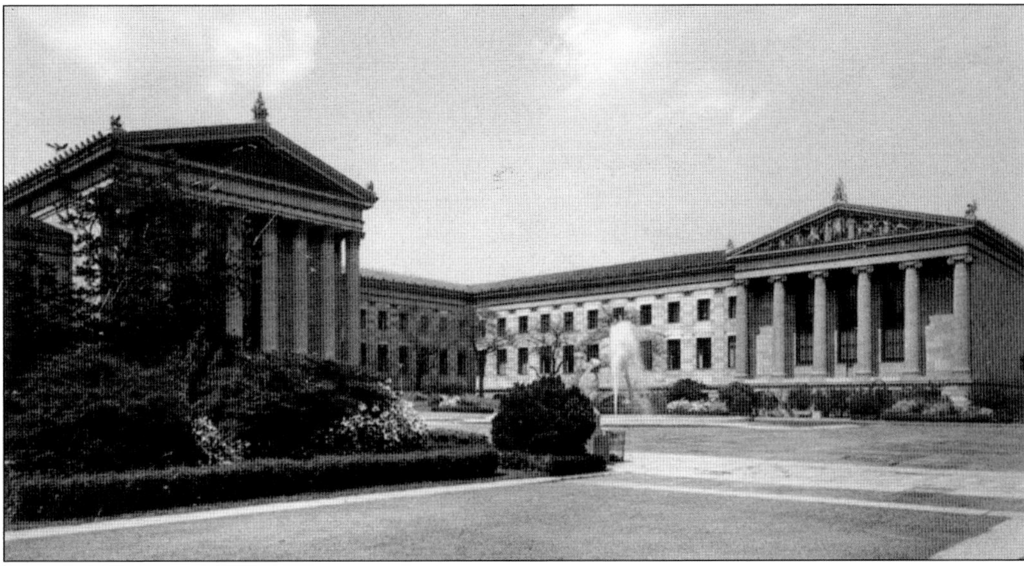

When dedicated on March 26, 1928, the museum was one of the crowning achievements of the City Beautiful Movement. Of special interest are the polychrome terra-cotta figures in the tympanum of the north wing's pediment, designed by sculptor C. Paul Jennewein in 1932. This was the first major use of this type of decoration in over 2,000 years. A total of 13 classical figures—including Zeus, Aphrodite, and Eros—are visible. There are no sculptures in the south wing's pediment. (United News Company.)

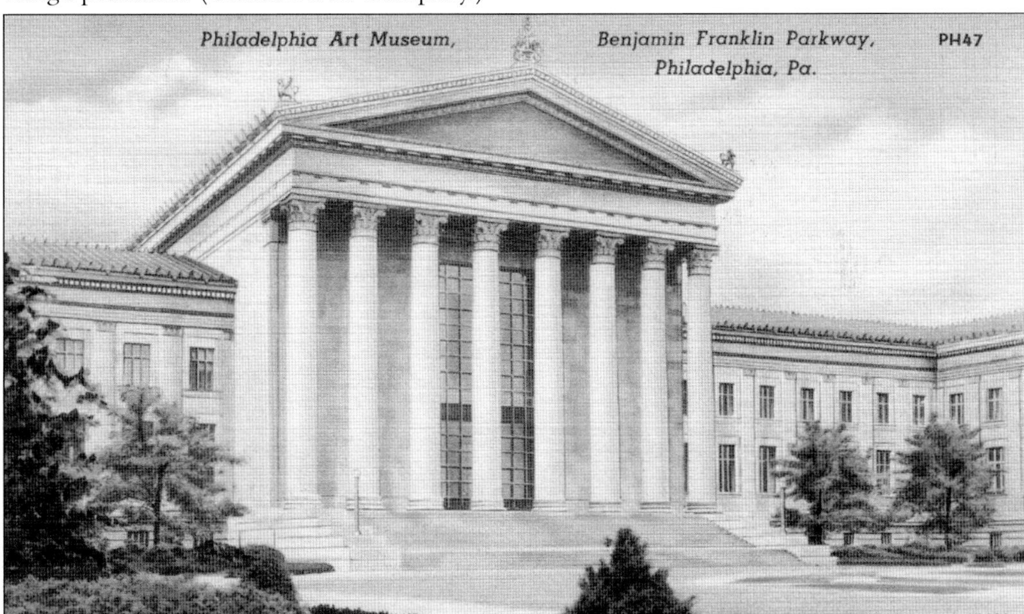

The central portico of the museum is portrayed in this charming linen card. Work on the museum's two wings commenced first, in order to ensure the flow of city funds and private donations to complete the building's connecting central portion. The world's largest Classic Revival building when built, the museum accommodates over 200 galleries covering 10 acres. The exterior is faced with Minnesota dolomite, and the roof is covered with glazed blue tiles. (Central News Company.)

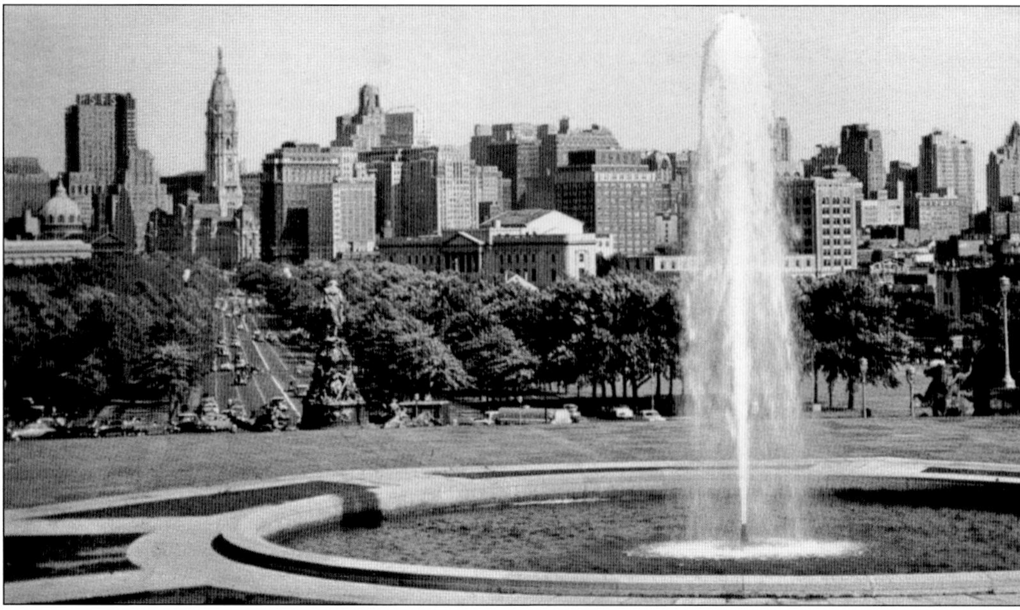

In the upper courtyard of the museum is the Henry M. Phillips Memorial Fountain, designed by Henry Mitchell and dubbed *Courtship*. Eight bronze reliefs depicting horses at play originally surrounded the basin, but they are no longer there. Incidentally, two virtually identical founts are on either side of the Washington Monument. The Ericsson Fountain was installed in 1934, and the Price Fountain was added in 1967 when traffic modifications produced Eakins Oval. (Art Color Card Distributors.)

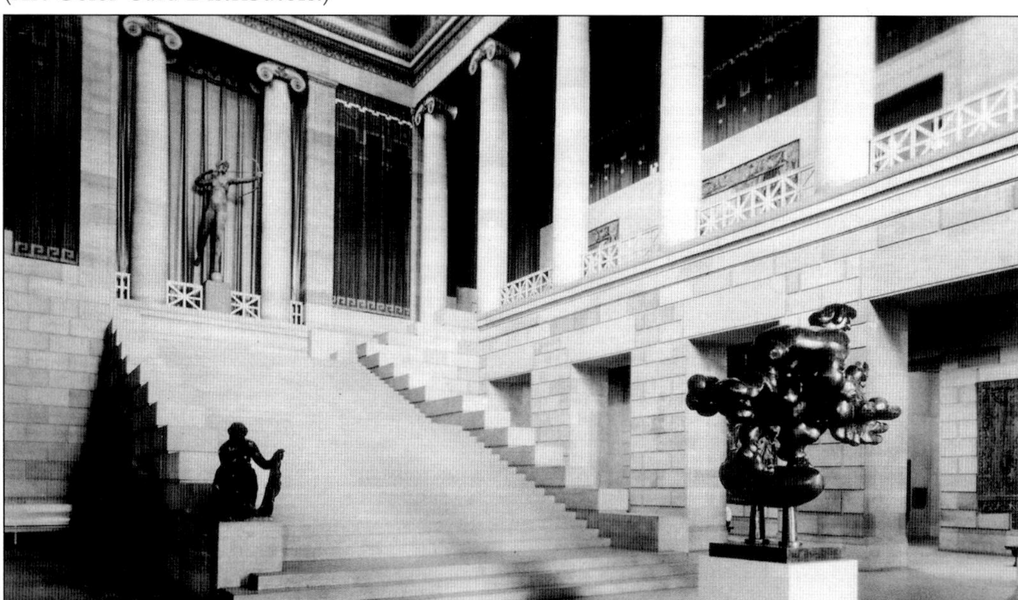

The statue of *Diana* overlooking the museum's Great Stair Hall once graced New York City's original Madison Square Garden. Created by Augustus Saint-Gaudens, it was the second version of the Roman goddess installed there as a weathervane in the 1890s. New York Life Insurance gave *Diana* to the Museum of Art after an unsuccessful search for a suitable home in New York. The hollow copper work is 13 feet high and weighs 1,500 pounds. (Philadelphia Museum of Art.)

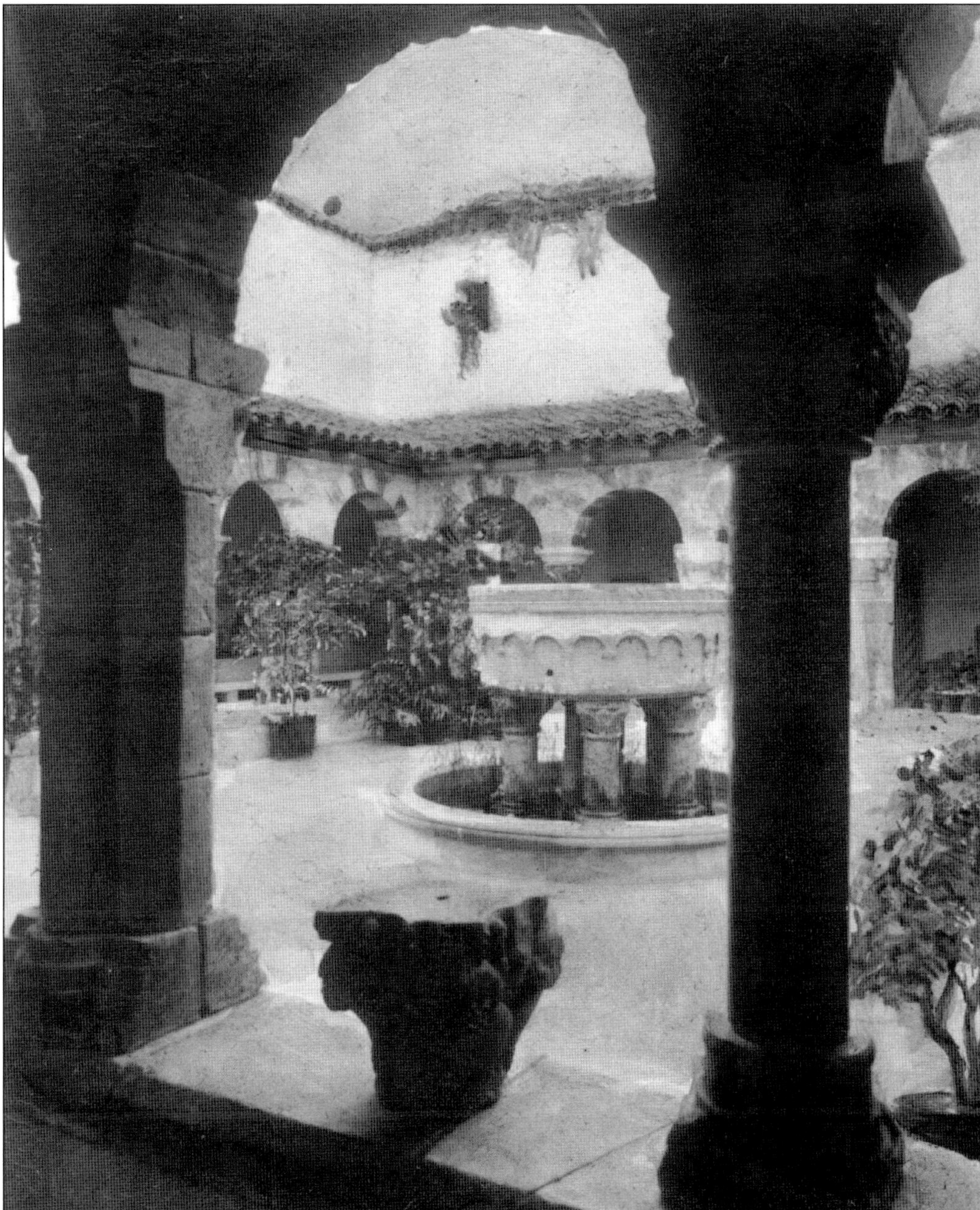

The museum has a series of highly esteemed period rooms from the 12th to the 20th centuries. Allowing visitors to "walk through time," these rooms and their architectural settings recreate environments spanning from a French grand salon to a Chinese scholar's study. This postcard shows a medieval cloister, one of the earliest period rooms acquired for the museum's outstanding collection of European art. Such cloisters were usually the space at the heart of a monastery where various events of the religious order transpired. This example is from the Abbey of Saint Genis Des Fontaines, Pyrenees Orientales, in southwestern France, and dates from 1270–1280. The center of the room features a 12th-century Romanesque marble fountain from the Abbey of Saint Michel de Cuxa in the Roussillon region of France. (Philadelphia Museum of Art.)

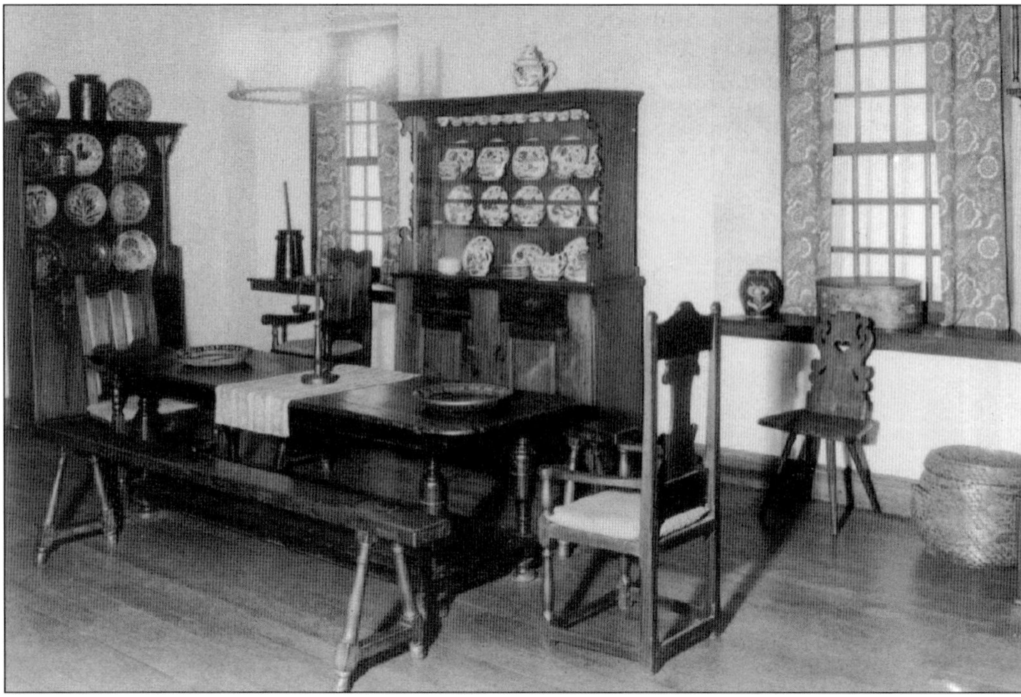

This early card shows the period kitchen from a house in Millbach Township, Lebanon County, Pennsylvania, from around 1752. Furnishings include walnut furniture, slipware, forged iron, pottery, and linen hangings. The room and its objects preserve the arts and architecture of Germans who came to Pennsylvania in the 1700s. (Philadelphia Museum of Art.)

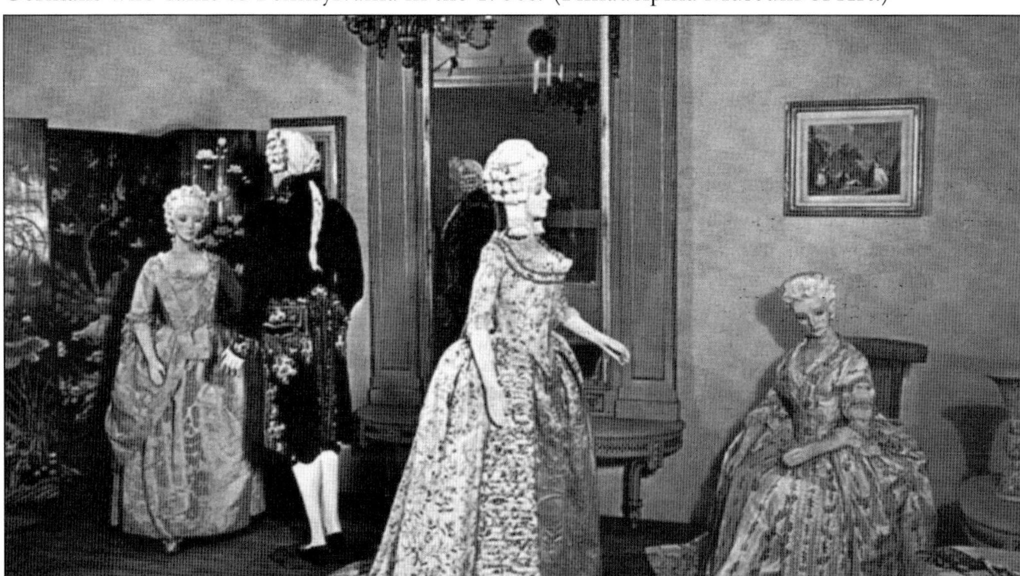

The museum's colonial costume holdings provide fashion historians an excellent resource to study historical American dress. The fashion wing and costumes from the 1770s are highlighted in this card. The wing was sponsored by the Fashion Group of Philadelphia, a local chapter of an international fashion organization. (Joseph F. Morsello, Philadelphia.)

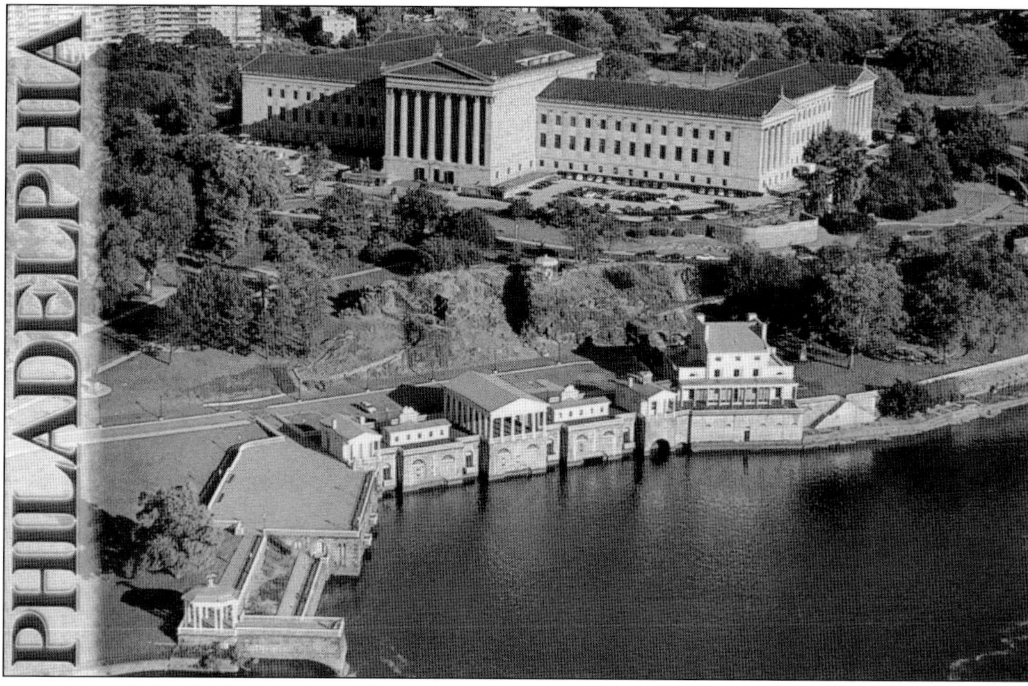

In 1683, Thomas Holme, the first surveyor general of Pennsylvania, produced for William Penn a map of Philadelphia on which he identified a hill by the Schuylkill River as "Faire Mount." In 1819, the summit became home to six reservoirs serving the Fairmount Water Works. After that facility was decommissioned, Fairmount was deemed a fine elevated spot for the city's new art museum, which would serve as the Parkway's western terminus. (United Souvenir & Apparel, Inc.)

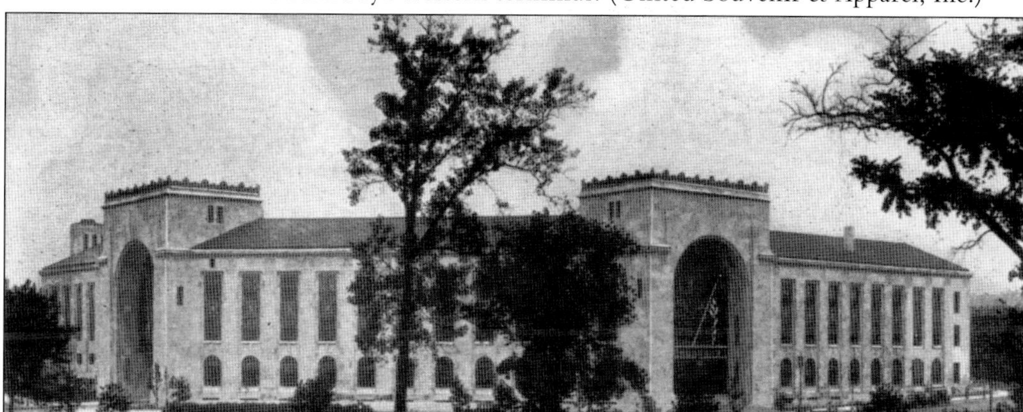

Finished in 1928 as the Fidelity Mutual Life Insurance Company building, this art deco edifice at Fairmount and Pennsylvania Avenues was later the Reliance Standard Life Insurance building. It is now the Ruth and Raymond Perelman Building, an annex for the Philadelphia Museum of Art that has provided six galleries of new exhibition space since 2007. (Unmarked postcard; courtesy Gus Spector.)

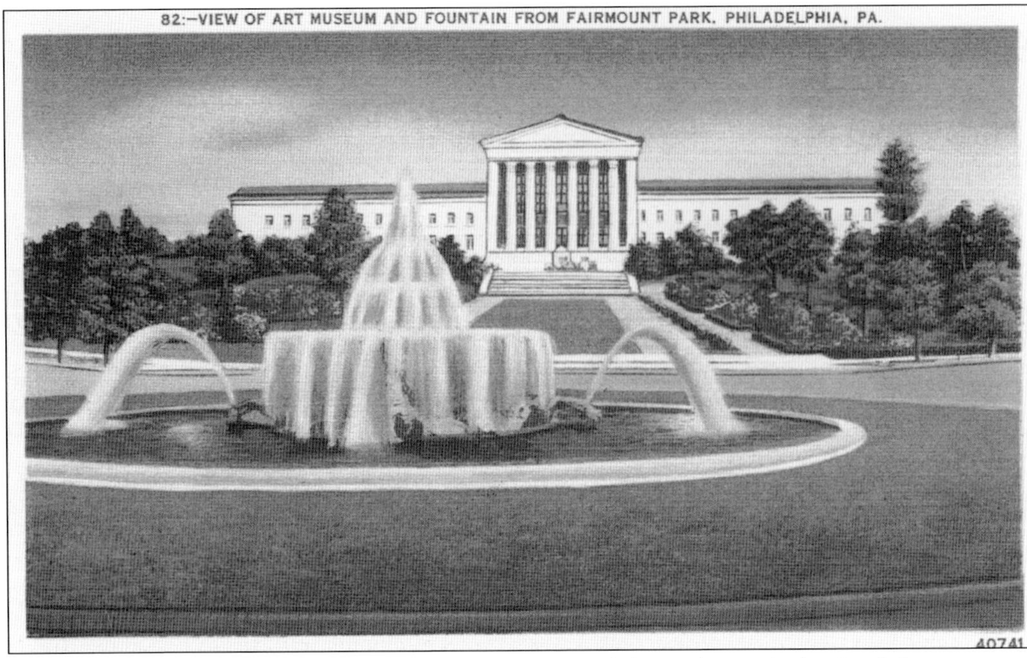

This picturesque 1940s postcard shows the *Fountain of the Seahorses*, in back of the museum. Colloquially called the Italian Fountain, the work was a replica gift from Italy on the 150th anniversary of the United States, but it arrived too late for the US Sesqui-Centennial International Exposition and was assembled at this spot in 1928. The travertine fount was painstakingly dismantled, cleaned, and refurbished in 2013. (Unmarked postcard.)

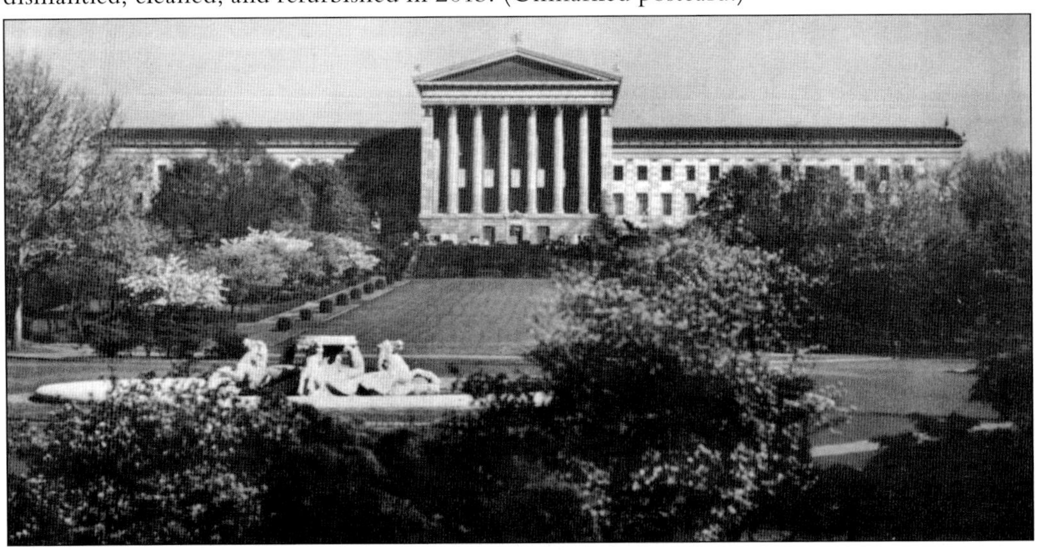

Absent from this shot are the many sculptures along the fairway leading down from the museum to the Italian Fountain. The statues are of soldiers and statesmen who helped create the United States during the Revolutionary War. This verdant area has been renovated as an entrance to Fairmount Park and is part of the Schuylkill River Trail, a bustling multiuse footpath to Valley Forge. Also, the Anne d'Harnoncourt Sculpture Garden is in this vicinity. The one-acre terraced garden extends the museum's galleries to the outdoors and offers a sampling of sculpture to both art lovers and onlookers. (K.F. Lutz, Philadelphia; Mike Roberts Color Productions.)

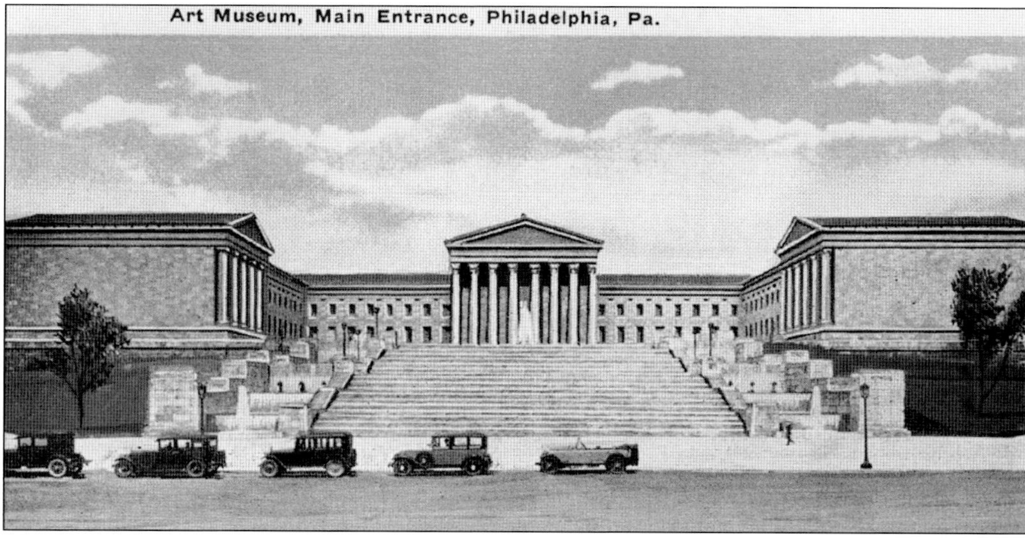

The top of the art museum's front steps offers a commanding view of the Parkway and the Philadelphia skyline. While already exceptional, the 72 stone steps achieved worldwide prominence with the 1976 release of the film *Rocky*. Since then, visitors from all corners of the globe have come to run triumphantly up the ascent, as Sylvester Stallone did in the Oscar-winning movie (and four of its sequels). In March 2014, *Rocky* was shown inside the museum for the first time. (P. Sander, Philadelphia.)

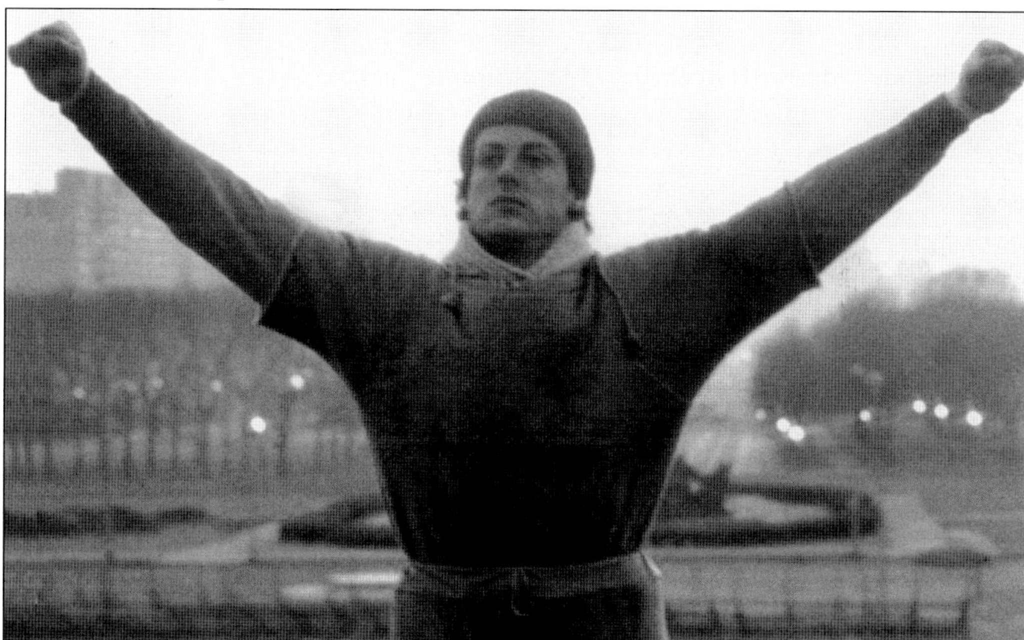

Sylvester Stallone, as Rocky Balboa, has his hands raised in exultation in front of the art museum; the Ben Franklin Parkway is behind him. Besides Stallone himself running up the museum's steps, the closing credits of 2006's *Rocky Balboa* showed various everyday people running up the famous "Rocky Steps." Plus, a bronze inlay of sneaker footprints, beneath the name "Rocky," was placed at the top of the steps, which have been called "America's Most Famous Steps." (Author's collection.)

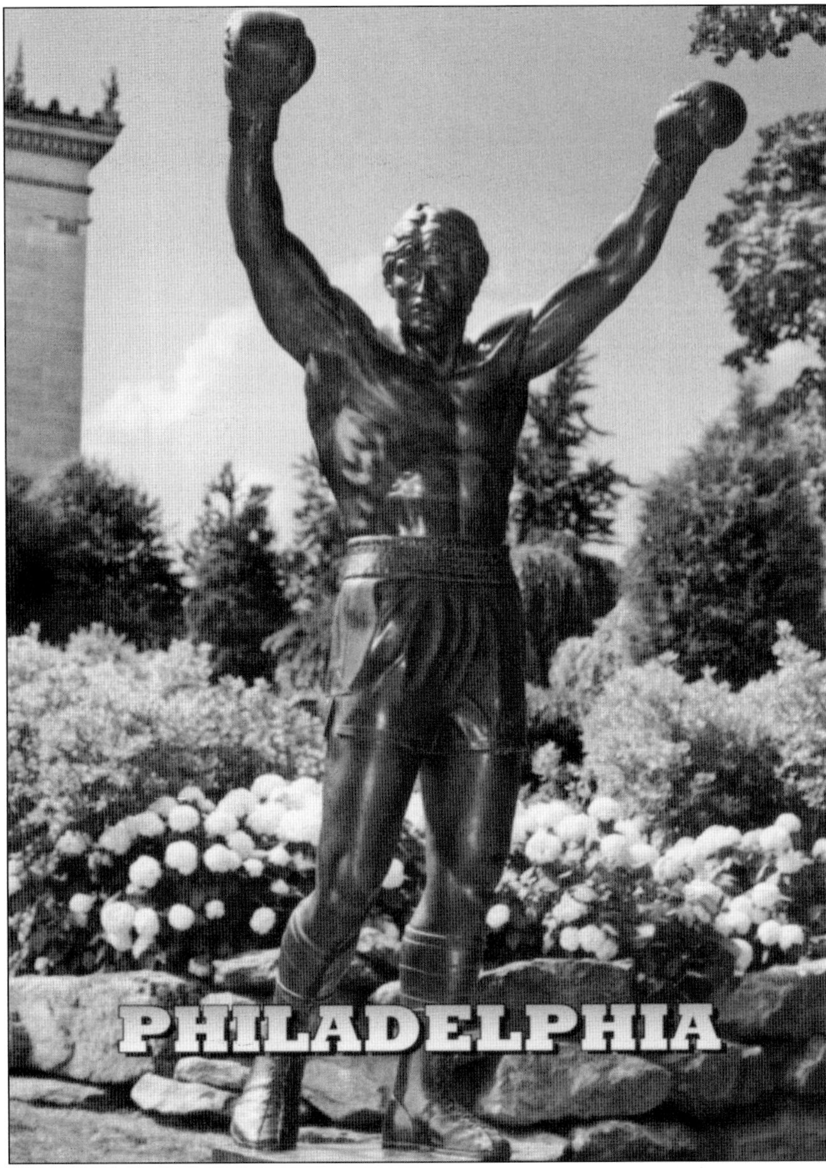

Formally titled *Thunder in His Heart*, this brawny bronze statue of Rocky Balboa was unveiled in the museum's upper exterior courtyard for the filming of *Rocky III* (1982). Sylvester Stallone then left the work to the City of Philadelphia, but cultural officials considered it merely a movie prop. After the public flooded newspapers with pro and con mail, the city's art commission decided that the sports complex in South Philadelphia was the proper environment for the sculptured fictional heavyweight. The controversy was rekindled in 1987, 1990, and 1993, when the statue was returned to the art museum steps for movie productions, but it was returned to South Philadelphia each time. The city finally relented and moved *Thunder in His Heart* to the bottom right of the steps in 2006. On September 8 of that year, Sylvester Stallone came to Philadelphia to dedicate the work at its new setting. (The author of this book was there on that most memorable afternoon.) The Rocky statue is one of Philadelphia's biggest attractions, and it is a quintessential photographic opportunity for streams of tourists from everywhere. (Peter Gridley, Impact Photo Graphics.)

Ten

Beyond the Benjamin Franklin Parkway

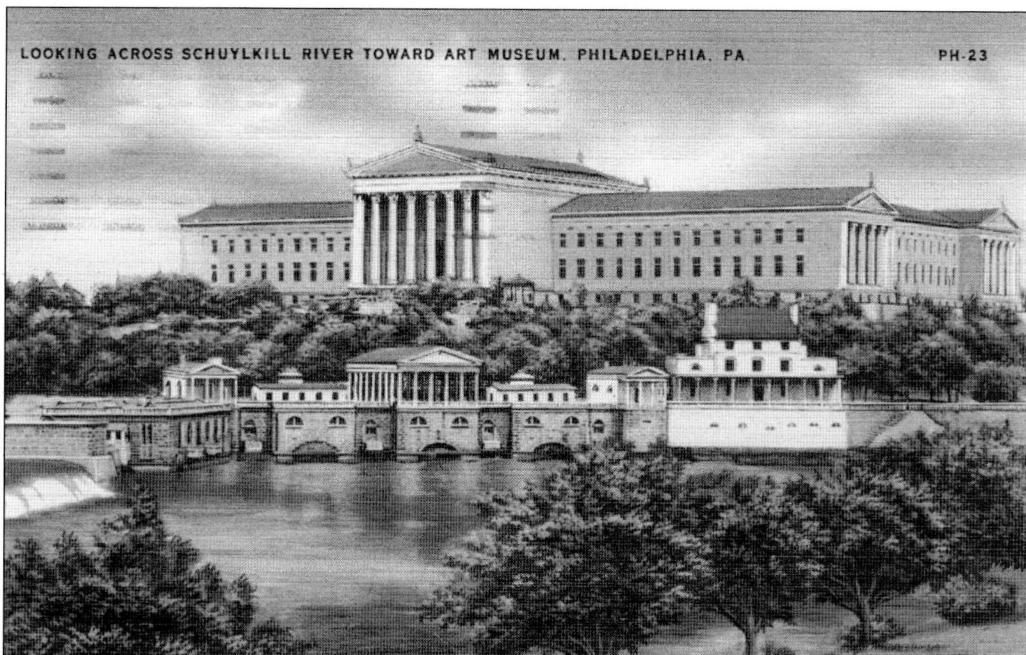

This eye-catching card exhibits two of Philadelphia's most exemplary structures: the Philadelphia Museum of Art and the Fairmount Water Works. Predating the museum by over 100 years, the water pumping station was an international tourist destination almost from the day it opened in 1815. No trip to Philadelphia was complete without seeing the manicured grounds, advanced machinery, and Roman temple–like buildings of the Fairmount Water Works. (Central News Company.)

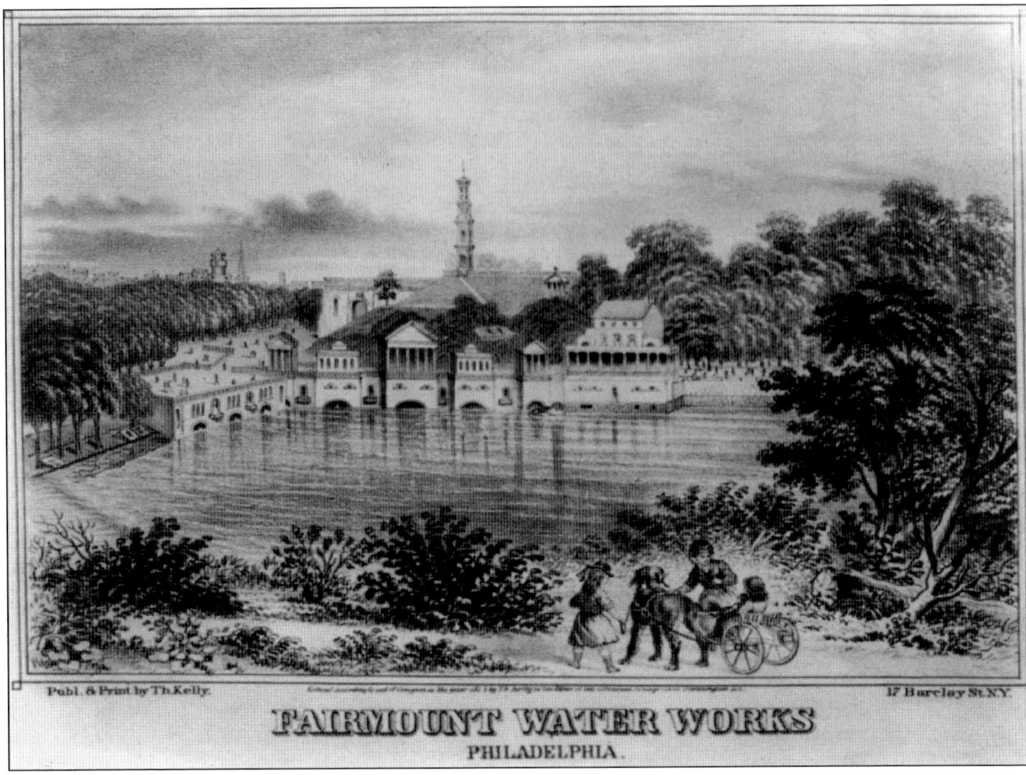

Philadelphia's initial waterworks at Penn Square had proven inadequate for the growing city. In 1811, engineer Frederick Graff recommended that the east bank of the Schuylkill River would be a good place for a new waterworks, and he was then charged with designing and constructing the facility. This lithograph, published in 1874, features a tall water distribution standpipe that was also an ornamental tower. (Library of Congress.)

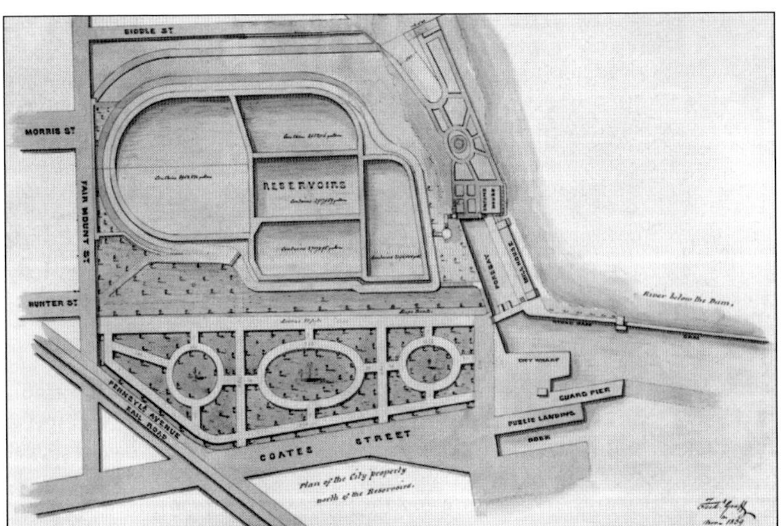

Graff drafted this plan of the fine promenades and water-settling reservoirs of the Fairmount Water Works in 1839. (South is toward the top.) The art museum now sits where the reservoirs were, and the surrounding landscape has been very much modified through the years. (Library of Congress.)

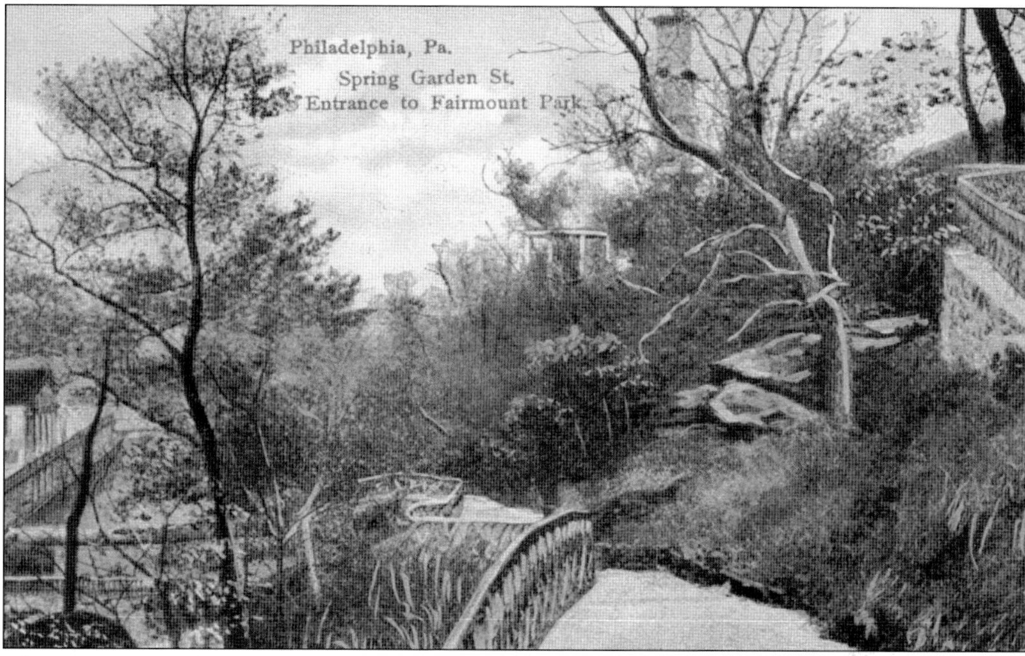

The Spring Garden Street entrance to Fairmount Park is shown in this 1909 view. On the left is the waterworks' forebay, which directed water to the waterwheels and pumps. In the background, faintly, is the decorative water standpipe, built in 1861 and brought down during the art museum's construction. The image highlights the trail that climbed to the reservoirs; these days, a restored pathway to the museum runs there. (Unmarked postcard.)

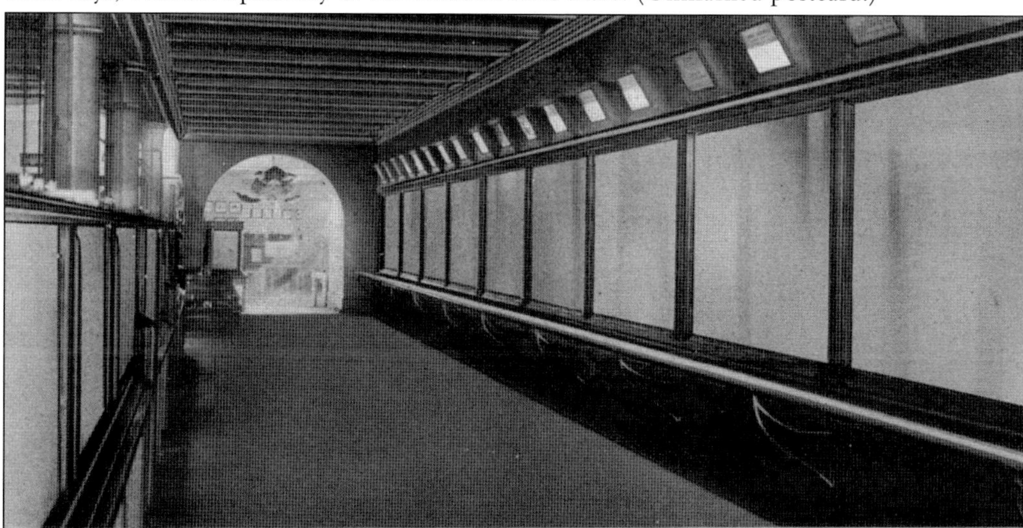

SEA WATER ROOM OF FAIRMOUNT PARK AQUARIUM

After modern water treatment plants began operating elsewhere in Philadelphia, the Fairmount Water Works closed in 1911, whereupon an aquarium opened there. By 1929, the Fairmount Park Aquarium was possibly the world's fourth-largest aquarium and supposedly had the best tropical fish collection in the United States. Seals and sea lions frolicked in the forebay at first, but they became ill, and the forebay was subsequently filled in to become Aquarium (now Waterworks) Drive. (Gus Spector.)

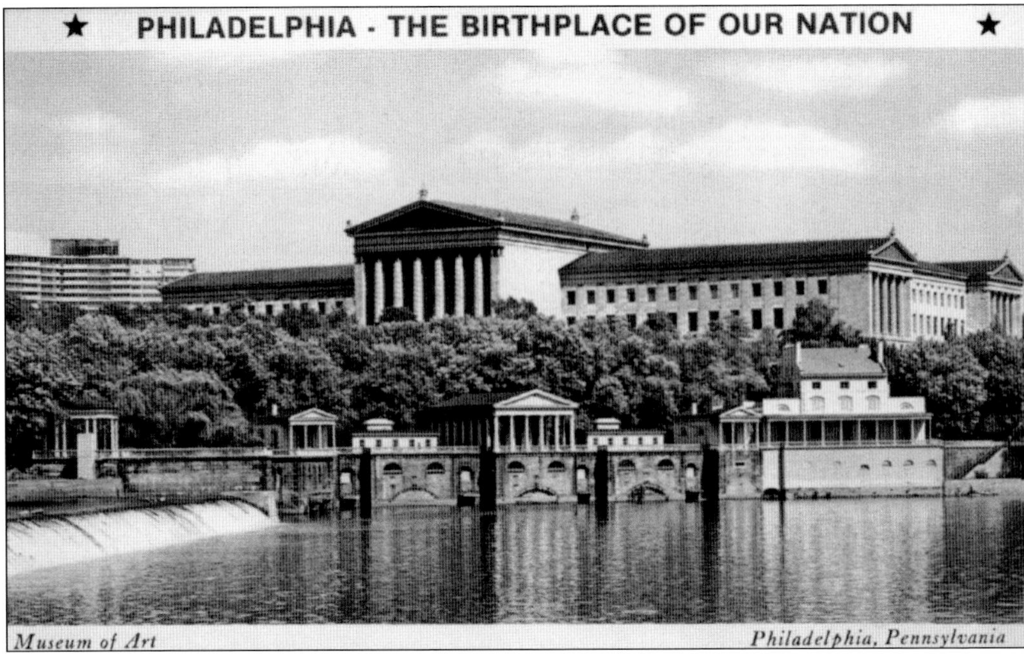

The Fairmount Aquarium shut its doors in 1962, a victim of politics and indifference. An Olympic-sized swimming pool was then installed inside a onetime waterworks building with funds from the John B. Kelly family. It lasted until Hurricane Agnes devastated the site in 1972. The place now operates as the Fairmount Water Works Interpretive Center, an interactive facility focusing on the Delaware River watershed. Additionally, the original engine house now holds the Water Works Restaurant. (K.F. Lutz, Philadelphia.)

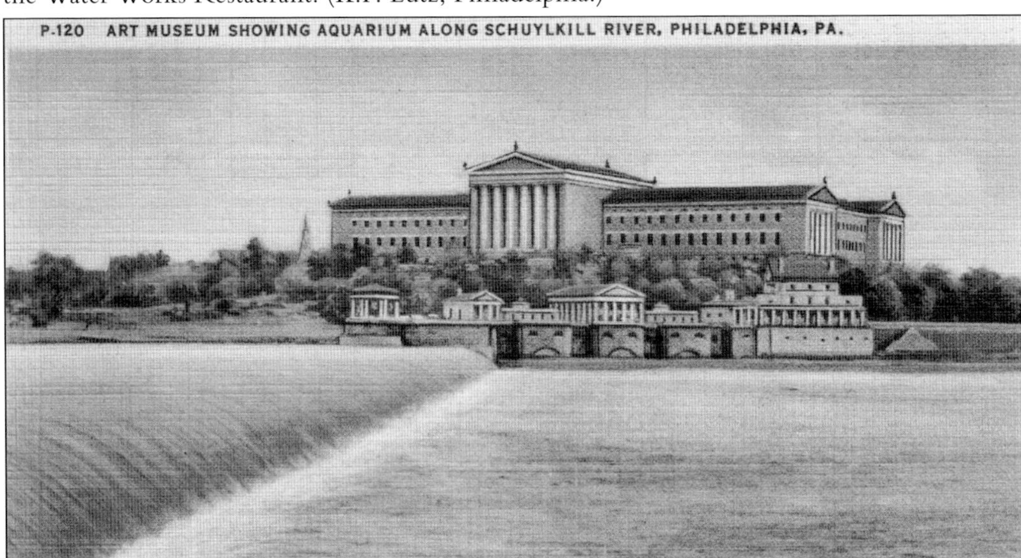

The city invested $400,000 to build a dam across the Schuylkill River for the Fairmount Water Works. Completed in 1822, Fairmount Dam forced water into a forebay leading through the pump house and several waterwheels that powered pumps that raised water to the basins on Fairmount Hill. Fairmount Dam, actually a 1,204-foot-wide diagonal spillway, was the longest dam in the world when it was made. (Lynn H, Boyer, C.T. Art-Colortone.)

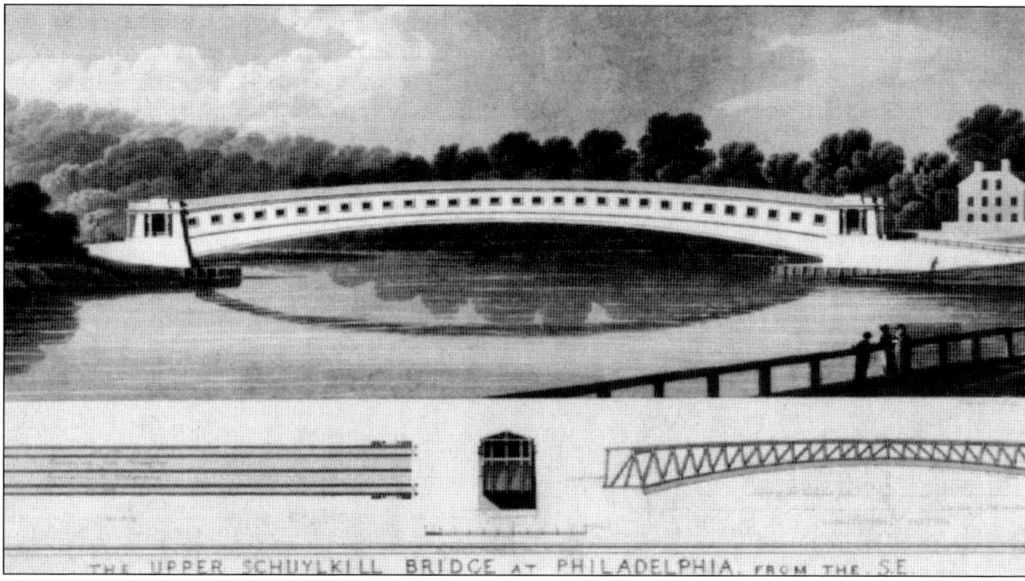

Parkway traffic can head west over the Schuylkill River into West Philadelphia, where another local attraction, the Philadelphia Zoo, is located. Today's Spring Garden Street Bridge crosses the river where three notable spans in American bridge-building history once stood. The first, built in 1812, was the Upper Ferry Bridge, a 343-foot bridge devised by German immigrant Lewis Wernwag. The "Colossus of Fairmount" was heralded as the longest clear-span wooden bridge in the world. (Library of Congress.)

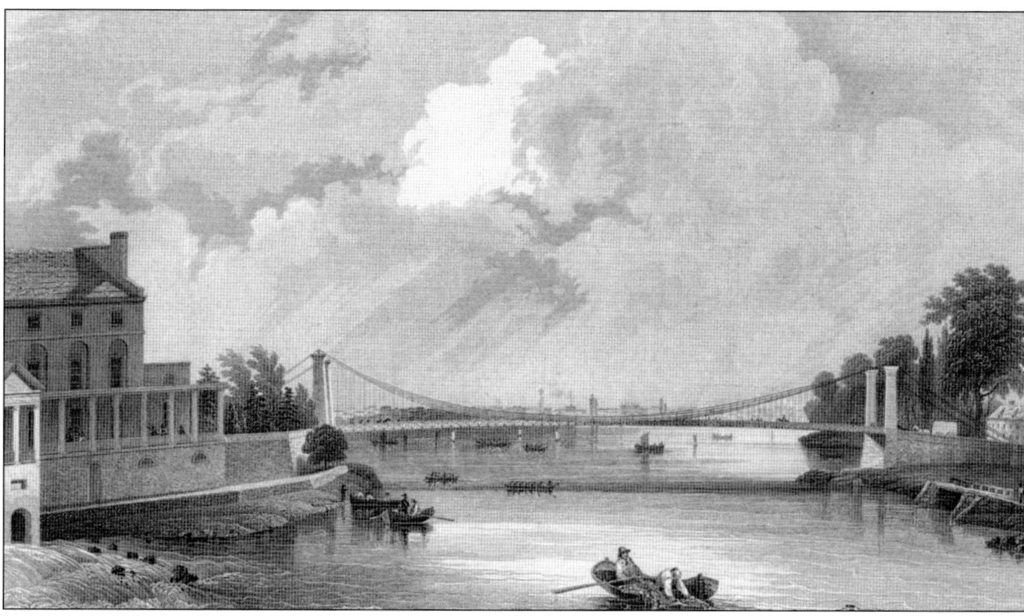

Wernwag's colossal bridge burned in 1838. Replacing it in 1842 was the Fairmount Wire Bridge, designed and fabricated by Charles Ellet Jr. The 27-foot-wide span had two sets of five cables with wire rope suspenders. This was the first cable-wire suspension bridge for general traffic in the United States, 41 years before the Brooklyn Bridge. This image is an engraving drawn around 1842 for *Graham's Magazine*.

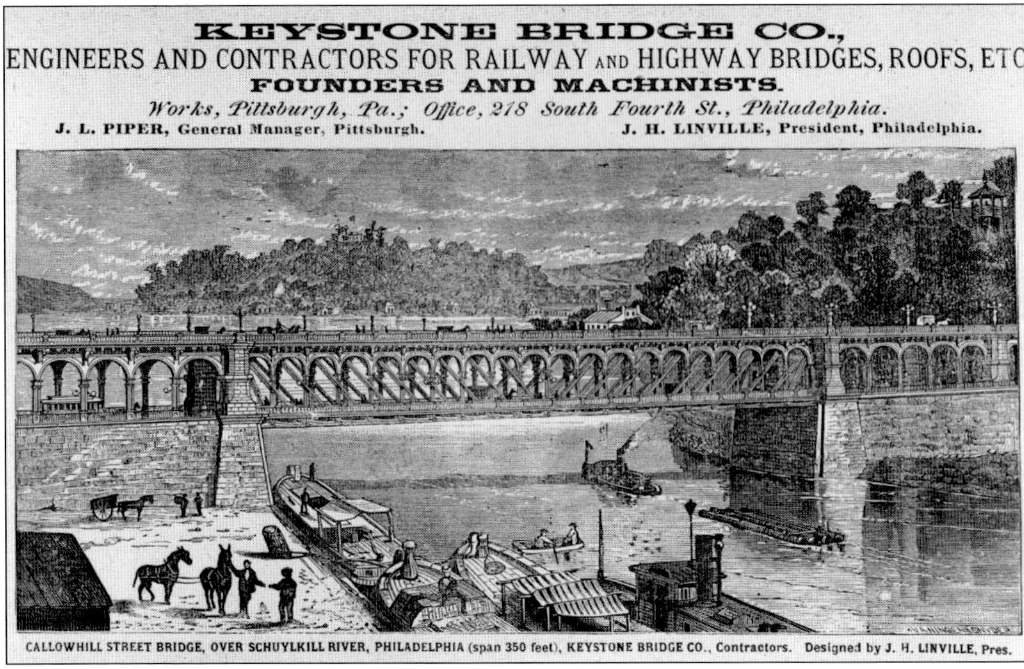

A stronger, double-decked steel truss bridge was erected from 1873 to 1875. The lower deck carried Callowhill Street, and the upper deck carried Spring Garden Street. The Keystone Bridge Company issued this promotion in 1875. This bridge lasted until 1964, when the girder span currently carrying Spring Garden Street into West Philadelphia opened. A lower bridge conveys traffic to Martin Luther King (formerly West River) Drive on the Schuylkill's west bank. (Library of Congress.)

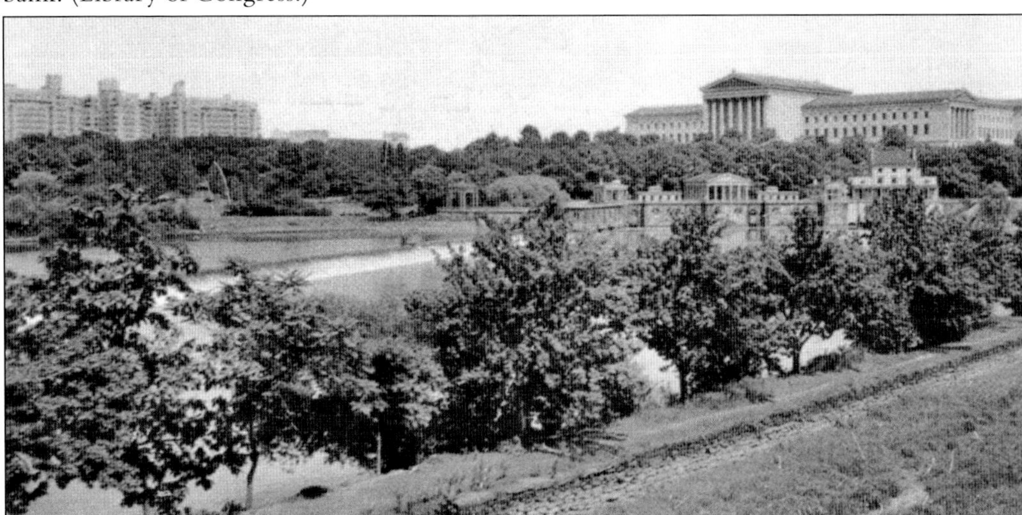

The western bank of the Schuylkill River provides a superb vista of the Philadelphia Museum of Art, the Fairmount Water Works, and Fairmount Dam. This is a photographic postcard taken about 1959 not far from the Philadelphia Zoo along West River Drive, just after the Schuylkill Expressway was built beside the river. The beauty and serenity of West Fairmount Park was forever ruined by the callous routing of this busy highway through West Philadelphia. (Charles F. Williams, Philadelphia.)

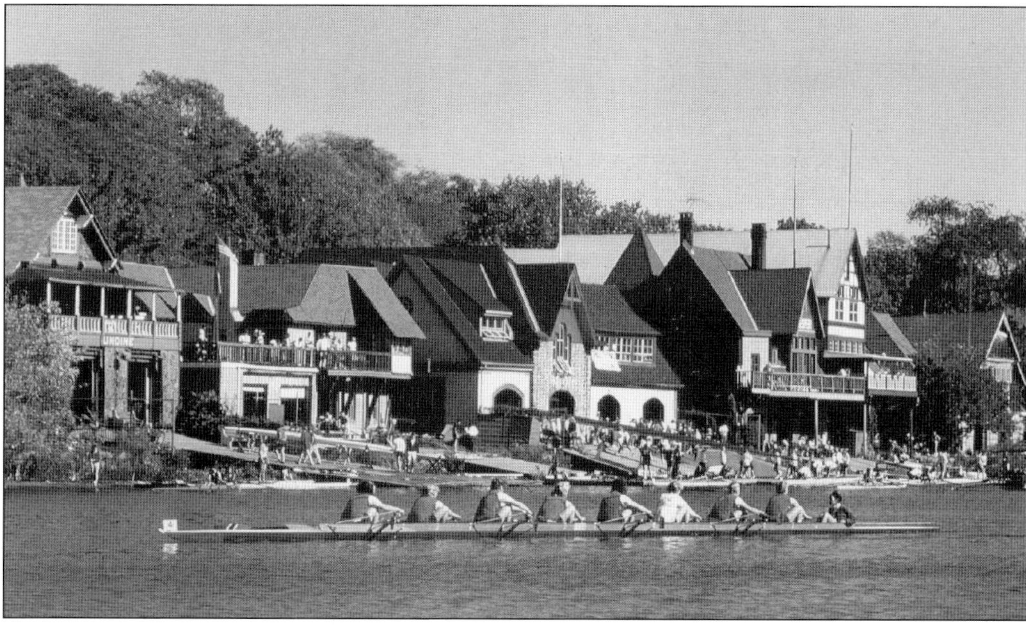

The Schuylkill River has enabled Philadelphia to host some of the most well-known rowing competitions of all time. The river was the site of global rowing races during the Centennial International Exposition of 1876, at which the Centennial Regatta was the first international rowing contest. Moreover, the earliest recorded organized rowing regatta in America occurred along the Schuylkill on November 12, 1835. (Unmarked postcard.)

Boathouse Row is among the most recognizable places in Philadelphia. The turreted, Victorian-style boathouses—the nation's oldest architecture of this type—were built by private rowing clubs starting in the 1850s. These associations make up the "Schuylkill Navy" of Philadelphia, which organized in 1858 and is now the oldest amateur athletic governing body in the country. (WYCO Products.)

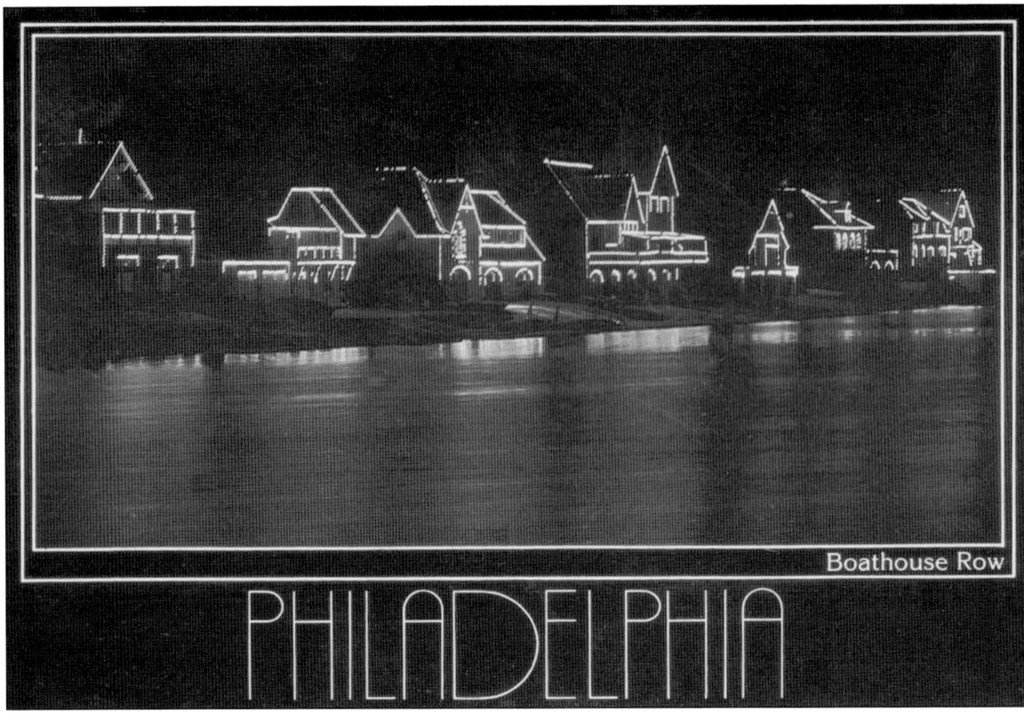

This is a Philadelphia scene known across the country: the houses of Boathouse Row outlined with hundreds of tiny lights reflecting off the Schuylkill. The lights were added in 1976 as part of the city's US bicentennial celebration; a better lighting system was installed in 1985. About 20 years later, the Fairmount Park Commission inaugurated a more versatile and energy-efficient LED lighting system. (Frank Burd, Philadelphia Post Card Company.)

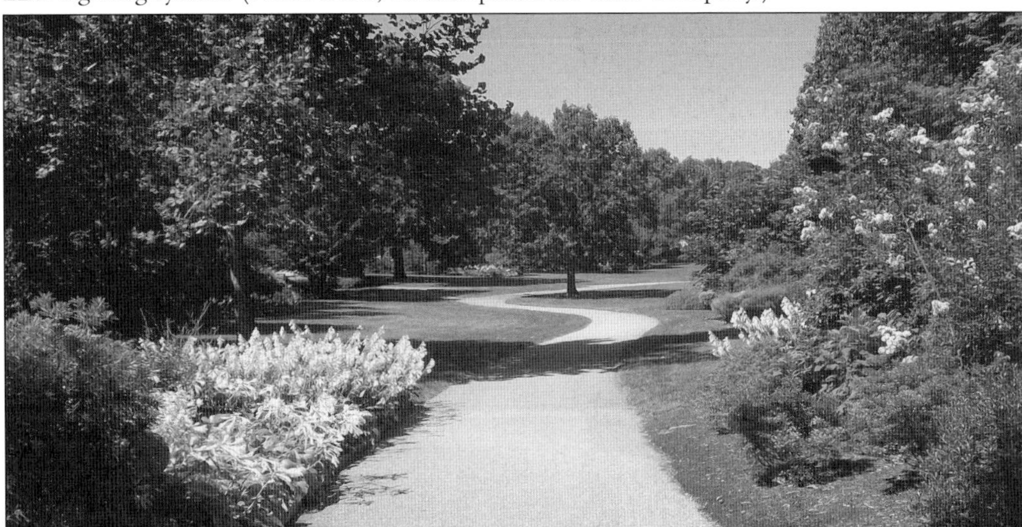

Behind the Philadelphia Museum of Art is Philadelphia's Azalea Garden: four acres of azaleas and rhododendrons intermingled with irises, tulips, and hundreds of blooming annuals and perennials. Designed by landscape architect Frederick Peck, the landscaped garden was donated to the city by the Pennsylvania Horticultural Society in 1952 and has become a favorite backdrop for weddings and other occasions. (Photograph by author.)

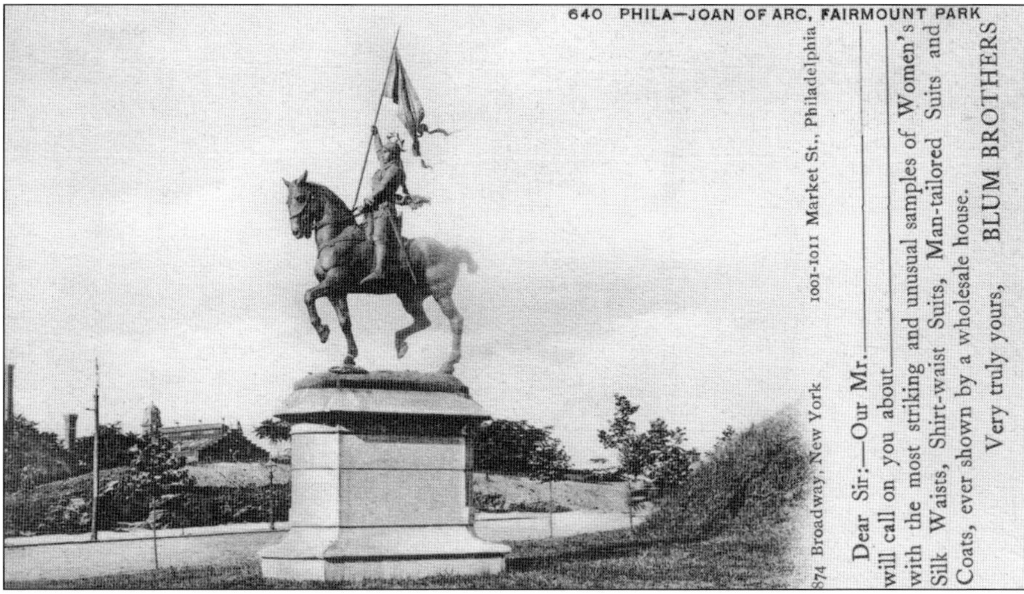

The Joan of Arc statue is perhaps the finest example of French bronze statuary in America. The monument was cast in 1874 by Emmanuel Frémiet and originally stood in Paris. In 1890, the Fairmount Park Art Association purchased it to set by the Girard Avenue Bridge. Unappreciated there, the statue was moved to East River Drive in 1948 and was then gilded. This Blum Brothers advertisement card shows it at the Girard Avenue location. (Unmarked postcard.)

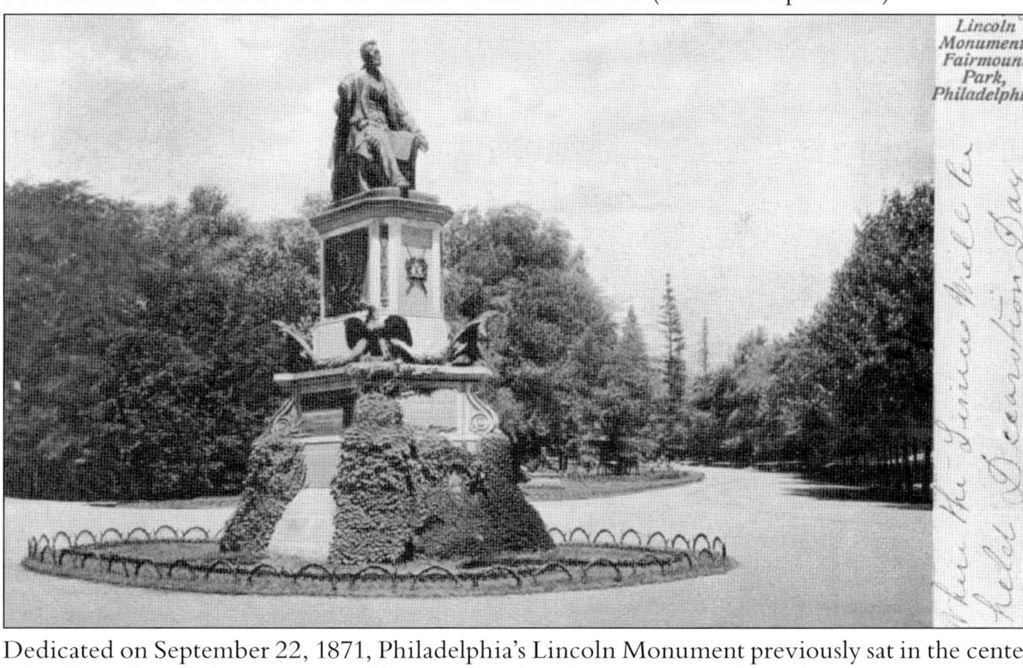

Dedicated on September 22, 1871, Philadelphia's Lincoln Monument previously sat in the center of Kelly and Sedgely Drives until being moved to the intersection's southeast corner in 2002. Sculptor Randolph Rogers placed the Abraham Lincoln figure on a granite pedestal decorated with eagles, garlands, and a plaque of Philadelphia's coat of arms. This was purportedly the third statue of Lincoln in America, and one of the earliest pieces of public art in Philadelphia. (Philadelphia Postal Card Company.)

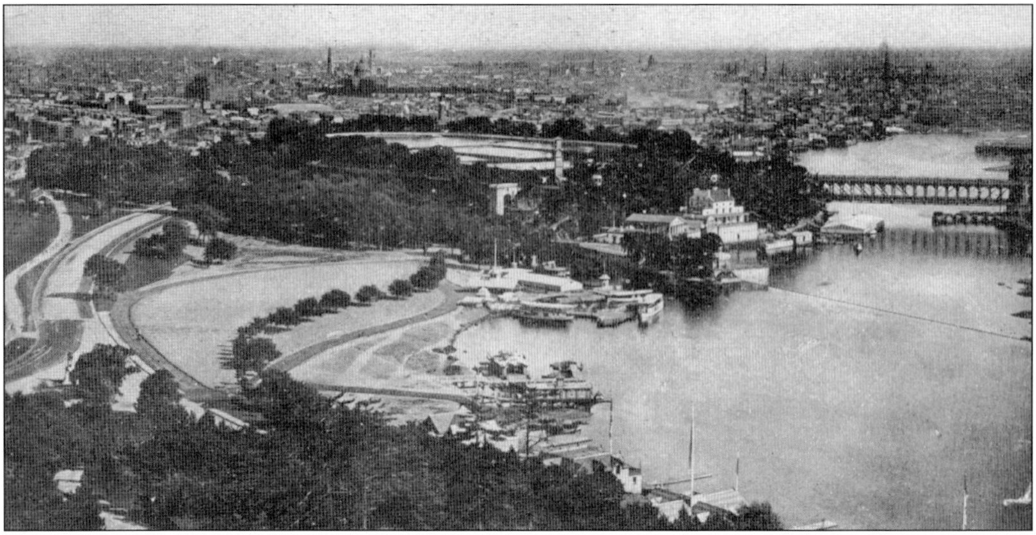

This late-19th-century prospect of downtown Philadelphia was taken from a 238-foot observation tower that was once above Lemon Hill, an estate the city purchased in 1844 as a preliminary step in creating Fairmount Park. (The tower was erected for the 1876 centennial and was later moved to Coney Island.) Reservoirs of the Fairmount Water Works appear where the art museum will one day rise. The Parkway would displace the many indistinguishable homes and workshops behind the basins. (Unmarked postcard.)

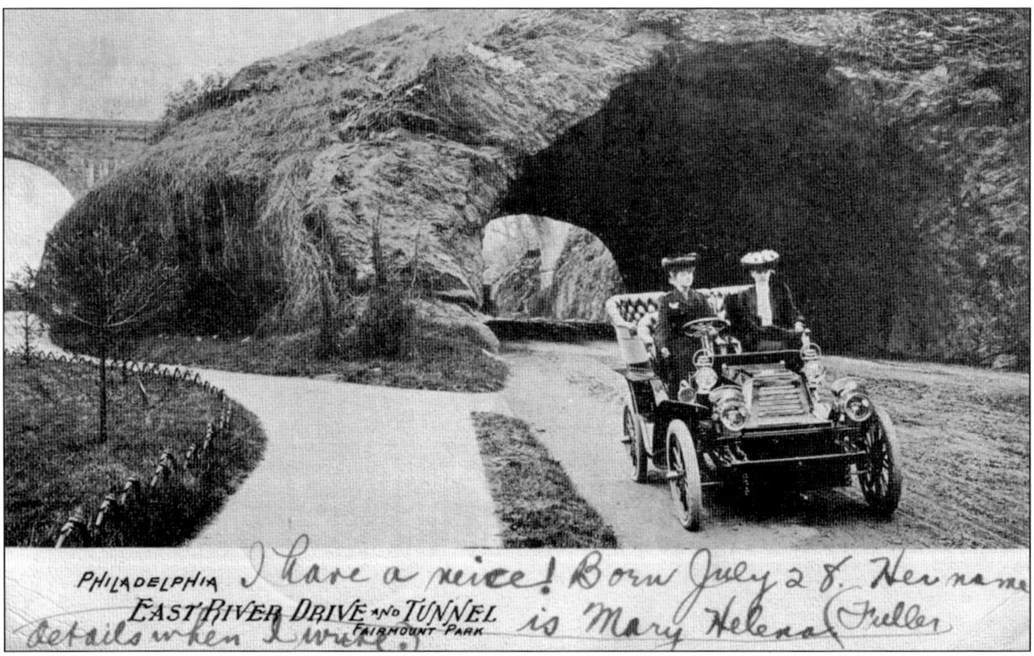

Two ladies have stopped their motorcar on East River (now John B. Kelly) Drive after going through the short tunnel of Promontory Rock in this popular postcard scene. In 1871, engineers burrowed through the outcropping of rock to unite two distinct parts of the drive. Since this postcard has a 1907 postmark, the Benjamin Franklin Parkway is definitely not their destination. However, Philadelphia's grand boulevard would soon begin to take form about two miles to the southeast. (World Post Card Company.)

BIBLIOGRAPHY

Brownlee, David Bruce. *Building the City Beautiful: The Benjamin Franklin Parkway and the Philadelphia Museum of Art*. Philadelphia: Philadelphia Museum of Art, 1989.

Carreño, Richard. *Museum Mile: Philadelphia's Parkway Museums*. Philadelphia: Writers Clearinghouse Press, 2011.

Completing the Benjamin Franklin Parkway. Philadelphia: Central Philadelphia Development Corporation, 1999.

The Fairmount Parkway: A Pictorial Record of Development from Its First Incorporation in the City Plan in 1904 to the Completion of the Main Drive from City Hall to Fairmount Park in 1919. Philadelphia: Fairmount Park Art Association, 1919.

Fairmount Park, Philadelphia. Philadelphia: Fairmount Park Guard Pension Fund Assn., Inc., 1946.

Introduction to the Philadelphia Museum of Art. Philadelphia: Philadelphia Museum of Art, 1985.

Kelsey, Albert. *The Proposed Parkway for Philadelphia: A Direct Thoroughfare from the Public Buildings to the Green Street Entrance of Fairmount Park*. Philadelphia: The Parkway Association, 1902.

Vitez, Michael. *Rocky Stories: Tales of Love, Hope, and Happiness at America's Most Famous Steps*. Dry Books, Inc., 2006.